Becoming a Heavenly Tribal Messiah

Heavenly Tribal Messiah Collection 2

| ACTIVITY HANDBOOK |

Becoming a Heavenly Tribal Messiah

Heavenly Tribal Messiah Academy

PREFACE

What is the heart of parents like? Let us say there are parents with five children, and that one of the five children did not come home for days. What would the heart of those parents be like? The Bible tells us the answer to this question with a parable: "What do you think? If a shepherd has 100 sheep, and one of them has gone astray, does he not leave the 99 on the mountains and go in search of the one that went astray? And if he finds it, truly I tell you, he rejoices over it more than over the 99 that never went astray." [Matt. 18:12–13]

Heavenly tribal messiahs are the central figures walking the path of true parents that will be recorded in history, for you are working hard to guide even one person to Heavenly Parent from among humanity, who are wandering like lost sheep without even knowing that the relationship between Heavenly Parent and humankind is that of Parent and children. How many valleys of circumstances have you crossed as you continued to dedicate yourself solely to your work, without taking time even to care for your own family? And how many hours, unknown to anyone else, have you struggled all by yourself to fulfill this mission? The path we walk, however, is the one on which we experience the heart of Heavenly Parent and True Parents on our way to perfection, and so we march forward toward our goal in silence.

This is a handbook that summarizes all the practical knowledge that you may require when you work alone in your mission area as a tribal messiah. Blessed central families have a paramount goal to achieve in your respective locality, namely the restoration of your own tribe, but the fact is that you may be working with many unanswered questions troubling you. The heavenly tribal messiah mission, in particular, is very different from the witnessing activities we carried out in the past in terms of its contents. Moreover, there is a limit to how much you can ask for help and guidance from church leaders, who have many of their own tasks to fulfill for the providence. Accordingly, this handbook is being published to help blessed central families to fulfill the heavenly tribal messiah mission by yourselves.

The writing staff of this book based our research on True Parents' words about the heavenly tribal messiah. We delved deeply into the course followed by True Parents in consecutive order, from the providence of restoration and the age of home church to the heavenly tribal messiah movement.

Moreover, we analyzed leading examples of heavenly tribal messiah work that were reported to the international headquarters from around the world, in order to deduce their success factors and to find the best way to adapt those success factors to the present situation of the providence. Methods of carrying out activities are diverse and subject to change. Even though you may have the same goal, you each have to decide on your own method and draw up alternative plans in accordance with the situation of your own locality. In this book, however, we tried to find the answers by limiting ourselves to methods that can be applied in all situations, while taking into account the circumstances of different nations. Though this book may be insufficient in various aspects, we will continue to revise and supplement it to make it a better handbook of guidelines for your work.

This book is the second volume in the Heavenly Tribal Messiah Collection, and Chapter 1 is a summary of True Parents' words on the identity of heavenly tribal messiahs and the direction of their tribes. It explains about the original dream of forming tribes that Heavenly Parent and True Parents tried to realize, based on True Parents' words. Chapter 2 contains the various tasks that blessed families need to fulfill before they make the resolution to carry out heavenly tribal messiah activities and embark on that path, since the preparation period is most important in any activity. Chapter 3 is about the process by which a blessed family can organize a tribe. It expounds in consecutive order on the tasks that blessed central families need to carry out, such as starting with the offering of jeongseong, holding Blessing ceremonies, and educating their tribe until they can become the owners of their local society. Chapter 4 lists the activities that blessed families need to carry out after organizing their tribe. After a tribe is formed, it must be guided quite delicately in order for it to continue to exist and prosper for all eternity. This chapter contains necessary contents that can be applied locally in educating tribe members and guiding tribal communities.

The contents of this book are designed to present a consecutive and comprehensive framework for heavenly tribal messiah activities and to convey the knowledge necessary in carrying out those activities. We hope that heavenly fortune will be with all members who read this practical handbook, so that you can complete the mission of organizing a tribe of 430 couples and be successful also in educating and guiding them. We are absolutely confident that you, the proud heavenly tribal messiahs of the Unification movement, will complete your given mission without fail. We earnestly hope and pray that the grace of Heavenly Parent and True Parents will be with you all.

February 1, 2018
Family Federation for World Peace and Unification
International Headquarters

CONTENTS

PREFACE 4

Chapter 1 The Start of the Mission

Section 1 The Ideal of One Human Family and Heavenly Tribal Messiahs 15

Section 2 The Three Great Kingships and Four Great Realms of Heart 20

Section 3 Realizing an Ideal Family in Resemblance to Heavenly Parent 25

Section 4 The Way of a Tribal Leader 27

Section 5 National Restoration and Establishing a Hyojeong Culture 29

Section 6 True Parent, True Teacher, and True Owner 31

Section 7 A Life Built on Love for Heavenly Parent, Love for People and Love for Nation 34

Chapter 2 Developing an Environment

Section 1 Unity and Cooperation within the Family 43

Section 2 The Pastor's Support 56

Section 3 Cooperation from Members 65

Section 4 Building the Culture 76

Chapter 3 Formation of a Tribe

Section 1 Creating a Spiritual Environment 93
Section 2 Declaration as the Messiah and
           Invitation to the Family 109
Section 3 Gathering Candidates 123
Section 4 Inviting People to Family Federation Events 138
Section 5 Invitation to the Blessing 148
Section 6 Love and Attention 169
Section 7 Educating Spiritual Children 179
Section 8 Leading the Local Society 186

Chapter 4 Maintaining a Healthy Tribal Community

Section 1   Spreading the Passion for Heavenly Tribal Messiah
            Activities 201
Section 2   Recording the Tribe's History 208
Section 3   Establishing a Tribal Vision 213
Section 4   Organizing the Tribe 219
Section 5   Leadership and Tribal Ministry 228
Section 6   Creating an Environment 237
Section 7   Education System 241
Section 8   Pastoral Visits and Counseling 299
Section 9   Forming Disciple Groups 323
Section 10 Outreach 326

Section 11 Business and Finance 332
Section 12 Caring for Tribal Families 343

Appendix

Appendix 1 Revised International Standard for a Completed Heavenly Tribal Messiah Mission and Minimum Requirements to Receive Certification as Heavenly Tribal Messiah Victors
.... 355

Appendix 2 Heavenly Tribal Messiah Activities Checklist 364

Appendix 3 Using the Online Genealogy Service 375

Bibliography 379

A GLOSSARY OF KEY TERMS 383

Chapter 1

The Start of the Mission

The Secret to Successful Heavenly Tribal Messiahship

Dr. Lek Thaveetermsakul,
Cheon Il Guk special envoy to Thailand

In October 2012, soon after True Father passed away, we held a UPF-Asia International Leadership Conference in Songkhla Province. The purpose of this event was to present a model for peace movements and interfaith peace Blessings that were to take place in southern Thailand.

However, one member of our staff said that she had a dream about True Father. She said he appeared to her in the dream and entered the auditorium with a broad smile. The large auditorium was filled with adults who were listening intently to Divine Principle lectures. True Father was sitting next to her and said, "Thank you, thank you," to the participants and began speaking. After hearing about this dream, I was sure that True Father would always be with us.

While listening to the story of our member's dream, I recalled the video of the last prayer True Father gave before going to the spirit world, about the mission of heavenly tribal messiahs. I determined to bless 430 couples before Foundation Day as an offering to Heavenly Parent and True Parents.

▼ Dr. Lek Thaveetermsakul and his family   ▼ Dr. Lek and his wife officiating the Blessing Ceremony

I promised myself that at least one blessed member should fulfill True Father's unfinished work so that the words that he left behind would not be wasted.

Early in November 2012, I brought together our young members to tackle the goal of restoring at least 500 couples. Even these young students resolved to take part in this effort. We decided to invite them also to participate in the Interfaith Peace Blessing Ceremony that would be held on December 1–2, 2012.

On the day of the event, more than 1,000 people filled the grand ballroom of a hotel in Khon Kaen, Northeast Thailand. It was the first event in Thailand for which we determined to break through our limitations. Exceeding all of our expectations, 650 couples attended the Blessing Ceremony.

Discussion Questions

"

First, may your family receive Heavenly Parent's and True Parents' blessings.

One, what do you think about heavenly tribal messiahs?

Two, heavenly tribal messiahs are seeking to build a world with blessed-member communities.
What do you believe that world would look like?

Three, if you become a heavenly tribal messiah and need to find more spiritual children, in what area would you need to prepare yourself?

Four, what do you consider the three main elements for heavenly tribal messiah activities?

"

Section 1 The Ideal of One Human Family and Heavenly Tribal Messiahs

If human beings had not fallen, humankind would have overcome the boundaries of race, religion, and national borders and become one family under Heavenly Parent. The people of this world would have inherited Heavenly Parent's good lineage and tradition and built an ideal world where they lived united with their brothers and sisters. However, human beings fell and Satan stole the ideal world, which Heavenly Parent had long dreamed about.

First, humankind has lost its original parent, Heavenly Parent. Therefore, it is humankind's destiny to meet the Messiah, who is the Savior and True Parents, who can guide it on the path back to its original parent, our Heavenly Parent.

Second, Satan stole Heavenly Parent's first son. Originally, Heavenly Parent wanted to raise Adam and give him the authority and right of inheritance to rule this world. However, due to Adam's Fall, he was stripped of the elder-son position that he should have inherited. Therefore, between Cain and Abel, Adam and Eve's children, Heavenly Parent had to search for an object partner that could remain focused on Heavenly Parent. Adam and Eve's first son, Cain, became a subject partner who worshipped the secular god. Therefore, Heavenly Parent established Abel as the symbol of goodness, and through a life of worship he carried out the providence in search of Heavenly Parent. The population of the human world then developed upon the division between these two brothers. The division in the first family expanded to the world level in the form of an Abel-type view of life and a Cain-type view of life. This caused a struggle between brothers—good values centering on the conscience and egotism centering only on the self—in all areas such as politics, economics, religion and culture. Up until now, the human world has groaned under a torrent of conflict and war.

Therefore, humankind needs the True Parents who are the advent of the Savior, the Messiah and are descended from good ancestors. Humankind needs to engraft to the good lineage, love and heart of True Parents. Those who have received the Blessing from the True Parents are part of Abel's tribe centering on Heavenly Parent. In other words, blessed members have started on a path as good descendants who have found what Heavenly Parent had lost. First, blessed members are Heavenly Parent's hope. They should focus on people in the Cain realm and introduce them to Heavenly Parent and True Parents so that they can receive the Blessing and realize one human family, which is humankind's wish. By doing so, human beings will find their original parent, our Heavenly Parent, and end their wandering as orphans.

When Cain's tribe is restored, the relationship between the two brothers in Adam and Eve's family, the first ancestors, can be restored to its original position. There is no more room for animosity and conflict to exist between brothers. There no longer will be a clash between the values of Godism, centering on good, and egotism, centering on evil. The two brothers will have created a position of unity and harmony centering on one Heavenly Parent. In other words, the movement of the heavenly tribal messiah community is to create an ideal family with united brothers centering on Heavenly Parent. Thus, the providence of this community is to restore the fallen world and the family that resulted from the division between Cain and Abel, and unite it as one original community.

Therefore, what are heavenly tribal messiahs? They are the ones who seek to restore a community under Heavenly Parent, as God had intended through the original family of Adam and Eve. Due to the Fall, Adam and Eve's family was split between Cain and Abel. Heavenly tribal messiahship is the providence centering on the heavenly elder son, Abel, naturally subduing Cain with love, and their uniting as brothers.

To fulfill the ideal of united brothers, the families who have received the Blessing from the Messiah, the True Parents, should work to unite their Abel-realm children, including their second-generation children, and their existing spiritual children, with their new tribal spiritual children, who are the Cain children, by pursuing the heavenly tribal messiah mission. When these two groups of children, representing Cain and Abel, can unite, the tribe will become an expanded ideal family that can attend Heavenly Parent together. The tribal messiahs who established these two worlds, these two sons, become the parents of that tribe. This is the position in which the ideal of creation can be fulfilled; we are to become true parents and give birth to good children, as was intended for Adam and Eve's family at the beginning. Therefore, blessed members who have restored and united their Cain children and Abel children through heavenly tribal messiah activities can restore the authority of parents. They will stand in the position of authentic true parents who attend True Parents, embrace both Cain children and Abel children, and inherit Heavenly Parent's heart.

When a husband and wife who are heavenly tribal messiahs restore the authority of parents, they simultaneously restore the authority of the king, which allows Heavenly Parent to reside within their physical bodies. Only then can the incorporeal Heavenly Parent have a corporeal body. This completes the incorporeal and corporeal substantial worlds. This position fulfills the three great kingships: the kingship of Heavenly Parent, the original king of this world; the kingship of parents, the current parents who restored their two sons, Cain and Abel; and the kingship of children, who are to inherit the kingship of the future world. When these goals are accomplished, human beings can live an eternal life as heavenly citizens.

In conclusion, the title "heavenly tribal messiah" signifies a couple's right to claim the position of becoming Heavenly Parent's body and the providence of restoring the positions of Adam and Eve before the Fall.

We dream each day of creating one human family centering on Heavenly Parent in a peaceful world in which there is no war or starvation and in which guns and weapons are melted down to make plows and plowshares. Our families, our tribes, our nations should unite with True Parents in front of Heavenly Parent's Will and ride on great waves toward fulfilling the dream of one world under God that Heavenly Parent has longed for.

Section 2 The Three Great Kingships and Four Great Realms of Heart

Originally Adam and Eve should have grown to maturity, received the marriage Blessing and formed a beautiful family. Humankind should have been built on that original family. When Adam and Eve received the marriage Blessing, Heavenly Parent, an incorporeal being, would have become one with them by residing within them. God's dream for creation was becoming a Creator with a physical form. God created the first ancestors, Adam and Eve, to multiply and give birth to future generations and have dominion over creation. Therefore, the second generation, Adam and Eve, and the third generation, grandchildren, would form Heavenly Parent's kingship on earth centering on the first generation, Heavenly Parent. It was the purpose of creation to pass this tradition on eternally. Thus, blessed members should take Adam and Eve's position before the Fall when they receive the Blessing and build a family in which three generations—the Grandparents, parents and grandchildren—live harmoniously. In other words, a family's three generations should become one. Within that family, parental love, conjugal love, siblings' love, and children's love will achieve heartistic unity and form a model of heaven.

First, conjugal love is important.

In the beginning, God hoped that Adam and Eve would mature and fulfill His ideal of becoming one with Him. That is why the scriptures record that, after He created Adam, God took a rib and created Eve, after seeing that Adam was lonely. We must not interpret that Adam had a higher position than Eve, because God created him first. The point of this verse is to emphasize that by taking a piece of Adam to create Eve, God created them from one body. Therefore, the love between a husband and wife should perfect one another: An absolute subject partner creates an absolute object partner, and an absolute object partner creates an absolute subject partner. This is the order of creation. In other words, your wife is the only person out of all the women in the world who calls you her husband and accepts your value. Only when that woman accepts you as her husband can you perfect your position as a husband. Likewise, when a woman's husband accepts her as his wife, she perfects her position as one. Therefore, you need to align yourself with your spouse, because your spouse has the authority to perfect your position. Putting yourself at the center does not allow your spouse to perfect you. The one thing that only you can do is fulfill your spouse's needs and help your spouse grow. When your husband or wife rises toward perfection, you also can rise at the same rate. The wife's level of perfection is not up to her but is up to how much her husband helps her grow. Thus, two people can become the ideal couple that God has dreamed of when they concentrate on perfecting each other and fulfilling each other's needs.

Second, it is important to have a parental heart.

Using a similar reasoning as that described above, parents' positions are not determined by the parents alone but are determined by the children when they call them their parents. As a result, the parents' value is established based on how much they enable their children to grow to perfection. Hence, even secular parents serve their children like slaves. Why is this? By enabling their children to reach perfection, they gain the title of "good parents." Their success as parents is evaluated in relation to how successful their children are. Therefore, the reason God has carried out the history of human salvation is that human beings, who are His children, need to call Him their Parent in order for Him to perfect His position as a parent.

Third is the realm of children's love.

Children are in the position to become future parents themselves. Children who receive their parents' devoted love also give back love with a filial heart. When they do their best to love their parents, their parents give them recognition. Therefore, the parents hand over their right as parents to the parents of the future world, their children, who inherit the right to lineage, the right to inheritance, and, as grown children, the right of equal status, which places them in a position equal to that of their parents and gives them the right to participate as equals with their parents. Thus, the perfection of children does not come about by them claiming it on their own; rather, their position and value are established by being accepted by their parents.

Fourth, is the realm of siblings' love.

Adam and Eve committed the human Fall, and their family was divided through a conflict between Cain and Abel. Our original Parent, God, hopes that the brothers will unite and return to their original Parent. Thus, we need not only to unite our own physical children but also to seek out their brothers in the lost realm of Cain and unite them with our children as brothers. In other words, brothers need to live for the sake of each other. An individual cannot create his own position, but when he goes the path to being recognized by his brother, the value of his individual position will be recognized and perfected. His value is determined when the brother can say, "My brother is a true person." You do not determine your own value. Individual perfection is achieved through other people, not yourself.

If this process were to be disrupted, the realms of heart, between a husband and wife, parents for their children, children for their parents, and siblings would be incomplete. Your family is the foundation to realize these four great realms of heart. One should expand and multiply the four great realms of heart that one learns in the family to one's tribe, society, nation, and the world. In other words, the three great kingships and the four great realms of heart perfect the family of Adam and Eve to its state before the Fall. Before the Fall, Adam and Eve should have fulfilled the three great kingships and the four great realms of heart and become the royal family, God's direct lineage. Therefore, the ultimate purpose of the providence is to restore fallen humankind and build the royal family. Blessed families need to complete this mission. Centering on the families that Heavenly Parent established, in an effort to establish an absolute standard, He needed models for a grandfather, grandmother, father, mother, a couple, and children. Korea, the nation of the chosen people, is oriented toward large extended families. Heavenly tribal messiahs should aim to leave behind a traditional history in which seven generations of Abel's tribe and Cain's tribe can live as one community.

Section 3 Realizing an Ideal Family in Resemblance to Heavenly Parent

What is an ideal family that resembles Heavenly Parent? As mentioned above, it is a family in which the three great kingships and the four great realms of heart are established. True lineage, true love, and true traditions are the mainstream in this family, which lives for the sake of others centering on Heavenly Parent's characteristics, for the perfection of the other and then the perfection of the self. In other words, the recognition and perfection of a husband's values come from not himself but his wife. It is the same for the wife. In this way, the wife creates and perfects her husband's value. It is the same for the perfection of the wife's value. Therefore, there is no perfection in the family for someone who demands others to follow. You must move centering on those who perfect you. Then you will receive recognition and can go the path of perfection. Ultimately, the other person determines one's perfected value. Thus, to reach perfection, one should strive to perfect other people.

This law applies to parents and children as well. This is because children are the ones who perfect the position of parents. Therefore, when parents perfect their children, they are going the path of sacrifice to perfect the parents' position. From this point of view, why did God create human beings as His children? After creating them, God was to perfect them and become their Parent. Therefore, why do we need to do heavenly tribal messiah activities? The perfection of your family can rise to the level of heavenly family perfection when you perfect Cain's tribe. If there is no Cain tribe, one cannot perfect one's family because Satan can invade. However, if the Cain realm is restored, they become a defense mechanism against Satan and protect the Abel tribe. Therefore, restoring one's tribe is not a burden but a movement for hope. We all should have this wish. All humankind is meant to form one family under the original Parent. On that foundation, we can perfect a people, a nation, and the cosmos.

Section 4 The Way of a Tribal Leader

As mentioned, tribal restoration is the path to perfecting our families. First, all our blessed members in the Family Federation, called to take part in the path of the Blessing, are central families centered on Heavenly Parent. In other words, blessed families are in the position that inherits the status of Adam and Eve's family before the Fall. Therefore, the path we must take is building a model of an unfallen family and becoming an example to other people. Moreover, we should not try to perfect only our own families. When we expand and perfect larger numbers of our tribe, our own family can receive protection and reach perfection. Blessed families should constantly invest in and sacrifice themselves for the sake of their neighbors and tribe, and receive recognition from them. This is the path to perfecting your family through others. Blessed families should fulfill the needs of the members of their tribe, who are their spiritual children, and practice a movement of true love to complete their spiritual children's shortcomings. When one does this, their tribe members will recognize them and say, "Our heavenly tribal messiah has an exemplary family centered on God." Then that model should expand and one's masterpiece of a lifetime will manifest as a tribal community. Therefore, that family will restore the model of the unfallen family of Adam and Eve and will receive the name and authority of the crowned chief of the tribe.

Section 5 National Restoration and Establishing a Hyojeong Culture

True Parents said that when there are 12 families that have victoriously restored their tribe centering on Heavenly Parent, God can work in that nation. Through the tribes of heavenly tribal messiahs, the number 12 brings the completion of restoration to fruition: Jacob's 12 brothers, the 12 tribes of Israel centering on Moses, Jesus' 12 disciples, and the 12 children centering on the returning Lord. In other words, blessed families who have paid indemnity and changed their lineage through the Blessing have received the right of God's children. When blessed families succeed in restoring the authority of the 12 tribes, their country also can achieve restoration. For the first time in human history, the parent–child relationship between God and human beings has been restored to those in the position of a blessed family. God finally can reside in an original tribe which fulfills the national realm and can open the way to the ideal kingdom of heaven. Within this, families in the state before Adam and Eve's Fall can emerge and unite with God. Then a hyojeong culture, in which people give and receive with their original hearts, can be established.

Section 6 True Parent, True Teacher, and True Owner

What kind of work should the tribe's chief do? True Parents said that human beings should become three great subject partners.

The first of the three great subject partners that you must learn to become is the true parent. Centering on true parents, one should establish three object partners through the grandparents, parents, and children and perfect a family united with true love. Heavenly Parent intended to give the ideal of heaven to Adam and Eve after He created the universe. Likewise, parents also have a right to inheritance. It is a right to Heavenly Parent's blessings. Heavenly Parent blessed the lineage of Abraham, Isaac and Jacob. For families centering on Heavenly Parent who rid themselves of the Fall, God will forever bequeath His blessings through their future generations. In other words, the position of a true parent should pass down Heaven's tradition and love, centering on Heavenly Parent, and inherit

Heavenly Parent's unfinished work. Therefore, a chief should take the path of offering the Blessing to his own family and heavenly tribe and pass on the lineage and tradition as well.

The second subject partner you should seek to be is a true teacher. This represents taking the path of perfection and receiving recognition as a teacher by helping one's students to excel beyond the teacher himself. Children perfect the parents' position, and the students perfect the teacher's position. The greatest teachers are a family's parents. This is because the children learn and inherit everything about their parents' lives. A true teacher's position can be obtained through the school. A teacher's position can come from one's siblings or friends. Therefore, you should take care to note that the responsibility for raising true children lies with the parents first. The children in each family should learn true behavior and habits from true parents and through the tradition of daily hoondokhae centering on Heavenly Parent, and they should be able to share Heavenly Parent's teachings with others. Children who grow up receiving education of goodness in their family automatically connect it with their school education. Within the perimeters of the school, teachers should fulfill a role like that of parents in a large, God-centered family and should nurture and teach their students as true children with the heart of true teachers. Therefore, teachers first should possess the heart of a true parent. Moreover, through family and social life, people learn by sharing practical skills between their siblings and their friends. If you treat your friend with the attitude of a teacher and give freely, your friend will treat you like their teacher, according to the amount you have given.

The third subject partner you have to become is a true owner. After the Creation, God established human beings as the owners of the world by telling them to be fruitful, multiply and have dominion over all things. As Heavenly Parent's children who inherited the universe and the earth, we should become owners who love nature, our society, our nation, and our world. Therefore, true parents, true teachers, and true owners are not separate but integrally connected as a trinity.

When you meet a true owner, you naturally have found a true teacher and a true parent. The three great subject partners expanded with parents' love is an ideology of living for the sake of others. We need to teach not only knowledge but also all the characteristics that our broad society possesses. Thus, we should form a heavenly tribal messiah community with the three great subject partners and live for the sake of our brothers and sisters, for the sake of our local society, for the sake of our country, and for the sake of our world. In conclusion, heavenly tribal messiahs automatically need to become owners, teachers, and true parents. Centering on the three great ideologies, we should carry out heavenly tribal messiah activities and connect them with love.

Section 7 A Life Built on Love for Heavenly Parent, Love for People and Love for Nation

When human beings are born, they should love Heavenly Parent, their original parent, love the brothers Heavenly Parent gave them, and love the world He created. *Aeguk* 애국: (Love for Nation) means to love the extended cosmos centering on Heavenly Parent. It refers to the vast nation where heaven exists.

Aecheon 애천: (Love for Heaven) means to love Heavenly Parent. It also means to resemble His characteristics and follow His Will. Thus, it establishes Heavenly Parent at the center of our lives. As it says in the scriptures, the first commandment for human beings is ① "You shall love the Lord your God with all your heart, and with all your soul, and with all your mind." [Matthew 22:36–40] The first thing for fallen human beings to find is their lost parents. To separate themselves from the satanic world and resemble Heavenly Parent's perfection, human beings should live in close proximity to their Heavenly Parent, giving their mind, life, and will for Him. The people of the world, who have been orphans, have found their parents through the True Parents. Therefore, they should become one with their parents and heal their hearts.

Aein 애인: (Love for People) means to love humankind. Love for people teaches that humankind should live as one family by loving one another on the foundation of love for God. The next verse from the scriptures describes the second commandment: ② "And a second is like it, You shall love your neighbor as yourself. On these two commandments depend all the law and the prophets." [Matthew 22:36–40] Beginning with one's characteristics that most resemble Heavenly Parent, one should connect through those attributes to one's family and love one's relatives, one's neighbors, one's coworkers, one's countrymen, and humankind. Love for people refers to achieving one big human family by loving those of a different nationality, religion, race, and culture than one's own without discrimination.

Therefore, ③ on the foundation of love for God and love for people, love for nation teaches one to love one's country, which includes God, people and nature. It refers to the utopia of Heaven that fulfills an ideal world of peace and unification. In the Korean concept of the word "*Aeguk* 애국", to have love for ones nation means to have a nation that has sovereignty, territory, and citizens—there can be no true nation if there are no people who live in it and love it. Humankind centering on God should align its direction with that goal and have interdependence, mutual prosperity and universally shared values. People live for the sake of others in this world. It is a world in which people long for one another, share with one another, and are centered on a love that lives for the sake of one another.

To complete their mission, heavenly tribal messiahs need to engraft members of their Cain tribe to their family, creating unity between their Cain children and their own children, who are in Abel's position. Therefore, two brothers that were previously divided can meet, attend Heavenly Parent as the parent in an original tribal community, and take the path to becoming authentic true parents. A heavenly tribal messiah should build a family and a tribal community in which Heavenly Parent can enter and live together in a corporeal and incorporeal substantiation. Heavenly tribal messiahs need to restore and expand 12 tribes in their nation to form a nation for Heavenly Parent.

✤ Discussion Topics

1) What do you think about heavenly tribal messiahs?

2) Thinking about the heavenly tribal messiahs you know, what kind of perspective do they have?

3) What kind of plans do you have for teaching your children or grandchildren about faith, and what kind of achievements would you personally like to leave behind?

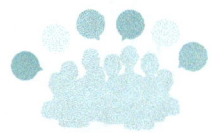

Chapter 2

Developing an Environment

The story of Rev. Bakary Camara, regional group chair of FFWPU of Africa

I am the regional group chair of FFWPU-Africa. Africa is in a growth stage. Its society is gradually maturing, its economy is progressing, and it is actively accepting outside civilizations. The public's level of interest in the Family Federation and its new teachings is rising as much as anything else. Blessing activities are easily increasing at an explosive rate, and the level of response that those in leadership have, as soon as they hear the Word, has been surprisingly beyond our expectations. Moreover, Africa is

◀ Archbishop Dr. Johannes N. Ndanga and Africa Group Chair Bakary Camara

an area where tribal culture has been well preserved until now. Recently, as I have been conducting Blessing activities, I have felt more eager than ever to offer up great achievements to True Parents. However, it is important that this not be a temporary movement, which means it needs more structural development.

We are studying the methods used in Asia and Japan and applying what we learn about their strengths and weaknesses to our systems. Even today, the national leaders in Africa send me many questions about our Blessing events. Every day I have a busy schedule leading various events, but I often spend time thinking about what the best ways are. Today I am visiting a town in Uganda to oversee a Blessing event. How much sacrifice has been made for this providence to bear fruit? As I look toward the horizon with an earnest heart in front of Heavenly Parent, I pray, "Heavenly Parent, may You bless Africa!"

◂ Africa Group Chair Camara with Family Federation leaders

Introductory Questions

"

What are the religious, cultural, and social backgrounds of the people in your local area or nation?

Analyzing the environment of the area in which you live, let's think about what can be done to create an environment to conduct heavenly tribal messiah activities.

"

Section 1 Unity and Cooperation within the Family

1.1 Oneness in the Family Is the Starting Point

By attending True Parents, the family becomes the focal point and model that realizes the four great realms of heart (parents' love, conjugal love, children's love and siblings' love) and the nucleus for the expansion of heavenly tribal messiahship. All the members of the tribe will look to the heavenly tribal messiah's family to develop their faith and find the direction in which they should go forward. That is why, at the beginning stages of heavenly tribal messiah activities, Satan may try to attack the family members, disturb the unity, and incite words and actions to cause the responsible person to lose their ground. Many blessed families probably have experienced this already, but there are also many families who have experienced conflict and hardship just before deciding to take part in these activities or in the beginning stage of these activities. You must know that difficulties like these are the spiritual works of Satan. This is because for Satan, the restoration of the original family means the loss of the base that he created through the downfall of the first family and the loss of his firm grip on humanity. That is why, when you decide to go the path of a heavenly tribal messiah, Satan may try to use your family, whom you love most, to make you lose your motivation and prevent you from taking responsibility. Therefore, the most important thing is for the entire family to center around one goal and offer jeongseong and do hoondokhae, in order to create absolute unity within the family and support the family's resolution to do heavenly tribal messiah activities.

1.2 A Harmonious Home Is the Foundation for a Victorious Tribe

The work of the world is the work of the individual human being, and the work of the human being begins in the family. As the saying goes, "If the family is harmonious, everything will be achieved." Thus, through a harmonious family, anything in the world can be achieved. If the family is in peace and harmony and unites around one goal, the strength and power of that family will be beyond our imagination. It is not an exaggeration to say that the success or failure of all things depends on the harmony within the family. In particular, the providence of heavenly tribal messiahship is a phenomenon in which one has to establish one's family as a model and then go on expanding to the tribe. On the other hand, if the family consistently fails to unite, the members of the tribe lose the pivotal center point and the example or template for the expansion of model families. Heavenly tribal messiah activities are not simply the pursuit and establishment of a model perfect family. In the beginning, we must use the power and strength of the unity of our families to help fulfill the needs of the Cain-tribe families. The reward of your family members' sacrifice is that they will experience the heart of Heavenly Parent and taste the amazing grace of entering that world. Through completing the wider range of the four great realms of heart, your family will go on perfecting itself as a family that resembles Heavenly Parent. From this perspective, we can see that the mission of heavenly tribal messiahship begins from a life of sacrifice in which the world does not notice you and goes up to the point at which your family is in a special position and stands in the spotlight. That is why families who begin the heavenly tribal messiah mission must attend Heavenly Parent, who is the original parent, in their family and establish a principled standard that will steadfastly lead them to live a model life.

1.3 Preparation for New Members

Heavenly tribal messiahs are parents who take care of many children. They especially have to take care of the Cain-realm children. That is why parents first should offer jeongseong and prepare the environment, just as they would when they are welcoming a newborn child. A sibling is someone who helps the parent and prepares the environment with joy in order to welcome a newborn sibling and someone who can share with their sibling all the love that they have received from their parents until now. A spiritual parent's welcoming a spiritual child is not just an encounter between two individuals. It is necessary for all the family members to prepare to welcome the spiritual child. First, you must have the same sense of affinity for the spiritual child as any parent who is welcoming the birth of a new child and guide your actions to make them part of your lineage. Second, you need to take responsibility to raise and nurture this new child as Heavenly Parent's child. Look at the surrounding environment of that person, and analyze and consider the spiritual and physical issues and needs of that new child. There is a need for careful consideration and preparation in many different aspects.

In order to welcome a new child, it is not just the parents who need to prepare. The biological second-generation children, as well as the spiritual children of the Abel realm who are already committed members, also need to prepare.

First, the biological children (or spiritual children in the Abel realm) must understand the heart of their parents who are nurturing so many children. This is because they might feel a lack of love, due to the fact that the love that they received from their parents is now shared—especially because the time and space that the parents and children spend together will decrease. This can lead to the children complaining about the church and their parents.

Second, you must educate your biological children beforehand, and let them know that they (and Abel-realm spiritual children) and the children of the tribe are in the position to restore the authority of the elder son. The best way to have the biological children (Abel children) understand about the parents' heavenly tribal messiah activities is to have them approach and relate directly with the spiritual siblings. When the biological children (and Abel-realm spiritual children) stand in the center of heavenly tribal messiah activities, they will come to experience Heavenly Parent's heart the most. I believe this is the best way to have them respect and understand their biological parents.

In conclusion, without the consent of the family, it is not possible to do heavenly tribal messiah activities for long. That is why the role of the biological children and Abel-realm spiritual children is important. It can become the formation of a great relationship to attend Heavenly Parent substantially in our families.

The method to welcome new members that was mentioned earlier is the best method. However, in the beginning stage, it should be a priority for at least the couple to be united. In the beginning stages you will begin to receive more strength and spiritual support when you can start to guide your spiritual children to participate in the activities with you. The biological children should at least clearly understand the reason for the parents' involvement in heavenly tribal messiah activities. It is wise in later stages, according to their level of maturity, to have them engage deeply in these activities.

1.4 Things to Note for Harmony in the Family

The following are lessons taken from interviews with families who have completed their heavenly tribal messiah missions, regarding how they were able to bring success.

① **The husband and wife first should become one, centered on the activities.** The era when people move and work as individuals is over. When the husband and wife work together, their witnessing contacts will be deeply moved and the spiritual children in particular will feel a sense of ease and relief. The focus of heavenly tribal messiahship is not one-on-one witnessing but for the family model to guide and lead the families of the tribe.

② **Have your biological children and Abel-realm spiritual children participate in activities, and have them take charge of some aspect of the activities, no matter how small.** Going beyond just the husband and wife, the biological children and Abel-realm spiritual children also participate. This is because the more your family as a whole takes part in activities, the more your tribe will trust you. It is good for biological children to participate in these activities together with you, from a young age, so that they get accustomed to them. Without the participation of your biological children, there will be a limit in how close the relationships between you and your spiritual children will become.

③ **Have a discussion concerning the activities during family meetings.** The family can become one through the process of discussing the activities, planning and dividing up roles. It is good for all the family members (including Abel-realm spiritual children) to naturally become members of the family ministry and develop a unified strategy. Therefore, responsibility and roles for the activities should be divided up among the family members.

④ **Refrain from allowing any disharmony within the family to be shown to the outside world.** The moment you start this family ministry, all the people around you will look at the actions of your family members. Negative behavior always will be noticed and talked about. This does not mean that you should act differently internally and externally. Controlling your anger leads you to the path to achieving morality, and having dominion over your thoughts is a way to cultivate your mind. In order to find ways to change any problematic stress practice changing your external environment or circumstances into some form of positive energy as a resolution method. As the central family of the tribe, your responsibility is vital, and as a model family, you should be good examples of heavenly tribal messiahs at all times.

⑤ **Devotedly follow the basics of a life of faith, including hoondokhae.** Heavenly tribal messiahship does not mean that you will achieve great providential results overnight. It means that you earn the respect and trust of the people around you through your basic life of faith. The training for this is done through the process of purifying the dark side of your heart through Heavenly Parent's and True Parents' teachings. In order for the Word to purify your heart, you must become more devout, practicing the Word in your everyday life. If all the members of your family carry out in real life the resolutions made through hoondokhae, all of you will grow closer to Heavenly Parent and True Parents. In the end, the purpose of heavenly tribal messiahship is for each member of the family and the tribe to experience substantially the process of resembling God based on the family.

> "If the family cannot harmonize,
> they cannot become a model."

Checklist for Your Family

1) How often does your family do hoondokhae?
   ① Every day ② Every other day ③ Twice a week ④ Once a week

2) How well does your family understand why you and your spouse are doing heavenly tribal messiah activities? (Pick the answer that is the average of the responses of the husband and the wife.)
   ① Very well ② They understand ③ So-so ④ They do not understand

3) How would you rate your family's willingness to do heavenly tribal messiah activities?
   ① 100 percent ready   ② More than 50 percent ready
   ③ Less than 50 percent ready   ④ Not ready

4) How well do your children understand the purpose of heavenly tribal messiah activities?
   ① Understand very well   ② Understand fairly well
   ③ So-so   ④ They do not understand at all

5) Do you have spiritual children? If yes, what kind of relationship do you have with them? (Calculate by taking the average of all your spiritual children together.)
   ① Parent–child relationship   ② Someone you witnessed to
   ③ Someone you are treating well   ④ You don't know them at all

6) How freely do your spiritual children visit you at home?
   ① Any time
   ② They come after letting us know they are coming
   ③ They only come if we invite them, otherwise they don't visit
   ④ They do not show up at all

7) What kind of relationship would you like to have between your family and your spiritual children?
   ① A parent–child relationship
   ② A relationship of faith
   ③ Help them out when needed
   ④ Like a close family member or sibling

8) What kind of relationship do your biological children have with your spiritual children? A relationship of
   ① Spiritual siblings ② Close relatives ③ Church members
   ④ Only close enough to exchange greetings

9) When you go out to do activities in your heavenly tribal messiah area, how well prepared are your biological and Abel realm spiritual children to work together with you (on average)?
   ① We are absolutely working together
   ② Might be possible if I persuade them
   ③ It will be difficult, even if I encourage them
   ④ I don't know

10) When you do heavenly tribal messiah activities, how do you prepare for financial issues?
   ① I can resolve these on my own
   ② I will work with my spiritual children to resolve them
   ③ I will look into it, starting now
   ④ I don't know

---

* If you have checked ① more than seven times, you are well prepared for heavenly tribal messiahship activities.
* If you have checked ② more than seven times, you just have to prepare a little more and you will do great!
* If you have checked ③ more than seven times, you should review your situation.
* If you have placed most of your checks on ④, a lot of jeongseong and reflection are necessary.

▼ Celebrating 50 years since the Furuta tribe met the Unification movement

Case Study: The Furuta Tribe in Japan

Motou and Kyoko Furuta (777 Couples) fulfilled their mission as heavenly tribal messiahs of the Furuta Tribe. This tribe's victory was possible due to the sincere dedication of Mr. Furuta's mother, Mrs. Mitsuko Furuta. When True Parents visited Nagoya during their First World Speaking Tour in 1965, Mrs. Furuta was so moved when she met True Parents directly, that she joined the church. She consistently conveyed the word to relatives and tribe members. As a result, she had 110 spiritual children before passing away at the age of 77 in 1996. Based on her absolute faith, her son, Motou Furuta, pursued tribal messiah activities and established a spiritual tribe up to the four great realms. Mrs. Furuta's absolute

▼ The Furuta family receiving special recognition from True Mother after completing their heavenly tribal messiah mission

faith toward God's Will became a model for all the families in the tribe, and her spiritual legacy is being passed down to the Furuta tribe's descendants today. Their tribe has produced four national messiah families, 36 church leader families and 12 second-generation leader families. In 2016, they accomplished the blessing of 430 couples, and currently in 2018, there is a total of 440 families in the Furuta tribe, including relatives and biological and spiritual children.

Section 2 The Pastor's Support

2.1 The Pastor and Heavenly Tribal Messiahship

The role of the pastor is crucial for blessed families to carry out their heavenly tribal messiah activities. Furthermore, the content and direction of the activities will differ, based on the pastor's leadership, so pastors have a responsibility to keep up with the ongoing changes in the mission in this new era.

    First, there is a need for change in how pastors relate with members. Until now, as pastors of the Family Federation, pastors focused on creating revival and development. However, from now on, they should actively support and work on developing members who can pursue heavenly tribal messiah activities. The pastors also, as a blessed members, should complete the heavenly tribal messiah mission. Furthermore, after retiring, they can come to be in the position to guide the heavenly tribal messiah family center, since all Cheon Il Guk citizens must establish hoondok family churches and heavenly tribes. They should think about the goal and direction of their church while taking into consideration this great providential flow. Furthermore, pastors should develop the ability to manage not just the church for which they are responsible but also the family centers that are pioneered by the heavenly tribal messiahs. This means that the abilities required of the pastor are now more extensive than ever.

Second, heavenly tribal messiahs should be absolutely united with their pastors and report regularly about what is happening in their heavenly tribal messiah activity. Based on this mutual trust, heavenly tribal messiahs should work at inherit pastoral skills for when they open and pioneer a family center later on.

Third, pastors should observe the standard of ministry of the blessed families in their region and gradually divide up roles in the ministry. A report with numbers should be presented monthly on the progress of heavenly tribe members becoming dedicated church members. The pastor, the local Family Federation members and the heavenly tribal messiah families should actively work and prepare so that, stage by stage, a heavenly tribal messiah pioneer family center can be established.

Fourth, if there is a heavenly tribal messiah family that has difficulty handling the ministry aspect, a biological child or Abel spiritual child from that tribe should fulfill that role. In order to do that, a few competent people should be selected and raised up through the pastors' training course.

In conclusion, we can say that the most important thing at this time is for the activities of the Family Federation chapter and heavenly tribal messiah center to harmonize appropriately.

2.2 The Role of the Pastor

As blessed families determine to fulfill the heavenly tribal messiah mission and begin actively working on it, the issue of how the local church pastor guides the activities of blessed families becomes important. As the heavenly tribal messiahs work to establish their own communities, they will need the cooperation and support of the headquarters and the pastor. Continental headquarters and national headquarters has been developing suitable policies for the missionary environment and situation of that nation. The Blessing activities, education and faith guidance of members will differ according to the leadership and course of action of the continental headquarters, national headquarters and pastor. There are several reasons for this. First, most blessed families have no experience with ministry. Second, there are differences in culture and in the church environment. Third, there is a difference in the level of faith and capabilities of the blessed families. The pastor of each region must analyze all these factors and prepare a management plan so that the blessed families in the region can carry out their activities. Pastors have to motivate people through their leadership and involvement, but if they do not have any experience, there will be many difficulties.

Blessed families have to attend their local church and, at the same time, find and establish their own community of spiritual children. However, members who do not have any experience in ministry inevitably will be confused in this situation. That is why the pastor, as the experienced one, should analyze the situation and get involved at the proper time to guide members to overcome their difficulties.

Pastors are responsible to help heavenly tribal messiahs in building their tribe by setting up pioneer branch churches (small groups) which they will work to multiply until it becomes a tribe. During this process, the attitude of the pastor is important. Pastors have to guide heavenly tribal messiahs with a firm heart so that they can pioneer their own branch church stage by stage. They should fully support the heavenly tribal messiahs' center until is it developed, be involved in the entire process until the tribe members become regular church members, and make a strong determination to ensure that the pioneer branch church can become self-reliant. In that process, the pastor should have the all-encompassing heart of parents that is willing to take on the main role. As we all know, the fact that a member establishes a pioneer church means that they have invested a lot of effort into it. If the pastor does not help them, it is easy for members to fight and give up. In this way, the role of the pastor is very important.

"The word must be spread everywhere in God's nation." According to True Parents' words, the church should be pioneered starting from the family to village units. The pastor has to support the pioneering of heavenly tribal messiahship from a long-term and holistic perspective.

On the one hand, the base of the members' lifestyle changes. There are times when they might move away to another region in the middle of pioneering one region. There are also situations in which the region that they are pioneering is not near their home but some other region where they have a connection. The reality is that witnessing is done centered on connections, so it is very difficult to change the region where people witness. Therefore, one region may be divided into many different areas. We predict an increase in cases of the pioneering regions being far from home or in different places. No matter what the situation is, the pastor should cooperate with other pastors to be aware of the pioneering situation of members, receive reports and actively support.

2.3 Branch Churches and Hoondok Family Churches

Blessed families should begin family church in their own homes. Centering on hoondokhae, the family church ministry can take root centered on the family. Then you can invite people from outside and gradually expand into a small group. True Parents have spoken about this from the beginning of the 1980s, calling it the "home church movement."

The current Family Federation is registered mainly as a religious or social institution, according to the cultural and legal background of the mission field and the general perception of the citizens and

Figure 2-1

society. However, in countries where there is a state religion or predominant religion, it is not possible to register a religious corporation. That is why legally the term "church" cannot be used. And even countries where religious freedom is guaranteed—for example, to non-Catholics and citizens who believe in other religions—there is religious resistance. That is why there is no risk in using the term "center," which is neutral and holds various meanings. The term to be used for the public can be decided in accordance with the continental headquarters so that it is suitable for the situation of the mission field. Therefore, members can begin ministry with an appropriate term for the public.

A heavenly tribal messiah family center is much like a church which exists for a small ministry in that it is a public space where a family environment can be created, while fulfilling the role of a branch church of the church to which they belong. If the conditions and environment of the place are inadequate, you may use a community hall or other public space. The heavenly tribal messiah family center ultimately should provide a public space where spiritual children and that region's blessed families can gather and live a grass-roots life of faith. Therefore, it means expanding the base where Heavenly Parent can be present officially. When a blessed family opens a pioneer church, which fulfills the role of a heavenly tribal messiah family center as a grass-roots organization, the family can settle long term with a Family Federation branch church.

No matter what field it is, pioneering is not easy. We see many instances in which pioneering ends in failure. In order to prevent failure in pioneering, support is important. That role needs to be shouldered by the regional church. Therefore, the family center pioneered by the heavenly tribal messiahs and the Family Federation regional and local churches should establish a proper relationship. This will be made possible by dividing up the ministerial and administrative roles between the regional church's pastor and the heavenly tribal messiah.

Furthermore, pioneer churches also face financial difficulties. It is ideal if the blessed families and spiritual children belonging to the tribe can support the center that is run by the heavenly tribal messiah (spiritual parents) with manpower and materials. When the center goes past the beginning stages of pioneering, it should focus on growth to normalize the functions of the ministry (Sunday service, meetings, events, education, counseling, hoondokhae, etc.). The family center is a small space, so it should actively make use of support from the local church (space, materials). In order for all this support to be possible and effective, the local church first has to attain a steady size.

2.4 Things to Note When Reporting

The way for pastors and heavenly tribal messiahs to be publicly connected is through reporting. The heavenly tribal messiah should report to the pastor first. Next we will discuss some things to note when heavenly tribal messiahs are pioneering the family center and how they should report to the pastor of the local church.

① All activities should be reported. As a public act, reporting means that the one who is reporting is in the public system. Reporting means that you let the pastor, who is in charge of the local church and who is in the Family Federation's line of report, know about your activities in general. There are various ways to report, but you can simply follow the policies set up by your respective continental and national headquarters. You must report to your pastor thoroughly about your heavenly tribal messiah activities and receive direction, interest, support and advice. This is because if you do not report, you cannot be connected to God and you cannot receive God's spiritual protection and True Parents' direction. The heavenly tribal messiah's center becomes official through reporting.

② The traditional ceremonies of the Family Federation are officiated by pastors who have received the Family Federation's official certificate of appointment. For a ministry, the most important thing is carrying out these ceremonies. These ceremonies in the Family Federation must be officiated by a church leader. For all ministry functions apart from these ceremonies, you can follow the policies of your continental and national headquarters. Heavenly tribal messiahs can carry out all other ministerial functions according to the policies, but only the church pastor has the authority to officiate the benediction for the Blessing. Whenever you hold a Blessing, the benediction has to be given by a current church pastor. It is mandatory for the pastor to officiate the ceremonies of the Family Federation, such as the benediction for heavenly tribal messiah Blessings, dedication ceremonies for second-generation children and buildings and Seonghwa ceremonies for blessed family members. The pastor has full authority in carrying out these ceremonies.

Section 3 Cooperation from Members

3.1 How to Overcome the Limitations of Members

It is not easy to maintain ongoing heavenly tribal messiahship activities with just the strength of one member or one family. This is because the process of establishing a tribe includes managing the guests, the Blessing ceremony and education after the Blessing, and this may require a lot of manpower. It is inevitable that there will be a limit to one family's capabilities in shouldering the responsibility for this whole process. Therefore, blessed families who are starting out the heavenly tribal messiah mission should divide up the work among themselves and become a source of strength for each other. Members can join forces and begin activities together, or someone who already has begun can cooperate with members and guide them. That is the reason for members joining forces and working together.

If we look at nations where heavenly tribal messiah activities are carried out actively, we can see that they have used a system of active cooperation. For example, blessed members still in the beginning stages of their heavenly tribal messiah mission would actively participate in Blessing Ceremonies and other events as part of the staff. They were also actively involved in the counseling and education of newly blessed members who are in the process of growing their faith. This cooperation among members was one of the keys to their success. Ultimately, this is similar to when parents cooperate in co-parenting because raising a child is difficult. Co-parenting can be a way for members who have limited capabilities to fulfill their mission as heavenly tribal messiahs more smoothly. Therefore, members should distinguish between co-parenting and individual parenting and divide up the roles among the members. In the field, the domain of co-parenting and the domain of heavenly tribal messiah individual parenting should be distinguished, and activities should be carried out accordingly. We have observed that those who have completed their heavenly tribal messiah mission successfully very carefully divided up and assigned activities to be done by the church or other members and tribe unit activities to be done together with their children. This means that even those who have completed their heavenly tribal messiah mission can get involved in other members' activities and give and receive support. In this way, those members who are in the very busy stages are able to manage the areas in which they need extra help. When we look carefully, we see that behind the success of any one family, there was a lot of help from other blessed families.

3.2 Theory of the Trinity

"Home group" is the term that was created to facilitate smooth cooperation among members. There is a need for systematic and administrative management of activities. This is because it is not easy for one blessed family to take care of 430 blessed families at the same time. Furthermore, it may take some time for the members of the tribe to become ready to cooperate for heavenly tribal messiah activities. That is why cooperation among blessed central members becomes very important. Even if you want to create a system for new members, if their level of faith is not yet mature, it is not easy to completely delegate much responsibility to them. Small group leaders may play the middle-man role within the tribe, but while they are still at a developing stage, they are limited. That is why, more recently, we have been using the term "home group" to refer to a small group of members who gather together. The home group system can be implemented in various ways to suit the situation of the mission field, but the most basic method is to have three persons support each other closely by forming a trinity. This trinity can be used in many different ways. For example, there can be trinities of members who are in the beginning stage of their heavenly tribal messiah mission, trinities among the newly blessed families within a tribe, trinities based on location, trinities based on roles, etc. A trinity system can be applied to various situations according to the goal. This will be discussed in more detail in Chapter 4: Maintaining a Healthy Tribal Community.

3.3 Division of Roles in the Trinity

If we look at True Parents' words, the concept of "trinity" encompasses the harmony of *cheon* (heaven), *ji* (earth) and *in* (people). *Ji*, meaning earth, also refers to the creation. If we think about *cheon*, *ji* and *in* as they relate to handling the work of the mission, *cheon* refers to handling God's work—in other words, conveying Heavenly Parent's Word and Will. It refers to the religious, spiritual and educational tasks. *In* refers to people, so it includes the work of gathering people, aligning them, training them and bringing them to unite. *Ji*, referring to the creation, means managing the economic work of the mission.

With this kind of meaning, we can say that from the perspective of the origin of creation, the trinity includes the three kinds of important tasks that exist in the world. The following paragraphs explain what it would look like if this perspective were applied to a trinity in the heavenly tribal messiah mission.

First, the families in the trinity form close ties and divide up the roles. Everybody keeps the basic principles of a successful community —interdependency (*gong saeng*), mutual prosperity (*gong yeong*) and universally shared values (*gong eui*)—as the background as they pursue their various areas of responsibility. The principle is for each person to take on a different task, and together they can naturally move toward one goal. This means there is a person responsible for religion and education, another person responsible for public and interpersonal relations, and lastly one person responsible for finances.

Second, the trinity establishes a foundation of jeongseong in setting a common goal and dividing up the roles. This contributes to the revival and development of the community. Everyone has a different role in the trinity, but centering on one goal at the same time, they should unite completely. Standing in the same position, they should move forward, helping, supporting and comforting each other. The one responsible for religion and education stands in the domain of ministry and therefore educates the guests with True Parents' words and focuses on their spiritual growth. The one responsible for public and interpersonal relations should reach out to and liaise with related organizations and VIPs in the area to find persons who can stand in the position of John the Baptist, creating the environment for witnessing. The one responsible for finances should resolve financial issues within the community and plan for ways to live a life of collaboration. If the trinity families in the field can display their expertise in their respective areas of responsibility and carry out activities, the process of establishing a tribe and the process of co-parenting will go smoothly. Furthermore, trinities will be established within the tribe and go through the same process of dividing up the work, so establishing a tribe will go smoothly.

Among the members of your tribe, find four persons who can work in each area of responsibility and establish a foundation to maintain the development of the tribe community. When you set up this kind of system, from there new amazing things will happen. True Parents have said that even if enemies try to attack tribe members, if three families are completely united, Satan's attacks will be repelled. Therefore, strengthening the system centering on a trinity is essential and necessary.

If we look at the process, it is a trinity, but the outcome is the four-position foundation. When three people become one, in the end one more person comes into being as the result, thus perfecting the number four and establishing the four-position foundation. If three families each establish trinities in their area of responsibility and complete those four-position foundations, this ultimately comes to be 12 families. In other words, if trinities in each area expand their foundation and establish four families each so that they can cover all four directions of north, south, east, and west, we have three families expanding into 12 families. Therefore, there will be four families in the religious area, four families in the social area, and four families in the financial area, establishing a total of 12 families.

3.4 Strategy to Establish Trinities

However, it seems that some members think the trinity system is very complicated. Below we have extracted helpful information on establishing trinities from people who have completed their heavenly tribal messiah mission.

① **Look for a trinity around you.** When members first determine to do heavenly tribal messiah activities, they look for people very far away or very carefully and seriously to be a part of their trinity. However, if we look at cases of people who have completed their heavenly tribal messiah mission, we can see that they began carrying out activities with people around them to whom they were close. It is important, in the beginning stage of your activities, to find the trinity prepared for you by God. The potential members of your trinity are not far away. Like iron being pulled to a magnet, they are nearby. There are surely members prepared by God near you. If you cannot find any members, you also can look among your Abel-realm spiritual children. If you still cannot find anyone, you have to find them among your co-workers and their families. If you don't have co-workers, you have no choice but to go at it alone. However, God already has made plans and preparations, so you surely will find people who will cooperate with you. By carrying out activities together with your trinity, you can rely on each other, lessen the burden and keep challenging yourselves.

② **Decide on a goal with the three families united and offer jeongseong.** God said that when three people unite and pray, He will answer the prayer. Therefore, through your trinity, God's

Will can be realized. It is important for the trinity, who are the central families, to first lead by example and offer jeongseong. A trinity is not just a cooperation system among members; it is the basic unit of all groups. Within the tribe as well, it is the basic unit for establishing a community, so everything must be open and transparent, and members within the trinity must become one in heart. What is most important is not just the union of people but establishing a heartistic union of people who attend Heavenly Parent at the center.

③ The three families divide up the roles. The roles must be divided into three areas: education (religion), interpersonal relations (politics), and society and finances (economy). If the roles are not divided, there is no meaning to having a group of three families. They must become one centered on a common goal, but each must take on roles in different areas. The family responsible for the area of education will lead the trinity. The central family is the one that is responsible for religion, spirituality and education.

④ They naturally should develop a close friendship and become one. In the beginning, do not emphasize only providential tasks. It will be good, in the long run, if you first try to become one by freely sharing your heart centering on the word. Establishing a family center and a tribe is a lifelong task, so your trinity will become your comrades for life. Therefore, you should share family matters great and small and remain comrades for life.

When you begin as a heavenly tribal messiah, it is difficult to lay a foundation on your own. There is a limit, in terms of lifestyle, because you have to bring your kids with you and in terms of your living area as well. It is the life of a refugee. Therefore, if your trinity has a house, at least you can eat porridge together and live together. That is how you begin. It is difficult for just one person to do it, so I am telling you to gather three people like brothers and work together. These three brothers decide on a direction, whether it be north, south, west or east, and see which one will be easier to break through; centering on that goal, carry out education. After that, expand so that 12 people can work on it as well. Instead of just one person laying the foundation, have three people or 12 people come together and lay the foundation one by one, and move forward like that. If you keep doing this, the time will come when everything will be swept up at once. [219-210, August 29, 1991]

The Kalisin Trininty in Thailand

Sangkom Netsopa (joined the church in 1991, blessed in 1995), Payungsuri (joined the church in 1990, blessed in 1992) and Walapon (joined the church in 1999, blessed in 2007) are from the Putai tribe in the Kalasin region of Thailand. Sangkom is the director of the HQ Family Department, and Payungsuri is a professional lecturer and responsible for education. Walapon is responsible for the finances (in charge of business). They have divided up their roles in this way. These three families have cooperated together and have maintained a very close relationship up to today. They work together at the Headquarters, but they also carry out activities in their hometown of Kalasin. They especially have led the Blessing movement extensively in Kalasin. They said that when their three families came together in August 2013 and decided to restore Kalasin through heavenly tribal messiah activities, they never imagined that the

Netsopa's family, Payungsuri's family, Walapon's family (from left)

Blessing would expand and spread this much. When they first began, they were just three families, but currently in Kalasin there are 21 families in total who have completed their mission of 430 couples. The following is a testimony from Director Sangkom.

"At that time, we each did our best in our respective roles, holding on to the desire to restore our hometown. At that time, we didn't even know that the term 'trinity' existed, but maybe God had already prepared our three families. If we did not have this foundation of a trinity, we would not have been able to accomplish the 430-couple heavenly tribal messiahship and would not have been able to establish the management system that we currently have." After this trinity was started, many members from both inside and outside Thailand have helped out and local administrative officers have actively cooperated. This all began from the prayer and determination of these three families.

Section 4 Building the Culture

4.1 The Power of Culture

Human beings are social beings, and there is an inherent culture in society. We can say that culture is the sum of values and symbolic icons shared by people. In a society where people live, cultures are formed naturally and are passed down. Therefore, the culture of the society you belong to prevents confusion of personal values, helps people interact mutually and facilitates personal decision-making.

Whereas culture can have a positive aspect, as mentioned above, it also can have a negative impact. This is because, with regard to growth and development, when one era ends and a new era comes to be, the cultural paradigm that cannot be accommodated in the new culture gets shut out. The old culture can act as a great wall when it is time for the new culture to be introduced. For example,

North Korea, which has a closed-off culture, is isolated from the international community and cannot accept a new culture. This kind of example can be found in many countries and regions with isolated religions. It is important to protect the indigenous culture and values of a people and country, but when a culture is faced with change and still hangs on to the past and does not have the cultural values that can embrace the world's people, that culture will perish.

The same applies to the Family Federation. We can say that, through heavenly tribal messiahship, our churches have expanded, pioneering and establishing educational programs and a culture of settlement. Through the power of this culture, members of the church easily implemented heavenly tribal messiah activities. However, if we are too busy managing the currently existing system of members without taking time to invest in the expansion and pioneering of the church, we will be limited.

Right now, there is a new paradigm, bringing about great change in the church, while the fourth industrial revolution is exerting a sweeping change on the world around us. The Family Federation of today is confronting many barriers in the social climate and obstacles in its activities and resources. In the mission fields where these walls have been broken down, a dynamic culture is being established. Just as the way we give and receive information has changed due to new information and communication technology, the method for witnessing also is changing. Therefore, it is important for our church community to change our methods for activities according to the changing reality and establish an environment suited to that change.

This also applies to the pastor's way of running the church. Whereas in the past, one pastor was in charge of one church, now it is possible to have a multidimensional model in which several pastors are responsible for several churches or several members are pioneering several areas. Therefore, we urgently need a new perspective on the identity of the church and a new ministry leadership model.

In the current society, church growth appears to be difficult and complicated. This can be a crisis for church communities, but at the same time, it also can be an opportunity. If you make the right adjustments to fit the direction of change, what was seen as limitations in the past can become advantages. One such example is that now we can use social media to reach out to guests as we like, even though they are far away and we can take care of several guests at once.

People who have the same interests naturally come to form a network and share information, and through this they come to accept the developed culture. That is why, in order to complete our heavenly tribal messiah mission, members who are carrying out activities need an active network. They need to meet and exchange information. It is only natural that this kind of network be established centering on members who are working hard to carry out activities. From now on, a culture of activity, movement and messiahship for world salvation must take root in the church community for the sake of completing the heavenly tribal messiah mission. True Parents are earnestly waiting for members to become owners of Cheon Il Guk, step out of the passive culture and establish an activity-oriented culture.

4.2 Activity-Oriented Culture and a Witnessing Community

Essential for the successful completion of the heavenly tribal messiah mission is building a witnessing-oriented and activity-oriented culture around ourselves. The stronger the influence of the culture, the easier it will be to carry out activities. Until now, we have been witnessing while receiving social pressure (primarily using a one-to-one approach to witnessing in the field). However, community witnessing (group witnessing) refers to making use of the strength of society. It is important to think about how we will establish connections to the people tackling society's issues (John the Baptist figures), how the Family Federation can make a principled approach fit for their culture, connect them with the pioneer family center and offer them education and the Blessing.

We have to consistently share information about the providential value of heavenly tribal messiahship and the direction of our activities with the people around us (current church leaders, people who have completed their heavenly tribal messiah mission, our Abel-realm spiritual children, biological children, blessed central members). It is especially good for symbolic items, tools, materials, etc., to be allocated and shared around. Make it possible for those who have completed the heavenly tribal messiah mission to testify about their meetings and their progress every Sunday during the service. Each church should have the vision to establish a pioneer center, and a culture of offering jeongseong and prayer together.

4.3 Building a Culture

In recent times, the Family Federation has been facing a great turning point in culture. One such phenomenon can be seen in the growth of our activities in Asia and Africa. A positive, activity-oriented culture—in which the motto "It will work out if we just do it" is a reality—is being established. There is a reason for the explosive growth of the heavenly tribal messiah movement in Asia and Africa. It is being carried out with the active cooperation of the community's leadership. This is a great change when compared to the providential history in the past. IAPP (International Association of Parliamentarians for Peace) and UPF (Universal Peace Federation) bring their contacts to participate in the ALC (Asian Leadership Conference) organized by the continental headquarters, where couples receive Divine Principle education. In Africa, there is education for representatives of religious denominations to learn the Divine Principle. The guests who attend these seminars are asked to participate in local activities within each of their own countries within the continent. They are people in leadership positions who influence the country and community. They have been moved by the Divine Principle and True Parents' life course, have changed their attitude, and now are actively supporting us in our activities. They return to their countries and support the members who are doing heavenly tribal messiah activities. They therefore participate in these events, testify about True Parents and lecture about the meaning and value of the Blessing at the Blessing ceremony. A culture in which government ministers, members of parliament, governors and provincial leaders are taking on the mission of John the Baptist has been established according to the plans of the continental headquarters. Furthermore, because of their influence these people can mobilize the nation and community and help us find and gather good families. Through this, the heavenly tribal messiah movement is taking root as a new culture for blessed families. It is considered an interfaith movement with the same values as the pure love movement, true family movement and peace movement.

Furthermore, the culture of the blessed families is changing gradually. In the past, when someone joined the church, they were left completely in the care of the church. However, now the loving care that members give their spiritual children is stronger. They are concerned about their future and their descendants and try to do witnessing from a long-term perspective. However, currently we have a culture in which three blessed families form a trinity and start out by helping the family with the greatest foundation in the area to achieve success. Then the two other families help each other out and complete their heavenly tribal messiah missions as well. A mature culture is being created in which all the local church members mobilize and help out during the heavenly tribal messiah education and Blessing ceremonies. The ultimate goal of the providence is the salvation of the entire world. Therefore, to separate and think only of your spiritual children and not those of other families is not the true culture that God desires to see.

"You must brighten your surroundings!"

4.4 Things to Note When Building a Culture

① **Unite centering on an experienced person (someone who has completed the heavenly tribal messiah mission).** Advice from an experienced person will be greatly empowering to you. When members who do not have an experience go out and try, it is easy for them to repeat the same mistakes in the process. This is because it is not easy to persuade another person to change their way of thinking. Therefore, in order to get results, you need many environmental conditions, wisdom, manpower, materials. It can be realized only when you are aligned with Heavenly Parent and True Parents' paradigm of the era and when there is an explosion of jeongseong. Therefore, the guidance of an experienced person is important to minimize trial and error. It is very important to listen to the advice and field study of the experienced person.

② **Utilize social media and maintain a close relationship.** People who are carrying out activities can experience difficulties at any moment. The outcome can vary greatly, depending on how you respond in that moment. That is why the experienced person's advice plays a big role. So in this case, you can get an immediate response if you use social media to communicate. It is important to actively use WeChat, WhatsApp, KakaoTalk, LINE or other social media and resolve these real problems immediately, so you can move on.

③ **Maintain a continuous relationship by centering on hoondok words.** The word is a cane that protects me. It is the record of True Parents' victory after having fought billions of Satans. The path of a heavenly tribal messiah is lonely, but you must be able to win over yourself by reading True Parents' record of victory. There will be times when there is no one to rely on or you face financial challenges or you are misunderstood and persecuted by society. However, by reading True Parents' record of victory, you will understand their heart and what they had to go through. God will be with you and give you wisdom to deal with your problems.

④ **When you cannot gain any energy from people within the church, meet with the prepared John the Baptist figure.** Even though blessed families are like treasures, if they are not connected to their own achievements, they will not be able to take initiative and lead by example. This is an advantage of the Family Federation's system for spiritual children, but it also can be a disadvantage. This is because they fall into self-centeredness when they see that there is nothing in it for them, instead of thinking about God's nation's commandment to witness to all corners of the earth. That is why in the Bible it says, "Your enemies will be right in your own household." [Matthew 10:35–36] There are times when your family members will not cooperate, but when the blessed families in the church who have been appointed as Abels do not help you in times of desperate need, you feel that you have hit the limit. Therefore, first you should frequently communicate with your pastor and give updates. Second, you should transmit information on a daily basis to support and inspire other blessed families around you who also can engage in heavenly tribal messiah activities. The blessed families who are pursuing the path of heavenly tribal messiahship must walk a model path for others to follow.

◥ Counseling second-generation members

Lee Gye-hyeong and Kang Deok-rye's family who used social media

I am Kang Deok-rye, and I am part of the 1,800 couples Blessing. I am very grateful for my spiritual children. This is because they are the driving force for creating our family and tribe. My spiritual children call me by the nickname "Mapo Omma" (Mapo Mom). This was in order for us to feel closer to and more intimate with each other. Every morning I read the *Cheon Seong Gyeong*, find a good paragraph, type it out and send it as a message to my spiritual children and tribe through KakaoTalk and social media. They see it instantly at 5:00 in the morning. There were times when I typed and sent long text messages, and my shoulders would be in a lot of pain.

It is always very rewarding when I combine True Parents' love and my jeongseong. and send out the message conveying my heart of "Let's start

◥ A workshop for second-generation tribe members

the day together with the word." Through doing this, my spiritual children receive the word every morning, and it became a good way to create a hoondokhae boom. The reason why I send these words to them consistently is because, just as the Bible verse states, "Man shall not live by bread alone, but by every word that proceedeth out of the mouth of God, [Matthew 4:4]" children need not only physical food but also spiritual food so that they do not succumb to temptation.

Among my spiritual children there are ten central families, and I communicate with them often. I convey to them True Parents' words and all the news from church, and we are pushing forward with many different projects. They then communicate with the spiritual siblings around them and share the grace. Through this kind of communication system, we connect to a channel of love and heart and live together with one another. I truly feel that when spiritual children see how hard their spiritual parents are working, they have no choice but to follow them.

❋ Discussion Topics

1) Can you describe your current heavenly tribal messiah activities?

2) If there is someone who is doing heavenly tribal messiah activities, have you tried to talk to that person?

3) If you cannot find anyone around you to talk with, what would you like your local church center to do to support you?

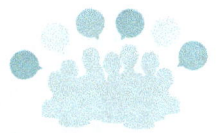

Chapter 3

Formation of a Tribe

Testimony by the Ronachit blessed central family from Kalasin Province, Thailand

My name is Ronachit Puttala, and I am the county governor of Kalasin Province, Thailand. Kalasin is my hometown, and I have been its county governor for a long time. I recently found out about the activities of the Family Federation, became interested in its teachings, received the Blessing and took part in various events. The teachings by

◀ Ronachit Puttala and his wife receive a gift from True Mother.

▼ Governor Ronachit Puttala greets gathered members

True Parents about the family are truly amazing. I met True Mother in Korea and was deeply impressed by her benevolence. I feel that the Family Federation is an organization that is crucial to the Kalasin Province. I was also very impressed by the passion of Family Federation members and am still playing an active role to this day. The message that the Family Federation for World Peace advocates really struck a chord with me. Moving forward, I will participate where I can and think about where I can offer a helping hand. Further, the members of the Family Federation do not completely understand the residents of Kalasin, so in this respect, I believe they are in need of my help. The members' passion and idea of living for the sake of others are all outstanding on their own. But, since I have been working as the county governor for a long duration, I know the ins and outs of this region very well and can be of great service. In any capacity, I would like to support the activities of the Family Federation to help them take root in my town, and to better the lives of residents. I would like to offer glory and gratitude to Heavenly Parent and True Parents for this opportunity.

Introductory Questions

"

What activities should precede having spiritual children or expanding my tribe?

If my activities came to a stop, what could be the cause of this?
How could I overcome this issue?

Of what significance are my witnessing contacts to me, and how do they see me?

"

Section 1 Creating a Spiritual Environment

1.1 Hoondokhae

We should live a lifestyle in which we begin each day with sincere reporting. It is crucial that one is imbued with a passion for witnessing. But the motivation should not begin with me but with Heavenly Parent. Our activities will bear fruit when our will is one with the Will of Heavenly Parent.

Next, it is best to start the day filled with True Parents' words from a hoondokhae session, and wrap up the day, after returning home in the evening, with another hoondokhae session. Activity is not accomplished with knowledge, but rather requires physical movement. When one becomes impassioned by the word, one can transcend reason and take part in God's work.

Unless you have passion that comes from being inspired by the

Word, you will be unable to encourage others to listen to the Word. Therefore, for blessed families to realize the heart of the Heavenly Parent, the providential significance of the True Parents, they must have the regular habit of hoondokhae. Just as one eats three meals a day for sustenance of the physical body, one must engage in hoondokhae morning and evening to nourish the spirit. This also will help to unite your mind and body so that you can live in vertical high-noon alignment without casting any shadow.

(1) The Significance of Hoondokhae

First, hoondokhae is taking the Word and making it flow like water. Therefore, the Word must be conveyed to those around you. When looking at the etymology of the word hoondok, it is composed of a Chinese character that includes the character for "speech" (言) and has the "river" (川) character on the side. The Word flowing along the river means that God's Word is like flowing water. The Word should not become a burden and be left to sink, but should be allowed to flow. The more it flows, the more momentum the Word gathers, and one's results form a large river or a great conquering army. The characters for *dok* (讀) include the character for "speech" (言) and the character for "sell" (賣). This means it is not something that is to be kept but rather is to be given to others. If you give the Word to 1,000 people, those people will never be at a loss. This is an eternal retail business.

Second, hoondokhae creates a standard for our lives, and it

becomes a mirror that reflects our lives. A life lived fulfilling one's duties of loyalty and filial piety, of saints in the world, and dedicated to building the kingdom of God on earth and in heaven is truly a precious life indeed. Each person must have a family standard in place to prevent a deviation from that standard. Going back to the garden of Eden, you would find it to be a place granted by and under the direct sovereignty of God. That is why hoondokhae was started to inherit the traditions of True Parents.

The words of hoondokhae are records of the victories of True Parents, and they include records of that victorious tradition. Until the cosmic liberation is attained, by applying such traditions to our lives we will be able to reflect on our lives on our own every day, and through hoondokhae we can realize our mistakes. Whatever the case, if we made a mistake, we must rectify that mistake by setting an indemnity condition centered on the family.

Third, hoondokhae is a tradition of the Unification Church that allows us to inherit and pass down the Word. The mother and father must set the example. Children who see their mother and father joyfully anticipating the start of hoondokhae will say, "We also should learn what our mother and father are learning." That way, one's family will be on the right path. Sons and daughters must be taught the traditions.

(2) The Methods of Hoondokhae

Messages that you feel are important or that make you want to ask questions should become your guideline in life. When doing hoondok, do not read the texts by yourself alone, but do it with a group of people and read the texts out loud. One person reads a page and calls out the next person to read the next page. Then the person who is called reads on. This is the tradition that should be established. The texts you felt were important or raised questions in your mind should become the guideline in your life.

One good strategy for hoondokhae is having the participants call out the next person to read the text. Then one-third of all the participants—meaning three persons, if there were ten persons in total—should ask questions afterward. If there is not enough time, fewer people can be selected to ask questions, and someone with knowledge can provide answers. This is more valuable than any lecture. Once a text is read from cover to cover three times, the meaning of its messages will be crystal-clear.

(3) The Reasons to Establish Hoondok Family Centers (Hoondok Family Church) Based on the Tradition of Family Hoondokhae

Premise: In the past, hoondok family church referred to holding a hoondokhae or worship service in a family. Today the scope of hoondok family church also includes the tribe. However, the term "center" is used more often around the globe than the word "church." Moreover, the word "church" has its limit in today's age of Family Federation. That is why the church in hoondok family church should be replaced with the center, and a hoondokhae within a family that is described in the following texts will be called family hoondokhae.

> You must unite with the victorious Messiah and sow the seeds of true life. This type of seed must be sowed within the family. Mother and the siblings are those seeds. That is the place where the ideal true love and true life of original Adam and Eve, who did not fall, began. I proclaimed the start of tribal messiah work in order to form that kind of families. [235-111, 1992.08.29]

> You have parents. You have your son, and you have all things. However, Adam lost all three of these things when he fell. These three things have to be reclaimed all at once and be offered back to God. The lost things must be returned to God first, and we have to inherit them from the parents. Only then will you be able to own your house and your own world. The foundation for this is family hoondokhae. This family hoondokhae should expand to the scope of tribe in order to form a hoondok family center (hoondok family church). [101-339, 1978.11.12]

(4) Indemnifying the Ideal of the Family Which is the Microcosm of World-Level Indemnification

The purpose of a hoondok family center (hoondok family church) is first to inherit the world-level indemnification course that has been walked by True Parents, who had to indemnify the failures of the children. The second purpose is to indemnify and restore the tribal realm of the Messiah that was lost by Jesus, and advance the messianic realm from tribe to nation, and finally, to the world.

> There is no advancement without indemnifying these two things. To resolve this, we have to go through hoondok family center (hoondok family church). No one can get to heaven without going through the hoondok family center. It is through your own hoondok family center that your tribe must shed sweat, blood, and tears, and receive persecution. Through this, you must understand the painful course that the Parents had to experience. You must understand that it is the task of the parents to do their best not to pass on their course of suffering to their children.
> [142-307, 1986.03.13]

(5) A Tribal Messiah Must Embrace Both Cain and Abel Types

A tribal messiah must embrace both Cain and Abel types. He must embrace his own tribe members and the Cain-type members. This is the case with the family of Joseph and the family of Zachariah from Jesus' point of view. The failure of these two families to unite led to the crucifixion of Jesus. We need family hoondokhae and hoondok family center (hoondok family church) based on the tribe. It is as if Jesus is standing tall, based on the foundation of unity between the families of Joseph and Zachariah. A nation can be restored if the people attend that tribal messiah and, furthermore, the national messiah.

That is why family hoondokhae should be established first in your Abel-type family. Then it can form the foundation for the tribal messiah who can unite the Abel-type tribe members and the Cain-type tribe members. Only then can the mission of a tribal messiah be considered finished. The Family Federation does not disappear simply because it has appointed tribal messiahs. The Family Federation will be required even after the billions of people are restored. It will be required until the day our minds and bodies are unified.

(6) The Stages of Forming a Hoondok Family Center and Tribal Messiah

Me (Individual Model) — Family (Family Model) — Tribe (Tribal Restoration) — Nation (National Restoration) — World

A hoondok family center has three stages of growth: from me as an individual to the family and then to the tribe. It signifies the stages of formation, growth, and perfection. A nation cannot be formed without tribes. Since a nation can be formed from tribes, we began our hoondok family center movement with the title of tribal messiah. This is the beginning of the kingdom of heaven. Then where will you be able to meet True Parents? You can meet them in a hoondok family center.

You must understand that Heaven is formed within you. If there is Heaven for your heart, there should be Heaven for your body as well. Your hoondok family center, or Heaven at the family level, can truly be formed when there is Heaven for the physical body. A heavenly environment cannot be obtained unless you can say that there is Heaven in both your heart and your body. When we say environment, it is the foundation of the hoondok family center that can connect you to the nation and to the entire world.

1.2 Meaning of Jeongseong

What is jeongseong? It is the basis for the unity of our mind and body, which is necessary because when we are in a group as a tribe and are not just individuals, all tribe members must unite with the heavenly tribal messiah so that we also can unite at the same focal point with Heavenly Parent and True Parents. Why do we need to offer jeongseong? It is because human beings came to have two separate minds due to the Fall. Before the Fall, human beings were united with Heavenly Parent in a parent–children relationship in which they could exchange questions and answers and interact with one another without any problems. Therefore, the Fall refers to the severance of communication between Heavenly Parent and humankind. Then how can we start communicating with Him again? We first need to study the condition by which Heavenly Parent can communicate with humankind. This condition is that Heavenly Parent embodies only goodness. Human beings, on the other hand, embody both goodness and evil. That is why Heavenly Parent cannot approach human beings. If Heavenly Parent were to enter a human being who embodies both goodness and evil, He would become a Being who created evil. Heavenly Parent can enter and work only through a person who embodies goodness. His own structure dictates this.

Therefore, our meeting with Heavenly Parent depends on us human beings alone, for there are no problems on His end. In other words, it becomes possible to meet Him when we maintain a state of 100 percent goodness by offering jeongseong. For this reason, the effectiveness and results of offering jeongseong depend on the questions "Why are we offering jeongseong? Centering on whom are we offering jeongseong? Are we offering jeongseong after emptying our minds and entrusting everything to Heavenly Parent?"

Fallen human beings cannot do anything without the cooperation of Heavenly Parent and the spirit world. Offering jeongseong regularly can be said to be the most basic thing in our lives. The second basic thing is to lead a strict life of reporting, thus creating a spiritual environment in which Heavenly Parent and the spirit world can work. The present is a time when all blessed families live with the realization that they are united with the spirit world. And when a blessed family is on the same level as the spirit world, the spirit world will work through that family 100 percent. The important thing is for us to work and to live our lives with a sense of responsibility so that offering jeongseong is almost as natural as breathing, so that we can be at the same focal point as Heavenly

Parent and miracles can be wrought. Once we achieve that, the spirit world will cooperate with us 100 percent. What is the hope of the spirit world? It is to realize the kingdom of heaven on earth, for only then can Cheon Il Guk be realized. Therefore, the spirit world must give support and work miracles to bring about the kingdom of heaven on earth, since it can dream of realizing the ideal of the kingdom of heaven only on the foundation of the actualized kingdom of heaven on earth. That is why miracles will take place when we are at the focal point. Just as you can start a fire by focusing sunlight through a magnifying glass onto a piece of paper, if you focus yourself in front of Heavenly Parent at a point where the spirit world can cooperate with you, a fire will be started at that very place. How delighted and grateful should you be about this? How could you possibly sit still and make no effort at all, if you live with this realization? You need to become people who report to and work together with Heavenly Parent and offer jeongseong every day. You have to make it a habit to begin each new day by offering prayers and jeongseong. filling yourselves with hoondok words, and renewing yourselves both physically and mentally.

(1) Types of Jeongseong

① Prayer Jeongseong

This is a method of making an appeal to Heavenly Parent in which you set the number of times to pray each day and make a list of things to pray about, such as your place of activity, the people you are to meet, John the Baptist figures, your Abel-realm spiritual children and the tribe members of the heavenly tribal messiah, and pray while picturing the subject of your prayer.

② Bowing Jeongseong

This is a method of offering jeongseong by setting a numerical condition to offer a certain number of bows a day. You can offer jeongseong in various ways befitting your current condition and the situation at hand. For example, you may offer one bow for each of your spiritual children, or if there is an upcoming event, you may set up a plan of offering 40 bows a day until the date of the event to accumulate spiritual energy.

③ Fasting Jeongseong

This method of offering jeongseong involves setting a numerical number for fasting, which can be breakfast fasting or one-day fasting or three-day fasting or seven-day fasting, and is accompanied by the offering of prayers. The members of a tribe may participate together—for instance, carrying out a breakfast fast in relay.

④ Other Forms of Jeongseong

Early morning prayer meeting, holy ground prayer meeting, praying after a cold shower, jeongseong through hoondokhae, participating in the praise session at a CheongPyeong workshop, etc.

> "It is not I who is doing this, but Heavenly Parent."

1.3 Cooperation between the Spiritual and Physical Worlds

You need to report to and discuss matters with the spirit world. You also need to adopt a method of offering jeongseong that is suitable to your tribe and establish it as a tradition in your family and tribe. Then your ancestors can cooperate with you, and you can work together in full force. Since we are entering the age of the great cooperation of the spirit world, you should act with confidence. Do you have your hometown land? It refers to the land where your tribe is formed. Just as you became a grafted branch in the same position as the incarnation of the perfected Adam, all tribes that are connected on the foundation of the heavenly tribal messiah join together like a clan that was born in the homeland of the heavenly kingdom.

When the blessed families become the ancestors, the spirit world can be united. The ancestors from the past will be resurrected from there, and the descendants of the future will be united there and will live together with Heavenly Parent forevermore. It is the heavenly tribal messiah's mission to create the family that Adam and Eve would have built in Eden had they not fallen. When you renew your hometown land, it will become the land that represents the historicity of your ancestors, your present clan, and your future descendants. The three types of hometowns—of the past, present and future—are connected centering on the tribal messiah. By establishing that the ancestors were born of the conditions of the heavenly family, the foundation can be laid for the liberation of the ancestors in the spirit world, liberation of the clan, and liberation of the descendants.

The spirit world cannot achieve this because it has no land, so it stands on Heavenly Parent's side centering on the tribal messiah. In short, the ancestors of the past, the people of the present and the descendants of the future are granted the boon to become directly connected o the heavenly kingdom. By being grafted on the condition of being born as the unfallen ancestors, you can be registered in the next world as members of the same tribe. In other words, if you create the ideal kingdom of heaven on earth on the foundation of the heavenly tribal messiah community centered on Heavenly Parent, when you go to the spirit world after living there, you will continue living in the same foundation of the heavenly tribal messiah community that is the kingdom of heaven in heaven.

Blessed families must become heavenly tribal messiahs and fulfill their responsibility. The ancestors in the entire spirit world are hoping for blessed families to set up the foundation as heavenly tribal messiahs and begin their work, and when they fail to do so, the ancestors begin to strike their own descendants, which is sad indeed.

Tribal messiahs are the saviors of their tribe. When they fail to fulfill their responsibility, they cannot create the hometown land where they can attend Heavenly Parent. No matter how much the spirit world wishes to be mobilized to help the physical world, it cannot be connected to the center if blessed families do not act. The ancestors are restless because they want to help the blessed families. How great is the mission of the heavenly tribal messiah? It is the best gift given to our tribes by Heavenly Parent and True Parents.

1.4 Advice for Leading a Life of Jeongseong

① **Strictly keep to the time that you have set to offer jeongseong.** When you offer jeongseong, it is a time when the spirit world joins with you to report together to Heavenly Parent, so it is good to set the time in advance. Once you have set a time, it is important to observe it absolutely.

② **If possible, offer jeongseong in a group, not alone.** You need to become used to offering jeongseong in a group, rather than doing it alone. When you offer jeongseong as an individual, it remains as an individual offering, but when a family or a tribe comes together to offer jeongseong, the community becomes aligned with one heart. Therefore, you can achieve better results when you offer jeongseong together in solidarity.

③ **Report to Heavenly Parent about your list of candidates.** You should write down the list of witnessing candidates and call out their names as you pray, so that their ancestors who have waited 6,000 years for you to find them and also those around them in the present can cooperate with you.

▼ The prayer altar in Kim Myung-dae and Cheon Ok-ja's home

Prayer with a Holy Candle by Kim Myeong-dae and Cheon Ok-ja's Family in Korea

Our entire lives, we have offered early morning prayers with the names of our children and witnessing candidates in front of us. We prayed every day without exception, and when time or the environment did not permit us to do so, other family members took turns to offer the early morning prayer. Reporting our daily schedule to Heavenly Parent before starting our day and carrying it out has become our tradition. It has now been 40 years since we began this morning prayer tradition. After giving birth to our youngest son, we resolved to offer jeongseong for the True Children and began doing so. Now our own children also are taking part, and our tradition of offering jeongseong through candlelight prayer is being continued through them. It could even be said that offering jeongseong through prayer

▶ A special gathering of the spiritual children

◀ A tribal messiah Blessing for part of Kim Myung-dae and Cheon Ok-ja's tribe

is an important part of our family tradition. Even when the parents are not at home, the children pray with holy candles. When you pray with a lit holy candle, a light also comes on in your heart and your soul is purified. There even have been times when we received revelations about things that would happen to our children. When we received such revelations, we talked to our children and asked them to be careful, and in that way we avoided dire situations several times. In this way our children have learned the importance of paying attention to revelations. We also use holy candles when we hold hoondokhae. When we pray and hold hoondokhae, we often receive inspiration about what we need to say to our spiritual children. I am determined to continue this tradition of early morning jeongseong and hoondokhae for all eternity. It will be the greatest legacy I leave to my tribe. And today, like always, I will pray earnestly before a lighted candle to be in complete accord with Heavenly Parent and True Parents.

Section 2 Declaration as the Messiah and Invitation to the Family

2.1 The Meaning of "Going into Battle"

The mental attitude toward completing the mission is important. The world responds differently depending on your mental attitude toward completing your mission as a representative of Heavenly Parent. It is important to report about your mission to Heavenly Parent and at the same time to announce it to others. Your announcement to the spiritual and physical worlds that you, a blessed central family, have appeared as the "messiah" in your local society becomes meaningful. Once the declaration ceremony has been performed, the side of goodness and the side of evil divide into two and engage in battle in earnest. This is because guiding a new life to Heavenly Parent is a spiritual battle. A ferocious war breaks out in which you have to fight fiercely against cunning and evil spirits. You need to know that the important thing in a war is not just to participate but to win. And in order to win in a war, you first need to gain ascendancy over your enemies. Therefore, you need to bring the victorious realm of Heavenly Parent and True Parents to the forefront to show others. Then you should boldly declare that you have become the commander and messiah of the region as a heavenly tribal messiah. In a territorial fight, your authority and position are determined when you separate goodness from evil and establish yourself. Therefore, you need to make a proclamation in that region by performing a Blessing ceremony. Through the Coronation Ceremony of God's Kingship of January 13, 2001, and the historic Foundation Day of January 13, 2013, Satan fundamentally lost his forces, but their remnants are still at large. Nonetheless, our current environment can be said to be completely different from what it was in the age before this one. We are living in the age of the True Parents of Heaven, Earth and Humankind, in which blessed families experience cooperation and amazing miracles, rather than persecution and opposition, wherever they may go. Hence, when you boldly make the declaration, the victorious realm of True Parents will bring heavenly fortune to the path you walk as a heavenly tribal messiah.

2.2 Declaration as the Tribal Messiah

True Parents walked the indemnity course of the individual, family, tribe, people, nation and world. Therefore, the blessed families of this age do not need to walk the indemnity course as True Parents did. True Parents said that blessed families are now going to be sent out as tribal messiahs who are in the same position as Jesus. Blessed families got married as newly reborn people, so they are connected to Heavenly Parent as individuals, families and tribes. True Parents walked the indemnity course in which everything was always connected to Heavenly Parent, but blessed families received the Blessing without having passed through such a course. Given that Jesus died before getting married, the Blessing signifies that blessed families stand in a position superior to his. That is why Satan no longer can make accusations against blessed families, for their lineage is connected to Heavenly Parent and True Parents. Therefore, Satan cannot accuse them on any level, from the level of individual to family, tribe, people, nation and world. This is because blessed families stand in a position of complete liberation where they can never be accused.

The declaration as a heavenly tribal messiah is Heavenly Parent's promise to support any blessed family whose lineage has reached a high level through the marriage Blessing, if that family shoulders its responsibility and steps forward. When a blessed family marches forward on the same standard as that of True Parents when they fought and triumphed against Satan in the difficult pioneering days, the spirit world keeps that promise made by Heavenly Parent without fail. Back then, we ushered in the age of tribal restoration despite opposition; now, the age in which we can achieve great developments without facing opposition and limitations has opened before us.

Why the term "messiah"? The name is very important. The savior is not the savior of power, the savior of money, or the savior of knowledge. The savior is the savior of love, the savior of life and the savior of lineage. Because we lost Heavenly Parent's love, life and lineage due to the Fall, the savior is the one who comes to restore them. The fact that blessed families are being sent out on behalf of True Parents to play this role of the savior, of the messiah, is significant.

To blessed families, the term "tribal messiah" is an amazing one. With that name alone, they can start out from a position and status that are more precious than even Jesus' own. Moreover, they have been given the authority to elevate even those people who used to oppose them and insult them to Adam's position before the Fall, all in the name of the tribal messiah.

Because True Parents fought against Satan and perfected the standard and responsibility of loving the cosmos and the world, blessed families need to love the lower stages, namely their nation, tribe, and family. On this standard, they must love their family members, just as husbands and wives love their spouses. Centering on the results of this love, they should be able to love their tribe and their nation. Since the cosmos and the world are already connected by True Parents, the victorious realm of blessed families who love their family, tribe and nation will then be connected to True Parents. If the family signifies the formation stage, the tribe signifies the growth stage, and the nation the completion stage. From the viewpoint based on the nation, the nation may be said to be the formation stage, the world the growth stage, and the cosmos the completion stage. Based on the world, the world would be the formation stage, heaven and earth the growth stage and Heavenly Parent the completion stage, and all stages are connected through love. In light of this principle of three stages, the principle by which they are connected and developed, you need to know how precious the standard of the tribal messiah is in national restoration.

"March forward in the name of the Messiah"

Blessed families come to have the name of tribal messiah, who is the savior of the tribe. How long did Jacob's family in the history of the providence wait for the coming of the messiah? They waited for thousands of years. In providential history, the Savior and Messiah could only be received after thousands of years of waiting, and yet his will could not be fulfilled. And then True Parents, the third Adam, manifested on earth. Through the toilsome course of True Parents, the history of the providence of restoration through indemnity was completed and a new age centered on Heavenly Parent was begun. The miracle of blessed families being appointed as messiahs to their tribe and being sent out as such is now taking place based on the sole fact that they have received the Blessing. This benefit of the age is truly tremendous. You need to know how precious tribal messiahs are.

2.3 Beginning Home Church through the Declaration Ceremony

The declaration ceremony as tribal messiah is also the opening ceremony of the hoondok family center (hoondok family church) that serves as the foundation for the activities carried out by a tribal messiah in his or her local society, the mission place, as the owner. In other words, it signifies the settlement of the foundation in the mission place, the foundation on which the manifestation and teachings of Heavenly Parent and True Parents can be propagated.

If what we have carried out until now in the Unification Church age is the home church movement, in the FFWPU age we need to start out centering on the hoondok family center (hoondok family church) based on the realm of the unfallen Adam's family. The culture of hoondokhae practiced in your homes leads to a heavenly tribal messiah hoondok family center. And when 12 tribes are organized centering on the heavenly tribal messiah hoondok family center, a people naturally comes into existence. Once the foundation is created on which the tribal restoration of numerous surnames like Kim or Park or Moon can take place, a nation naturally will come into existence. The tribal center will evolve into a people's center, a national center, world center, and cosmic center. That is why it is important to hold family hoondokhae at home, because it is the starting point.

A family hoondokhae begins with a couple. The foundation of family hoondokhae is a husband seeking the love of his wife and the wife seeking the love of her husband. Then the foundation can be laid on which parents and children can unite as one and brothers and sisters can unite as one, centering on their parents. On that foundation, Heavenly Parent can expand the providence to the tribal level, centering on that family.

This foundation expands to become the heavenly tribal messiah hoondok family center (hoondok family church). It is a community in which the families in the tribe that become connected centering on the family of the heavenly tribal messiah truly come together as a tribe of one great family. As parents, heavenly tribal messiahs should be able to love their tribe members more than their own sons and daughters, with the love they have attained on the foundation of family hoondokhae. Only then can they cross the boundary through which they can leave the world of evil and enter the original world. Without a hoondok family center, you cannot advance to the original homeland, and if you cannot advance to the original homeland, you cannot advance to the fatherland, and if you cannot advance to the fatherland, you cannot advance to the kingdom of heaven. To put it another way, when you realize a hoondok family center (home church), you can go on to realize the homeland, the fatherland, the world and the kingdom of heaven. Therefore, you should unite under a new culture and new movement through the hoondok family center (hoondok family church) and begin a new revival.

When you have met a witnessing candidate outside more than three times, you should be able to bring him or her to your home (family hoondokhae). You should let him or her meet your family members at home and see how a blessed family lives. And you should encourage your spiritual children and your own children to harmonize and form fraternal bonds with one another, so that they can feel true love that is even more stimulating than the love of the Cain world. When a witnessing candidate is invited to your home and is moved to see how you and your family live, you will be able to witness to him or her naturally without having to speak a word, and he or she will become your spiritual child. That spiritual child then naturally will witness to his or her friends, the friends of friends, and even brothers and sisters and parents later on. In short, witnessing to one person spreads out like sweet-potato vines. When all is said and done, inviting someone to your home to experience a new world and culture of love, thus creating the environment, marks the beginning of the hoondok family center.

2.4 Matters to Note in Making the Tribal Messiah Declaration

① **It is advisable to notify others through a declaration.** The declaration is a ceremony desired by Heavenly Parent. The ceremony is significant in that, just as True Parents manifested on this earth as the True Parents and Messiah of humanity, blessed families are making an appearance in their mission place and hometown as tribal messiahs. The messiah declaration ceremony adds historic meaning as a ceremony that declares to heaven and earth that you were given this mission from Heavenly Parent and that you are appearing as such. In addition, you should make this declaration ceremony a festival to which others, such as local residents and relatives, are invited. However, it is said that there is no freedom without results. There may be side effects if you have no accomplishments to speak of. Since you were enabled to stand in a position in which you can hold the declaration ceremony through the indemnity condition successfully set by True Parents, you should not forget to show modesty. And now, as the representative of Heavenly Parent and True Parents, you need to convey all the love that they were unable to give until now as their representative, by embracing others with a love that is several times greater than they have ever known.

② **A couple should have a sense of mission and responsibility as messiahs.** What True Parents have shown us is that they love Heavenly Parent more than anyone else. Theirs has been a path walked on behalf of Heavenly Parent to ease His bitter sorrow and to bring His enemy to voluntary submission through love. True Parents have shown this to us through their lives and through the traditions they have left behind. They are asking us to live our lives as they have lived theirs. Therefore, just as True Parents walked the path of restoration through indemnity to establish the parent–children relationship between Heavenly Parent and humankind and loved Him and took pride in Him, the first commandment of being a heavenly tribal messiah, which we should set as our goal, is to love and take pride in

Heavenly Parent and True Parents more than anyone else. The second commandment is to establish the standard of loving our tribe and the citizens of the heavenly kingdom. Heavenly Parent lost His children, humanity. Therefore, True Parents loved humanity on His behalf. We need to invest boundless love and forget having done so, in order to transform the Cain-realm children within our tribes into Abel-realm children, the children of direct descent, and connect them to Heavenly Parent so that we can attain the position of parents in the family of the unfallen Adam.

③ **We need to include the term "heavenly tribal messiah" in every event.** If we do not use this title and instead use some other name, though we may be able to alleviate the misunderstanding of local residents, our spiritual status will be notably diminished. Though it may not be easy to do so, we have to set the principle of using the title just as it is.

④ **If you have had a history of sacrificing yourself to serve the local residents before making the declaration as the messiah, the declaration becomes that much more meaningful.** There have been cases in which Japanese or Western members cleaned the streets in their neighborhood and visited centers for the aged to hold hoondok meetings. When their neighbors saw them doing these activities, they were witnessed to automatically. There are also many cases in which, through such selfless acts, our church came to be recognized as a good church by the local society and was even awarded plaques of appreciation. When your neighbors or relatives are moving house or have suffered some kind of loss, you should not forget to visit them and help them and love them. The most basic thing you can do is to carry out easy and simple acts like greeting others, being kind, finding out what others require of you and doing things for them as much as you can, cleaning the streets, or sending hoondokhae materials to others through social media. However, it is more important to go a step further and show your local society the substance of the true family movement centered on your tribe, and carry out work to right the deteriorating family culture and resolve the ethical problems and degeneration of adolescents through the pure love movement. If you approach others for your own gain or with the goal of making a profit, one day they may turn their backs on you. Christianity is now on a downhill trend because it has surfaced that Christian churches are witnessing to others for the sole purpose of increasing the size of their congregations. What people really want is for some kind of salvation in a part of their lives that they cannot resolve by themselves. That is why when you sincerely work to heal your local society by holding seminars and carrying out actual programs for families, when you resolve problems between parents and children and, furthermore, when you meet with leaders of the local society, such as mayors and county magistrates, and resolve those problems together, in less than three years your sincerity will win you much support from others.

What human beings lack right now are their parents. They miss their parents. True Parents! True Parents are the only people your true heart tells you to lean on and to embrace. Everyone yearns to do so. Everyone misses them. That is why now is the time when miraculous events will take place almost explosively if you so much as say one word to others. [2017.5.26]

▼ Speaking at the Naruko family church

The Tribal Messiah Declaration Ceremony by the Furuta Tribe of Japan in 1992

In accordance with the directions of True Parents, Rev. Motou Furuta brought together everyone in the Furuta clan and held a declaration ceremony. After the ceremony, the entire spiritual foundation of his local society was transformed. The local residents, who had vehemently opposed him before the declaration ceremony, adopted a more amicable attitude after it. Similar to the story in the Bible of how the walls of Jericho were brought down by shouting in front of it, Rev. Furuta realized through his experience that when you fulfill the mission of Heavenly Parent with absolute obedience, the world backs down of its own accord. The fact is that "messiah" is a Christian term and therefore a difficult term to be accepted in Japan, a society of many beliefs. However, it turned out that the

◣ Members of the Furuta tribe who attended the tribal declaration ceremony

term "messiah" was the term most feared by Satan. This incident showed that, when someone on Heaven's side makes a declaration using the term most hated by Satan, it may cause Satan to retreat far back, which is truly incredible. It makes you wonder if it was a miracle wrought by Heavenly Parent and True Parents. When True Parents heard this news, they were extremely delighted, and they blessed Rev. Furuta as the first tribal messiah of Japan.

Section 3 Gathering Candidates

3.1 Searching for a John the Baptist Figure

One widespread belief in Jesus' time was that Elijah, the prophet who had ascended to heaven, one day would come back to earth. This expectation is based on Malachi 4:5–6 in the Old Testament: "Lo, I will send you the prophet Elijah before the great and terrible day of the Lord comes. He will turn the hearts of parents to their children and the hearts of children to their parents, so that I will not come and strike the land with a curse." There are many references to Elijah in the Gospels [Mark 6:14–15; 8:27–28; 9:11; 15:36], almost as many as those found in the Apocrypha [Sirach 48:10; Enoch 90:31] and Talmud [Schekalim 2:5; Sotah 9:15; Baba Metsia 1:8; Edaioth 8:7].

Moreover, when asked about the return of Elijah, Jesus answered,

"Elijah is indeed coming first to restore all things. How then is it written about the Son of Man, that he is to go through many sufferings and be treated with contempt? But I tell you that Elijah has come, and they did to him whatever they pleased, as it is written about him." And then he revealed that the one who had come with that mission was John the Baptist [Mark 9:12–13].

The father of John the Baptist was Zechariah, a priest of the Abijah division, and his mother was Elizabeth, a descendant of Aaron. In Chapter 1, Verses 6 through 8, in the Book of John, it is written, "There was a man from God whose name was John. He came as a witness to testify concerning that light, so that through him all might believe. He himself was not the light; he came only as a witness to the light." In short, John the Baptist was sent to testify to the Christ.

John the Baptist began his work near the River Jordan by preaching a baptism of repentance [Luke 3:1–14]. He humbled himself and remained faithful to his role as the herald, carrying out the work of preparing the people to receive the Messiah, Jesus [Mark 3:1–11; Luke 1:17; John 1:31].

That is why he was teaching people to repent and baptizing them in the wilderness, telling them that the time to receive the coming Messiah was near at hand. He was creating a situation in which he could bring the nation and the people of Israel under control and dedicate them to God for the coming Messiah, the Son of God. In other words, from the horizontal position as their representative, he was fulfilling the mission of dedicating them to the Son sent by God.

John the Baptist had the responsibility to bring all the people of Israel and Judaism together and lead them to the Messiah. Since it already had been foretold in the Bible, the rabbis and priests of Judaism knew very well that John the Baptist had to testify to the Messiah before his coming. They did not doubt the fact that John the Baptist was the one who was preparing the Messiah's path beforehand. Therefore, they were all waiting with anticipation for the one to whom John the Baptist would testify as being the Messiah. If John the Baptist had found his way to the Messiah and testified that he was the beloved Son of God and the Messiah promised by Him, all those who had been waiting a long time for him would have united as one and established the foundations of the people and the nation.

This John the Baptist symbolizes the archangel Lucifer before the Fall. Lucifer was entrusted with the mission of leading the angelic world and guiding the young human ancestors, Adam and Eve, until they grew to maturity. However, he failed because he felt less loved and became jealous. The way to restore this through indemnity is to reverse the failure of Lucifer by taking the opposite route and resolving it through the mission of John the Baptist.

Therefore, based on the Principle, John the Baptist always must appear in the providence of the Messiah. The same is also true for the providence of the tribal messiah. There is bound to be a John the Baptist figure, prepared by Heavenly Parent in any society or mission place to fulfill his mission. The John the Baptist figure is usually a leader in that society, and though he may show doubts in the new teachings, once he becomes confident that he will be able to resolve all his worries as a leader, incredible things will start happening. Because he is programmed to recognize the potential of changes in the society faster than anyone else, he will actively step forward to help the heavenly tribal messiah resolve the urgent substantial problems of reality. In many cases, such figures are already prepared environmentally, spiritually and mentally through the work of Heavenly Parent even before they meet the tribal messiah. However, the heavenly tribal messiah may have to undergo hardships in the stage before they meet John the Baptist. Moreover, the person with the mission of John the Baptist is sensitive to the loss of love, as was shown by the fall of Lucifer. Therefore, he needs to be complimented continuously, and you need to make him feel that his work of creating a new local society is meaningful. More than anything else, the greatest blessing you as the messiah can give him is to connect him to True Parents, so that he can receive love on the fundamental level, and to teach him to know clearly about Heavenly Parent.

3.2 Background behind the Appearance of John the Baptist

The archangel Lucifer was entrusted with the mission of leading the angelic world and guiding the young human ancestors, Adam and Eve, until they grew to maturity, but he failed because he felt less loved and became jealous. The mission of John the Baptist to restore through indemnity Lucifer's failure to show obedience and submission was frustrated, and Jesus was unable to make people of the leading social class his disciples. Therefore, he had no choice but to approach those in the lower walks of life (fishermen, tax collectors and prostitutes) to find his disciples. This parallel history was passed down to True Parents, and the tribal messiah also cannot avoid it. Therefore, a John the Baptist figure must appear in the course of the tribal messiah to restore through indemnity the position of John the Baptist. When the messiah appears as the parent, John the Baptist also appears, and when children are created and educated, John the Baptist must cooperate with the messiah to restore his position through indemnity. Accordingly, when the tribal messiah declares his or her mission in the chosen mobilization area, a figure who stands in the position of Lucifer and John the Baptist in the higher class of that local society makes his appearance without fail. And when the tribal messiah makes the declaration and begins his or her work, the John the Baptist figure simultaneously realizes his mission spiritually and comes to stand at a crossroads, to choose whether he should support the messiah or oppose him or her. Upon the appearance of the messiah in a local society, John the Baptist comes to face the biggest conflict of his life. Tribal messiahs can complete their mission only if they stand on the foundation laid down by such figures and receive their support and cooperation. In the end, the core factor in completing the mission is the relationship between John the Baptist and the messiah.

3.3 Characteristics of a John the Baptist Figure

John the Baptist figures may come from various levels. They may be heads of state (presidents, prime ministers, premiers, national assembly speakers, etc.), central figures who represent the government (ministers, vice ministers, heads of organizations affiliated with the government, etc.), figures who represent the locality (governors, parliamentarians, heads of cities, counties, townships, neighborhoods, etc.), and figures who represent the local society (heads of major organizations, grass-roots leaders working under the government system, heads of NGOs, etc.).

The tribal messiah may have to undergo hardships before meeting John the Baptist. A characteristic is that, when a John the Baptist figure in a high position starts following an Abel-type course, it is highly likely that John the Baptist figures in the level under him will copy him automatically. However, starting out with a John the Baptist figure from the highest level is more suitable to a national leader or regional president, who works on the national level or higher, than a tribal messiah. The tribal messiah first must convey clearly to the John the Baptist figure his or her mission and the work he or she is trying to do.

First, you must clearly testify to Heavenly Parent and True Parents. Then they can open the way by which you can be recognized as a heavenly tribal messiah.

Second, you must clarify that Heavenly Parent and True Parents love humanity, that they are carrying out the peace movement, and that they are advocating the true family movement to create One Family under Heavenly Parent. And you must proclaim that True Parents are at the center of the providence they are carrying out to establish the parent–children relationship between Heavenly Parent and humankind.

Third, you must have them learn the words of the Divine Principle, which will help them resolve all problems and form the original family, and emphasize that they need to go through the ceremony of forming a pure family by participating in the Blessing ceremony. You also must clearly implant the idea that you have come with the mission of heavenly tribal messiah.

Fourth, you must encourage the John the Baptist figure to work with one heart and one mind with the tribal messiah. To make him work more actively with you, you should discuss with him how the will of True Parents is to be fulfilled with regard to matters in your local region, and show him how passionate you are as a heavenly tribal messiah, so that he will be motivated by the fact that you are more worried about the local society and nation than he is. Thus, you should impress him and move his heart.

Fifth, you must make John the Baptist figures learn the Divine Principle thoroughly. There is a need to educate them intensively about the Divine Principle and True Parents' ideology, perhaps by persuading them to go to another country to attend a workshop, such as the Asian Leadership Conferences held for three nights and four days, where they can learn together with other people of a similar level. This is because we need to prepare them to give congratulatory addresses in all events hosted by us, where they can give testimonies to the local societies.

Sixth, you must try to cater to the needs of John the Baptist figures in every matter, and make it so that, when something happens within the tribe, the matter is discussed and decided by a meeting of John the Baptist figures. Thereupon, the sense of responsibility or the position of John the Baptist figures within the tribe will become that much more important. Then they will come to feel greater self-confidence and a heavier sense of responsibility.

Seventh, you should encourage the John the Baptist figures, the regional representatives, to stand at the forefront and testify to Heavenly Parent and True Parents. They also should testify to the heavenly tribal messiah, who is carrying out the peace movement and the true family movement in order to change the local region and resolve social problems.

Eighth, Have John the Baptist figures representing the local society (grassroots leaders, local NGO leaders and other leaders) at the forefront where they can work for you most devotedly. The heavenly tribal messiah must also help them in turn.

Ninth, the heavenly tribal messiah must have them working at the forefront to get a grasp of the local situation, and make plans together with them to carry out pure love seminars, the true family movement and the peace movement, and translate those plans into action with all earnestness. In carrying out the true family movement in particular, you should encourage them to recruit couples who can attend one- or two-day Divine Principle seminars, to make such couples take part in the Blessing ceremony, and to provide a roadmap of the continuous education for living as blessed families, including the 40-day separation period, the three-day ceremony, and what comes after that. In this way, they should be constantly encouraged to find and bring people to attend the seminars.

Tenth, the heavenly tribal messiah must check up weekly on the blessed families living in the region of the John the Baptist figure, the catalyst, to see whether they are following each stage faithfully. Whenever John the Baptist figures ask for your help, you should help them immediately and encourage them to do their best in leading their small tribal groups. This is because the success or failure of the heavenly tribal messiah's work depends on the small group leaders, the John the Baptist figures working at the forefront. John the Baptist figures who have become small group leaders should attend Divine Principle workshops repeatedly whenever possible, so that they can be inspired to follow the heavenly tribal messiah. When they take part in the small groups with zeal and dedication and begin to feel a sense of responsibility and also interest in what they are doing, that is when they are transformed from John the Baptist figure to small group leader, and in the end the groundwork is laid for them to become a regular Family Federation member. The heavenly tribal messiah should put effort into finding and establishing such figures in order to establish as many such small group leaders as possible.

In society, John the Baptist figures exist in many forms. It would not be an exaggeration to say that they resemble the character of

Lucifer. John the Baptist figures are highly skilled people in the leading class of society. Since they are active in their own way, they are revered as leaders. However, because they already recognize their limitations in resolving social problems, they are looking for the key to those solutions centered on True Parents.

However, they do not possess only merits. First, when they fail to see the vision and contents they desire, they may change overnight. Therefore, the best thing you can do is to show sincerity and have them participate continuously as you plan and work together with them and set an example. Second, sometimes they may ask for too much and put a burden on you. Therefore, you have to show them transparently how much sacrifice the blessed families are making through financial management and activities. Sometimes you must eliminate the misunderstanding that the center of our organization is financially well off. You must not forget that, in the time of Jesus, his followers tried to use him politically rather than seeking salvation from him. As for those figures particularly prepared by Heavenly Parent, in many instances they may have the ability but they may be staying immobile and not working for society even though they are worried.

In the path of a heavenly tribal messiah, there must be a John the Baptist figure. It is an important duty for you to find such figures through prayer and work, to train them by setting an example before them, to touch their hearts through transparency, to move them through sincerity, and to make sure their ties to Heavenly Parent and True Parents remain solid at all times.

3.4 A Strategy for Dealing with John the Baptist from the Position of Abel

① **Resolve the difficult problems faced by John the Baptist.** John the Baptist is a leading figure in your mission place, and as such he has many worries. The solutions to many difficult, unsolvable problems in the world can be found in the teachings of True Parents and the various projects of FFWPU. The fastest way to move John the Baptist is to present him with the solutions to the problems gnawing at him as a leader.

② **Propose a vision and persuade him to become one with you.** You should propose visions befitting your mission place and become one with him centering on the visions he never would have come up with. In addition, if he does not have a clear grasp of the core problems of his locality, you should speak to him using statistics and suggest the solutions to those problems and the direction of the movement. By your doing so, the leader in the position of John the Baptist should feel moved to express his agreement positively and of his own accord.

③ **Win his approval and blessing.** When you win the approval of the John the Baptist figure, he can introduce and recommend you to local residents as the leader who will guide them in the direction desired by all. When he feels moved to promote projects and activities to local residents, you should encourage him to take part in them with a sense of responsibility.

④ **Listen to the opinions of John the Baptist figures and make good** use of their external foundation. Many people like to talk about themselves. They like to boast of their abilities, their money, their family, their children, and themselves. Therefore, before approaching a John the Baptist figure, become familiar with his or her achievements and let them know that you appreciate what they've done. Once your relationship with them has grown closer, you can talk about True Parents and our movement, emphasizing our activities that are closest to their own field of expertise. You can keep them informed about upcoming programs and invite them to attend them. After some time, you can invite them to a presentation of Divine Principle. Finally, you can ask for their support in organizing seminars or programs in their area.

⑤ The work of bringing people together in the mission place is very important, and if the John the Baptist figure is in charge of that work, the heavenly tribal messiah must play the role of the head priest. The John the Baptist figure should remain in his position as a leading figure; however, the role of the head priest, the teacher, should be fulfilled by the heavenly tribal messiah as Abel, so that the range of his or her authority remains firm and unshaken.

⑥ When the John the Baptist figure abandons the existing values of his group and begin following new teachings, he may find himself in a difficult situation in the society to which he belongs. When he is in such a situation, he must be given constant encouragement and love. Since the fall of the archangel was caused by his feeling less loved, you must not let John the Baptist forget his sense of ownership. Despite everything, you need to lead him naturally and flexibly. Sometimes you will be supportive of his ideas, and sometimes it's necessary to follow the rules of FFWPU to the letter. After the Blessing ceremony, the way to lead the group centered on the John the Baptist figure is to guide it toward gradual changes with John the Baptist at the apex of the group, while at the same time choosing those candidates to focus on and nurturing them to grow faster than others. If you rely too much on John the Baptist, there is the danger of the entire group being swayed by him alone. Therefore, when you are dealing with John the Baptist figures, you must first educate them about the Divine Principle thoroughly so that they learn quickly about the positions of Cain and Abel and the heart-based order of rank within FFWPU. On the other hand, if you cause him to neglect his leadership of the group before he is fully educated, that may work as a negative factor in his individual relationships with the group members, and you may have trouble nurturing them one on one.

⑦ Guide the John the Baptist figure into the position of the elder son within the tribe. Historically, John the Baptist testified to Jesus but failed to attend him. Therefore, his failure to attend Jesus even after testifying to him must not be repeated. You must educate John the Baptist to lead the community as the elder son, while accepting your guidance. The only way to do that is through the truth of the Divine Principle. By continuing to educate him and love him, he can come to realize True Parents'

▼ Hospital director Dosinpool leading hoondokhae with employees

sincere love for humanity and accept them as the Messiah, the Savior and True Parents.

▼ The Dosinpool family distributing True Father's autobiography

Sanguon Dosinpool (hospital director) of Kalasin Province, Thailand

I am Sanguon Dosinpool, the director of Lub Hospital in Kalasin Province. My spiritual parents are the Ampal family, and I was blessed in January 2015. I was deeply moved by the teachings of FFWPU. After that, I met True Parents in Cheon Jeong Gung, and I came to have a high regard for them. Moreover, I came to recognize True Parents as the Messiah spoken of in the Unification Principle, and I resolved to practice the faith of FFWPU and actively participate in its activities. Though I had attended Divine Principle lectures several times, not all of my questions were answered, so I began to study the *Exposition of the Divine Principle* on my own. In addition, I gradually learned about Heavenly Parent and all parts of the Divine Principle by questioning leaders and receiving their answers. I also came to have a deep understanding of the points of contact between the teachings of Buddhism and the Unification Principle, and I realized that there are many similarities between them. I have a vague feeling that this Unification Principle is the new truth long awaited by our Buddhist society. I plan to fulfill my responsibility as a leader of the local community and also as the leader of my home group. As yet, blessed families are not much aware of home groups and have not entirely learned how to practice the faith of FFWPU, but I believe that things will improve with time. In particular, a great advantage we have in the Kalasin region is that the home group leaders are also the local society leaders. I admire them for taking pride in fulfilling their roles under FFWPU and for not neglecting their duties and participating in its activities, despite their busy schedules. I also plan to devote myself to carrying out those activities more actively, whenever I can make the time.

Section 4 Inviting People to Family Federation Events

4.1 The Significance of Inviting Guests to Events

In order for heavenly tribal messiahs to complete their mission, they first have to bless the residents in their area. Therefore, it is important to host an information session in the beginning stage and invite guests. There are diverse events hosted by Family Federation, and it is good to invite guests to these events so that they gradually can understand our values and vision. If we look at the case of David and Patricia Earle, who are successful heavenly tribal messiahs in England, "We have been carrying out activities as a couple for 25 years, from 1991 until now. We merged FFWPU, UPF and WFWP and have been carrying out activities so that we can approach all kinds of people." It does not have to be an information session on the Blessing. Through any event, guests can be introduced to the Family Federation's basic vision, true family movement and True Parents. This is because through these events, participants can lose their ignorance and prejudice against the Family Federation, develop a level of trust and come to accept future invitations from the leader.

Most of the invited guests at the events are either people with whom the blessed family has made a connection directly in their area of witnessing or someone who has been connected through a John the Baptist figure. The bonds you have with your guests are an important variable, because the deeper the bond, the higher the chance that they will be satisfied with the event and participate in future programs.

4.2 Managing individual differences

There will always be individual differences among guests. They will have different interests, problems, levels of education and different backgrounds of origin. Some guests will connect with you to establish a relationship; others will connect to resolve their problems; some guests have interest in the ideology and vision of the Family Federation, and others try to use the foundation of the Family Federation. The situation is different by culture and region, so there is a need for adequate—and often times flexible—explanations about the Family Federation." Heavenly tribal messiahs should get publications and materials from the church and learn how to explain about the Family Federation. Pastors should prepare pamphlets that are appropriate for the beginning stage of activities.

4.3 Building Rapport with Guests

Rapport refers to a bond of heart. It refers to a state in which one person's heart is connected to another's. Thus, it signifies the state in which our hearts are communicating with each other. If you build rapport, feelings of goodness and trust will arise and you will be able to express everything that is in your heart.

The following section explains how to build rapport.

To understand yourself and others, answer the following questions.

What are your strengths?
What are things you need to work on?
What kind of person do you want to witness to?
In what aspect have you been successful at witnessing before?
In what aspect have you experienced failure at witnessing before?
Do you feel capable to witness?
If not, what can you do to become more confident?

You must be able to answer the questions above. Second, you must trust and respect the other person. Third, you must have a genuine interest in the other person. Fourth, you must open your heart and get rid of your prejudices, stereotypes and defensive attitudes. You should be able to make the other person feel that you are interested in them.

When you are engaging in a conversation with another person, keep the following points in mind.

① Face the other person at a 45 degree angle or less.
② Stay close and lean very slightly in the direction of the other person.
③ Use expressions, voice and words that convey interest and warmth.
④ Respond appropriately, verbally and non-verbally.
⑤ Give your undivided attention, and do so with enthusiasm and the will to engage in the conversation.

To sympathize means to understand, share and feel a person's emotions, thoughts and experiences from their perspective. This means understanding the world from their perspective.

- Have a clear perception of the other person's current state.
- Try to understand from the other person's perspective.
- Do not judge or evaluate the other person, but accept them as they are.
- Share the other person's feelings, but maintain your objectivity.
- Show the other person that you want to help them.
- Respond positively to the other person's sincere conversation and emotions.
- Relate similar experiences that you have had.

❈ How to Engage in a Conversation

① Introduce yourself by name and how you like to be called.
② Decide a time.
③ Determine if they are a visitor, a customer, a person with a need, a person with a complaint, etc.
④ Find a special characteristic and compliment them.
⑤ Set a goal.
⑥ Listen and observe and find the main point.
⑦ Find a solution to the problem and lead the way.
⑧ If the current situation were to change, what would your future look like?
⑨ Sympathize with the answer they offer and welcome them.
⑩ Summarize.
⑪ Summarize the tasks that need to be resolved.
⑫ Do not try to convince or explain but guide them to find the answer that is within themselves.
⑬ Take the problem and solution that the person has found and set a goal.

4.4 Strategy for Inviting Guests to Events

① **Recruit guests by visiting and inviting them.** There is a need for family visits as well as inviting them to information sessions. The most effective way is to have the John the Baptist figure recruit people in the area in groups. However, you need to educate the John the Baptist beforehand. And you must absolutely follow up by introducing the guests to True Parents. Many people until now have been afraid to introduce True Parents to people whom they meet for the first time. This is because the social prejudices have been ignoring the truth. However, in today's realm of grace we should explain about True Parents in a direct way and convey to people about True Parents' sacrifice and love for the sake of humankind. Through doing this, we can defeat Satan and True Parents' victorious realm of grace can move the guests' hearts so that they no longer can oppose us. The amazing things happening in Africa and Asia can be credited in some part to this. Furthermore, you must explain the foundation and activities that True Parents have established worldwide and convey the truth that they have contributed to world peace. You should emphasize that the community needs to change through the peace movement, purity movement and true family movement, and guide people so that they can participate in those movements. You should encourage them to participate in Divine Principle seminars and do your best to run these programs so that participants can be moved. Apart from this, there is also the method of choosing a set area and having the blessed families visit all the houses in that area without leaving anyone out. However, this is very difficult in advanced countries, because their customs and traditions discourage people from visiting strangers at home.

In our current era, it has become possible to meet John the Baptist figures and have them lead their group to us. We are able to attend meetings and seminars in the greater community and build a relationships by stages with John the Baptist figures who play a leading role in the greater community and then invite them to our seminars. The issue is jeongseong and the deep struggle to become one in heart with Heavenly Parent and True Parents. As you carry out activities in your area, you can pray that Heavenly Parent will guide you and help you meet the appropriate John the Baptist figures.

② **If possible, build a personal relationship with your guests.** There are large-scale Blessing ceremonies taking place, through which you can accomplish your heavenly tribal messiah mission. You may have a John the Baptist figure helping you to recruit many couples for the Blessing. However, after that, you should take care of your guests through building personal relationships and be aware of their situation after the Blessing ceremony. Maintaining a personal relationship comes with many emotional and physical difficulties, but the process to becoming a spiritual parent is the process of creating a deep bond, so you should not forget to focus on this personal relationship. You should listen to what they are interested in, share closeness and love, accompany

▼ Christian Peace Blessing in Zimbabwe (June 29, 2017)

them to our events, recruit them as staff, and have them become a part of the community. One of the main reasons why people fail to become members is because we let them remain in the position of guests for too long. After a new member hears the Divine Principle and receives the Blessing, and when the thing that they were pondering and wondering about every day is resolved, they want to practice it and feel the change in themselves. It is important to have them actively join in, so that they can quickly put those things into practice. Furthermore, you should have them create a mission for themselves and have them participate in events. After the event, it is very important for them to encourage themselves and be acknowledged through personal testimony. Furthermore, all positive evaluations and results should be connected to Heavenly Parent, True Parents'

▼ Interfaith Peace Blessing in Zambia (May 25, 2017)

course of suffering, and the Divine Principle in action in our daily lives. If this is lacking, even with closeness and love from people around, it will be difficult for them to overcome the conflicts and challenges they will face. Therefore, you should give love to your guests, but at the same time you should reinforce the fact that your love comes not from yourself but from Heavenly Parent and True Parents. Ultimately, faith means grafting them onto True Parents.

The Unity of Africa's Traditional Tribe Culture with the Family Federation's Blessing Movement

A frica is a continent where traditionally a tribe-oriented culture is prevalent. The tribe leader influences the tribe's religion, politics and finances. The tribe-oriented culture has been seen as a weakness, with modernization on the way, but there are those who feel that if the weaknesses of the tribe culture can be supplemented, there is no real need to collapse the community structure.

In the midst of this situation, a Zimbabwean religious community tribe leader, Archbishop Johannes Ndanga, learned about the culture of the Family Federation, accepted True Parents as the True Parents of humankind, and sent out a proclamation to hundreds of thousands of believers and over 3,000 churches connected to his organization. In Senegal, the religious leader Cheikh Mansour Diouf testified to True Parents in front of 400,000 of his followers and is holding Marriage Blessing Ceremonies for all of them. In South Africa, Prophet S.B. Radebe, as the leader of the Revelation Church of God, has been promoting True Parents all over Africa consistently. Large-scale Marriage Blessing Ceremonies and education activities are being held within the already established tribe structures. God's heavenly tribal messiah activities are being grafted onto Africa's tribal culture. What are the differences with the tribe culture of the East? We are still looking into the differences, potential and similarities. However, God's work is not carried out by human strength alone. We have come to know that there are prepared John the Baptist figures.

Section 5 Invitation to the Blessing

5.1 The Significance of the Blessing

The family is the nest of love and the root of happiness. When the family is unstable, one's existential value, joy and happiness are lost. Therefore, protecting the family unit is the key to protecting our existence and the starting point to protecting our society. Anyone can express their concern about and say what must be done about this. But what is needed at this time is to find a way to establish strong, true families and begin specific campaigns for the sake of the world Heavenly Parent desires. From this vantage point, the Blessing ceremonies, which are taking place as a part of the true family movement, substantially restore God's true love to the families that have lost it.

The following explains the significance of the Marriage Blessing

Figure 3-1) Blessing Categories

	Type	Explanation
1	Blessing for Single Candidates	This is a Blessing between unmarried first-generation members or between unmarried second- or third-generation members who have been matched by their parents or a matching advisor. This also includes candidates who wish to be re-blessed according to the policies of their nation's headquarters.
2	Already Married Couples' Blessing	This is a Blessing for couples who are already married. They understand Heavenly Parent's Will and wish to renew their family life by joining the Family Federation and being reborn as Heavenly Parent's children through the marriage Blessing.
3	Spirit World Blessing	This Blessing is officiated at the CheongPyeong Heaven and Earth Training Center in Korea. It is for two individuals who have already passed to the spiritual world. When the CheongPyeong Heavenly and Earth Training Center announces that such a Blessing will take place, a spirit person's family members or their descendants on earth can register them for the Blessing.
4	Single Person Blessing	This is a Blessing for an older person who has not married or who was widowed before joining FFWPU. The person participates in the Blessing Ceremony alone, with the commitment to receiving the Blessing later with their original spouse, or with a newly matched spouse.
5	Spiritual World and Physical World Blessing	This is a Blessing for an older person who has not married or who was widowed before joining FFWPU, and who has already received a Single Person Blessing. In this Blessing, an FFWPU member on earth is blessed to a person in the spirit world.
6	Comfort Blessing	This is for two individuals who were widowed after starting family life. With True Parents' permission, they may be matched and blessed as a couple for the duration of their earthly lives.
7	Special Grace Blessing	The Grace Blessing is for those who lost their connection of lineage by falling after receiving the Blessing, but are then restored through Special Grace and the forgiveness of Heaven.

Ceremony.

- A ceremony of salvation: purification from original sin (full authority of the True Parents)

- Rebirth, resurrection, and eternal life: inheritance of true love, true life, and true lineage
- Restoration of a human being's original state cleansed of any connection to the Fall
- A ceremony to make a new start as an ideal family
- Contributes to the movement of peace among humankind (interracial, interreligious, and international)
- Conversion from Satan's realm to God's realm
- Liberation of Heavenly Parent from His resentment at having no true family
- Already married couples also can receive the Blessing and move toward the ideal of creation
- The foundation for building the ideal of Cheon Il Guk
- The cornerstone for the building of one family under Heavenly Parent

The marriage Blessing is not just a social formality to commemorate the union between a man and a woman. It is a ritual in which the couple pledge their determination to Heavenly Parent, the original Parent of humankind, to build a true family centering on Him. The first commandment for true families is fidelity between the husband and wife. The second commandment is the viewpoint of striving to perfect oneself by first enabling the perfection of one's spouse. The wife cannot recognize her position and value as a wife on her own; this is possible only through her husband. Out of countless men, only a woman's husband can address her as his wife.

In other words, people cannot perfect their positions on their own. This is the same for the wife's position and the husband's position. Therefore, after the marriage Blessing, you should live for the sake of your spouse. It is our natural responsibility to make up for the shortcomings of our spouse instead of blaming them. Your own position is perfected depending on your spouse's level of perfection. Thus, the marriage Blessing is a ritual that restores human beings to the state of Adam's perfected family before the Fall. When a couple receive the Blessing, each person resolves to enable their spouse's perfection and to become one centering on Heavenly Parent.

The Family Federation's large-scale Blessing ceremonies identify with and support this will. Young men, women and couples all over the world take part in these ceremonies; therefore, they generally are held in the form of large-scale international Blessing ceremonies. This movement is taking place in 187 countries around the world. It is a hope-filled event that is contributing to the realization of one human family under Heavenly Parent.

This is the understanding and standard that heavenly tribal messiahs should have in mind as they prepare for the marriage Blessing ceremonies that their tribe members will participate in.

It is necessary for Blessing candidates to attend introductory education. In Cambodia, one- or two-day Divine Principle workshops and lectures about the true love movement are taught. The one-day workshops summarize the Principle of Creation, the Human Fall and the Principle of Creation, and present speeches about True Parents' life course and achievements and the significance and procedures of the Blessing ceremony. The schedule also includes listening to the testimonies of local people who have received the marriage Blessing—speaking about how it changed them and gave them a happier family life. Once the workshop is completed, the staff register the information of those who wish to take part in the marriage Blessing and collect a registration fee.

Afterward, all the church members work together to thoroughly prepare the Blessing ceremony. Right before the event, John the Baptist figures and church members divide into teams to visit the Blessing candidates' families. They respectfully and casually review the main points of the event, so that the candidates will know what to expect.

5.2 The Significance of the Membership Application Form and the Blessing Application Form

Blessed families must implement the following three things: put up the Family Federation flag; attend True Parents' picture; and fill out and submit a church membership registration form. They must do all three of these things.

(1) The Significance of the Membership Form, True Parents' Picture and Flag

The flag represents the Family Federation. True Parents' picture symbolizes the hero of salvation. The membership form means having one's name entered into the register. That is the beginning of all things.

To place True Parents at the center and attend True Parents means that one's home has become one with True Parents. The flag is the symbol of the worldwide Family Federation. The flag also represents myself and my couple. It represents our family, our tribe and our nation. When we put up the flag, it holds the same significance as when the Israelites were able to avoid death and revive by painting blood on their door at the time when they were leaving Egypt and all the firstborns were being slaughtered.

When Moses and the Israelites were bitten by the snake and were dying, those who saw the copper snake survived. In the same way, when Satan's world was about to collapse, those who believed in Jesus lived. If you attend True Parents' picture and have been registered, you will be protected from Satan. It will change the realm to which you belong. An embassy is the symbol of friendly relations between two nations. The embassy is established in another country, but the sovereignty and territory of the building where the embassy is located are recognized as that of the nation that the embassy represents. In the same way, a space separate from Satan's realm is being declared. That allows those inside that space to receive True Parents' protection.

5.3 The True Family Movement and Blessing Explanation Sessions

Blessing information sessions explain the significance of the Blessing and convey the value and hope that each family can become a family blessed by Heavenly Parent and True Parents. The true family movement is interreligious and interdenominational. We do not pressure people to convert their faith, but we allow each person to change, if they choose to do so. However, it is good to have an interreligious Sunday Service that people of all religions can attend, at a time of day other than that of their own Sunday service.

A true family is created when the parents, husband and wife, children and siblings unite, centered on unchanging, absolute love. They are a family that upholds absolute sex and establishes the model tradition of love by living for the sake of others and perfecting oneself by helping others to become perfect. Introduce the true family movement before the marriage Blessing, and remind them of the significance of a blessed family.

Participating in the true family movement means that true families practice absolute sex and true love by taking part in activities in the community to build a true society, nation and world. Therefore it is a movement that offers couple therapy, parent–child therapy, programs and seminars to create ideal families, to raise the value of the family to that of the original value of the family.

The true family movement has the following four spheres of activity: There are three main movements: the movement for pure love and absolute sex; the movement to create true families; and the movement for realizing happy families in order to establish a happy society and peaceful nation through realizing true families.

First, there is the pure love and absolute sex movement. These days, many young people think they are free to pursue sexual pleasure as they please. This kind of selfish love and desire results in them not keeping purity before marriage and leads them to pursue other desires, ultimately making them miserable. The pure love and absolute sex movement seeks to overcome the limitations of the existing sexual ethics and establish absolute values on love and sex.

Second, there is the movement to create true families. The heart that makes us human and love is not understood by the head but through experience. The movement to create true families is one that seeks to have all the members of the family experience and perfect the four great realms of heart and love. Through the four great realms of heart we establish the culture in which we attend True Parents, who are the causative parents, and a world of heart where their attributes are spread so that I can perfect myself by helping others to perfect themselves. The movement to create true families hosts couple and parent–child programs.

Third, there is the movement to create happy families. This is the movement in which Family Federation members and tribe members feel value from working together in a supportive community, establishing a school, teaching, learning and sharing each other's expertise area, and volunteering in the community. This can include cooking classes, entrepreneurial training, classes to learn skills so that hobbies can supplement job skills, etc.

Fourth, there is the movement for national salvation. The collapse of ethics and morality has become a serious social issue. As a result, the nation and world are being driven into a whirlpool of chaos and confusion.

These issues in the society, nation and world can be solved through the resolution of family issues. The true family movement is facilitating that path by restoring the ideal of the true family centered on true love. It transcends race, religion, denomination and national borders. By spreading worldwide, it will be a movement of national salvation that builds a peaceful world through the foundation of happy families. The Blessing ceremony, as a part of this, will connect the root of families to Heavenly Parent and be the foundation for a new beginning for families as God originally intended.

5.4 Planning a Blessing Event

First of all, the venue (main event hall, stage, changing room, VIP waiting room) and hall decorations (plan card, hall, stage, master of ceremonies' seat) should be prepared. The following table (Figure 3-2) shows the tasks that are necessary when holding a Blessing event.

Figure 3-2) Blessing Event Preparation Tasks

	Section	Details
1	Pastor	Oversee the entire Blessing for already married couples
2	Planning and running the event	1. Planning and assigning tasks 2. Conducting the event 3. Checking the tasks and the schedule for the Blessing ceremony 4. Order of the ceremony and proposed banner 5. Compiling the budget and settling accounts 6. Making a manual (program cue sheet) 7. Reporting the results
3	Administration	1. Blessing administration 2. Registration of Blessing documents 3. Orientation for the officiant's assistants and preparing materials
4	Materials for the Ceremony	1. Orientation for ceremony staff (attendants, people who sprinkle holy water) 2. Preparing ceremonial materials for the event (holy wine, holy water, holy wine cups, veils, corsages, bouquets, gloves, attendants' gowns, folder with affirmation of vows and proclamation of the Blessing) 3. Delivering, using, collecting and managing the ceremonial materials 4. Music CD to use for the Blessing ceremony
5	Officiators	1. Reception room and changing room 2. Reception room hospitality 3. Prepare glass of water, etc., for the stage
6	Stage Preparation	1. Set up platform and stage 2. Stage ushering 3. Stage protocol
7	Sound Preparation	1. Prepare microphones 2. Prepare music for the event 3. Prepare video for the event 4. Take photos and videos
8	Ushering Support	1. Reception, registration, orientation 2. Ushers in the ceremony hall 3. Prepare refreshments 4. Standby event support

The following table (Figure 3-3), (Figure 3-4) shows the things to prepare for a Blessing ceremony event and the roles of the Blessing ceremony staff.

Figure 3-3) List of Things to Prepare for the Blessing Ceremony

Section	Item	Quantity	Comment	Comment 2
Preparation beforehand	Officiators' corsages	2		
	Affirmation of vows, proclamation of the blessing case	1		
	Flower bouquets (2), glass of water (1)	2 each		
	Tray	1		
	Corsages (for MC, guest who does representative prayer, congratulatory remarks, etc.)	10		
	Tray for use during exchanging of rings	1		
	Officiants' gloves	2 pairs		
	Hosts' gloves	10 pairs		
Task	Attendants, people who sprinkle holy water	10 couples	Senior couples who have received the Blessing	Decide the number of staff according to where the officiators will stand
	Staff for holy wine can also be staff for holy water Officiators' assistants	2 people (2nd gen)	Blessed family 2nd gen (single)	People who have kept their purity
	Ceremony staff standby waiting room			

Section		Item	Quantity	Comment	Comment 2
Preparation beforehand	Selection criterion	Holy wine, holy water	According to the number of participants		
		Holy wine jug (ditto)	″		
		Holy wine cups, holy water bowls (ditto)	″		
		Holy wine ceremony card (ditto)	″		
		Attendants' gowns (ditto)	″		
		Pamphlets (order of ceremony) (ditto)	″		
	Other	Placard, signboard			
		Prepare changing room for ceremony staff			
		VIP ushering			
		Congratulatory remarks			
		Filming and photography			
		Ushering inside the ceremony hall			
		Prepare rings		Rings of representative couples	Representative couple: Collect and prepare them beforehand
Task		Staff (ceremony staff)			
		Lunch (restaurant)			
		Men, women (veil, gloves, bouquet, corsage, etc.)			
		Gloves for attendants			

Figure 3-4) Blessing Ceremony Preparation Materials and Tasks

Role	Officiators' assistants
	• 2 people needed • Female 2nd gen • People who have kept purity • Age under 24 years old • People who have no grounds for disqualifications in their life of faith • Height 165~170cm
	Ceremonial clothes: • 2 Pink dresses • Hair should be done the night before or early in the morning • Make-up can be done at the same time as the brides and grooms • Hair should be be worn up
Role	Officiators' assistants
	Things to prepare • Wooden trays: 3 (for affirmation of vows, proclamation of the blessing and when preparing the rings) • Hand towel: 2 (for the officiators to use after the holy water ceremony) • True Parents' gold holy water bowls): 2 • Holy water: 1 bottle • affirmation of vows case and content • proclamation of the blessing case and content • tray and prop for rings • 6 clothes pin: to keep rings in place • Officiators' flower corsages: 2 • Officiators' gloves • Prepare the waiting room and changing room for assistants and announce its location beforehand • 2 good quality, strong boxes

1. Wear the dress uniform, hold the holy water bowl and be prepared
2. Stand by place is the officiators' waiting room
3. When the MC announces for the officiant to enter, take the holy water and follow at a distance of 1 meter behind the officiators and enter at the same time (prepare towel)
4. After the officiators enter and during the holy water ceremony, stand on either side of them and assist with the holy water.
5. After the holy water ceremony is over, walk backwards and quickly leave the stage
6. After getting off stage, go to the waiting room and prepare for the affirmation of vows
7. When the MC announces that it is time for the affirmation of vows, put the affirmation of vows folder on the tray, enter the stage and give it to the officiators.
8. After delivering it, quickly leave the stage and go to the waiting room
9. When the affirmation of vows are about to end, enter the stage, get the wedding vow folder and leave the stage.
10. The MC will say, "It is time for the exchange of rings. Representatives couples, please come up to the stage." When he says that, prepare the to store event goods representative couples' rings and case and enter the stage
11. When the exchange of rings is over, quickly leave the stage and go to the waiting room
12. When the MC announces that there will be the proclamation of the Blessing, prepare the proclamation folder, enter the stage and give it to the officiators
13. After giving it to them, walk backwards to exit the stage and go to the waiting room.
14. After the proclamation of the Blessing is over, quickly enter the stage, get the folder and leave the stage
15. When it is time for the offering of the bouquet, be on standby. When the representative bride and groom offer the flowers to the officiators, stand on either side of them and receive the flowers. Then leave the stage and go to the waiting room
16. When the officiators are leaving the stage, get the holy water bowls, stand on either side of them and follow them off stage at a distance of 1 meter.

Role	Attendants
	1. Number: At least 3 couples but decided according to the scale of the event 2. Select couples by sending official memo to churches at various levels a) model families b) height 165. 3. Attendants are model older blessed couples who help guide the participants in the ceremony
	Preparations beforehand 1. Waiting room 2. Attendants gowns: red gowns 3. Female and male gloves for attendants **Lines** 1. Men. line up by height, check their attire (holy water attendants, staff attire, gloves) 2. Women. line up by height Position decided according to order of height **Rehearsal** • Gather 1 hour before the Blessing ceremony and hold a rehearsal **Order of Ceremony** Opening ceremony → prayer → entrance of attendants → entrance of officiators → Attendants exit stage → Officiators' message → holy water ceremony and affirmation of vows → Benediction → exchange of rings → proclamation of the blessing → congratulatory remarks → offering of flowers → Greetings of brides and grooms → 3 cheers of eok mansei ※ attendants enter → officiators exit ※ attendants exit → closing
	1. During the prayer, move to the waiting line and wait there (holy water assistants) 2. March in step to the music when they announce, "Entrance of attendants." Have the left and right lines march in with the two lines keeping together. Lead group should march slowly to keep together. 3. When the last line (at the end of stairs) marches on and everyone is in position, turn to face each other in order and stand still. 4. When the officiators enters the stage and passes in front of you, then you turn to face the hall. Don't bow when the officiators walk past you at this time. ¡ØHoly water assistant staff should wait where the attendants were waiting and then follow the officiators. 5. When the officiators bow to True Parents and begin the prayer, the attendants turn back and leave the stage. 6. The attendants should be on stand-by in the waiting room. 7. When the congratulatory song is over, reenter the stage and face the front. 8. During the offering of flowers, do not clap and during the three cheers of mansei, do not do the mansei. 9. When they announce, "The officiators will exit"(first) the attendants will face each other again. 10. When the officiators exit the stage and pass you, turn to face the back. (face the back of stage) 11. You will exit following behind the holy water attendants.

5.5 Program Order of the Blessing Ceremony

The order of the Blessing ceremony is as shown in (Figure 3-5). In the case of religious leaders from other faiths being invited, there can be an interfaith ceremony before the main event.

Figure 3-5) Program Order of the Blessing Ceremony

No.	Order	Conducted by
1	Opening remarks	MC
2	Cheon Il Guk Anthem	All together
3	Opening Prayer	One couple from the heavenly tribal messiah trinity
4	Entrance of the attendants	Senior family / Blessed family from church
5	Entrance of officiators	Officiating couple
6	Message	Officiators
7	Holy Wine Ceremony	Officiators
8	Holy Water Ceremony	Officiators
9	Affirmation of vows	Officiators and brides and grooms
10	Benediction	Officiators
11	Exchange of Blessing rings	Brides, grooms (this may be omitted for already married couples)
12	Proclamation of the Blessing	Officiators
13	Presentation of flowers	Representative brides and grooms
14	Congratulatory song	VIP
15	Congratulatory remarks	Special invited guest
16	Couples offer a bow to guests	Representative brides and grooms
17	Three cheers of eok mansei	Officiators
18	Recession of the officiators	Officiating couple

| 19 | Declaration of Closing Ceremony | | MC |

Figure 3-6) Ceremonies before and after the Blessing Ceremony

No.	Name of	Contents
1	Holy Wine Ceremony	• The Holy Wine Ceremony is a ceremony to cleanse the original sin of adultery and change the lineage of the participants from Satan's lineage to God's lineage. It is an indemnity ceremony in which human beings born in Satan's world can be reborn through True Parents. It is a ceremony in which the man and woman go through a process internally in which the woman, who fell first, is restored first and then gives birth to the man. • Adam and Eve did not become husband and wife and love each other as they were supposed to. They put Satan at the center, so this ceremony restores the order of love, which was reversed, to its original state. • It is a ceremony to inherit the new blood line centering on Heavenly Parent and cleanse the original sin and a ceremony to change our fallen bodies to center on Heavenly Parent.
2	Indemnity Stick Ceremony	• Holy songs, prayer, True Parents' words, event (couples bow to Heavenly Parent and True Parents; wife hits husband three times husband hits wife three times) • The reason for hitting three times is to symbolize the restoration of indemnity of the three stages (formation, growth, completion) and three ages (Old Testament Age, New Testament Age, Completed Testament Age). • God could bless Jacob, in order to raise up the Israelites, only after He had the angel strike his hipbone. Therefore, when the Israelites make an important pledge, they put their hand on their hipbone. Since the beginning of history, men and women have come to have resentment against each other because of the misuse of their lower parts. Therefore, unless they solve this resentment, a man and a woman cannot stand as a couple of original nature. The Fall was caused by the misuse of the lower parts, so the indemnity stick ceremony establishes the condition to restore this through indemnity. When the husband and wife, in the position representing Heavenly Parent, hit each other, the ceremony indemnifies their past mistakes, in both body and mind.

▼ Religious leaders participating in a holy water ceremony at an Interfaith Peace Blessing

3	Three-Day Ceremony	• This is the ceremony to begin conjugal life after the forty-day holy separation period. (This is the final stage for restoration as a couple.) It is a substantial ceremony to restore through indemnity on the family level the 6,000 years of God's suffering and True Parents' lifelong painful course of indemnity. It is the substantial ceremony of restoration to restore through indemnity the entire history of the providence of restoration. • The first day is the ceremony to restore the Old Testament Age (fallen Adam, Old Testament realm). The second day is the ceremony to restore through indemnity the position of Jesus in the New Testament Age. The third day is the ceremony in which the restored husband re-creates the wife. • As an indemnity ceremony to establish the conditions to be reborn through True Parents, it is a process in which externally the wife is restored first and gives birth to the husband.

"The Blessing is the most important moment in your life when your lineage is changed and you become Heavenly Parent's child."

5.6 The Rules of the Blessing Ceremony

▼ Representatives of different faiths in the holy water ceremony

① **The officiators will dress formally in holy robes.** However, according to the situation of the mission field and the policies of the headquarters, the men can wear navy-blue suits and the women can wear white formal clothes or other traditional attire.

② **It is best for the officiators to officiate together as a couple.** Through the officiating couple officiating the Blessing ceremony together as a couple, it can be a complete beginning for the blessed couples.

③ **By placing a picture of True Parents on the stage during the Blessing event, it becomes an event overseen by True Parents.** In the case of already-married Blessing ceremonies, the Blessing is to be received from Heavenly Parent and True Parents, but in this case, church leaders who are involved in ministry appointed by the headquarters in each nation have been sent out and authorized to officiate these Blessings on True Parents' behalf. In order to display True Parents' authority, it is good to place the picture in the middle or to the left of the stage so that the brides and grooms and guests will notice it. Explain that the Blessing is authorized by True Parents and that Reverend Moon and his wife are the True Parents of humankind and that we also must go a course to resemble them.

④ **The brides at the Blessing ceremony should wear a veil and gown, and the grooms dark blue suits.** However, depending on the situation of the mission field and the policies of each nation and headquarters, they may also wear their nation's traditional costumes.

⑤ **Keep the program order of the Blessing event.** You may shorten the order of the program, but you cannot omit the Holy Wine Ceremony, the Affirmation of Vows, the Proclamation of the Blessing or the Benediction (to guarantee the complete integrity of the event).

⑥ **Brides and grooms should participate as a couple, but they also can participate alone.** However, the heavenly tribal messiahs should provide the participating spouse with holy wine to take home for the spouse who cannot attend, or else the officiators should visit them and do the Holy Wine Ceremony. The Holy Wine Ceremony cannot be conducted unless both the husband and wife have consented to participate in the Blessing.

⑦ **Couples who do not follow through the entire program must participate in the ceremony again from beginning to end.** Participating in only some parts of the Blessing ceremony is not permitted.

⑧ The indemnity stick ceremony can be adjusted according to the officiator's discretion, but it must be held (before or after the Blessing event). Couples must participate in this indemnity stick ceremony, but it can be replaced by another ritual if someone has a health problem. It can be substituted by an exchange of promises in a question-and-answer format.

⑨ Brides and grooms participating in the Blessing ceremony must be aware of the 40-day separation period and the three-day ceremony after the Blessing. They must absolutely be educated before and after the Blessing. They should learn the reason why conjugal relations are not allowed for a period of 40 days after the Blessing and why they should be doing basic conditions of sincere jeongseong. They should be guided to do hoondokhae every days, read the entire Divine Principle book, read the entire autobiography of True Father, etc. Then the day before the three-day ceremony, it is good to call them again and educate them on the significance of the three-day ceremony.

Interfaith Peace Holy Blessing Festivals

Southeast Asia is an interreligious region. It is a mixture of Confucianism, Buddhism, Christianity, Hinduism, Islam and folk religions, and there is a different religion in each country. No matter the country, the religious leader is in a respected position. At wedding ceremonies, it is human nature for the bride and groom and guests to want to receive a blessing from a respected figure. However, it is not easy in any of those countries to have leaders from different religions attend one event at the same time or to plan an event where they can unite and express their actions based on a common goal. It is amazing that these religious leaders can come together and bless people at this moment of absolute destiny in life that we call the marriage Blessing. The fact that interfaith dialogue, harmony and unity are made possible through the Blessing ceremony brings people renewal and it is a beginning with a new perspective. Asia has been developing the interfaith peace Blessing ceremony by having religious representatives participate in the Blessing ceremony and give their words of blessing as the congratulatory remarks. The religious representatives stand on the stage together and sprinkle the holy water from there onto the participants during the "water of harmony ceremony," a ceremony of religious harmony which the participants find deeply moving. The interfaith peace Blessing ceremony, in which religious leaders are invited to perform this ceremony of religious harmony, has elevated the understanding of the direction of the Blessing movement to the interreligious community of Asia. People feel that the value of the ceremony they participated in was elevated. Religious leaders are well respected, so through them the Family Federation has been recognized and looked upon favorably and has gained the trust of the community residents naturally.

Section 6 Love and Attention

6.1 Restoration of the Realms of the Elder Son and the Parents

It is easy for new tribe members to respect their heavenly tribal messiah and follow his guidance and receive the Blessing. However, it is not as easy for them to actually accept their heavenly tribal messiah couple as their spiritual parents.

If the tribal messiah is to be accepted as a spiritual parent, first he needs to build a foundation of love through giving them love and attention.

Second, the tribal messiah's other Abel-type spiritual children need to play the role of John the Baptist. This will hasten the pace at which the Cain-type tribe members accept their tribal messiah as their spiritual parent. If the Abel-type tribe members refer to the tribal messiah as their spiritual parents, this will provide a way for the Cain-type tribe members to ask questions about what a spiritual parent is. This will give you a good chance to bring up the subject of the spiritual parent–child relationship.

Third, the tribal messiah needs to help the new tribe members understand the significance of Divine Principle through education. Abel-type members' respectful attention to the Cain-type members has to lead to the point at which the Cain-type members proclaim, "You are my spiritual teacher, and I will attend you as such." Continued education of the new members on the teachings of Divine Principle will surely lead to the moment when they accept the heavenly tribal messiah as their spiritual parent. You may have led them successfully to proclaim you as their messiah and receive the Blessing, but it takes more love, time, and efforts to get them to accept you as their spiritual parent.

Management of New Members: Help your new tribe members develop a sense of ownership through giving them love, sharing companionship, educating them on Divine Principle, getting them to participate in events, and involving them in other tasks. Even if you meet a candidate several times and invite him to your home, there are still a few more steps to be taken before that person will be ready to submit his application to join the movement and have his faith take root. You must let the new member feel love from different angles. It is important to remember that a new member should be treated as an unfamiliar face only the first one or two times he visits. Afterward he should be given responsibilities such as participating in service activities, joining the choir, taking part in a home group, coming to events and such. A focus should be given on him making new friends, giving him continued education in Divine Principle, letting him participate in events, and helping him develop a sense of ownership. This is the best method of loving someone. Someone who loves the church will surely develop into someone who is sacrificial. Giving him a mission, however small it may be, will help him develop a sense of calling, and he soon will have a sense of belonging and ownership toward the tribe.

6.2 The Path of Spiritual Parent and the Parent of the Tribe

It is difficult to have personal time with a new member if he or she was part of a large Blessing. In this case, extra efforts should be made to develop a personal relationship with each member.

First, pastoral visits are an important step after the Blessing. Weak personal relationships may lead to a member's attitude suddenly growing cold and distant . In particular, those tribe members who have received the Blessing without any previous personal connection may not feel the deep value of the Blessing. That is why a system of pastoral visits should be established as soon as possible.

Second, waste no time in establishing home groups and providing them with education. It is very difficult to manage a large number of people simultaneously. That is why it is a good idea to select 12 members from the tribe who show good leadership and assign 36 members to each of them. This will serve as a good management system. In addition, the heavenly tribal messiah quickly should raise 12 disciples and train them in how to lead hoondokhae sessions, manage people, and become the Abel-type leader. They also should receive training to unite absolutely with and testify to the heavenly tribal messiah who is their spiritual parent. Continued education and hoondokhae should take place on such a foundation. The heavenly tribal messiah should provide them with materials and hold regular seminars, encouraging all the members of the tribe to participate.

Third, the heavenly tribal messiah's direct children and Abel-type spiritual children (those who already have become blessed members) should be guided so that they quickly can stand in the position of the elder-son realm. They need to be able to support their heavenly tribal messiah. In order for a heavenly tribal messiah to perform the role of parent, the support of the people who already have been awakened is critical.

A heavenly tribal messiah should always strive to give more to all his children, sharing their pain and suffering as well as their joy, and giving words of blessing at any appropriate occasion.

Fourth, a heavenly tribal messiah should never be selfish and calculative in his relationship with his spiritual children. We all learned how to conduct ourselves through True Parents' teachings and life course. In the same way, it is important for us to be the shining example of true love, the kind of love in which you give and forget.

Fifth, the heavenly tribal messiah should convey regularly the

▼ 2015 year-end gathering by a heavenly tribal messiah group

providential news of True Parents to his tribe members. Spiritual parents need to convey to their spiritual children information regarding the providential news and victories of True Parents. This will strengthen the faith identity of the heavenly tribal messiah as a spiritual parent and also help nurture his spiritual children into active members who have enthusiasm for Heaven's providence.

The faith identity of tribe members as spiritual children can deepen only when the link of love between them and Heavenly Parent and True Parents strengthens. On the other hand, a spiritual child will have a greater chance of leaving if he receives insufficient love from his spiritual parents. True Parents infinitely poured their love to the blessed members.

Therefore, we should take after them and offer endless prayer and jeongseong, keeping with us a list of all of the tribe members and

▼ A heavenly tribal messiah Blessing in Thailand

praying for them regularly, and live a life of conveying True Parents' love to them through various channels. True Parents' teaching of making others indebted in love has an important value to us. We must remember that all tribe members are the result of love that we invested.

6.3 Test of Love, Victory of Love

The tribe members will continue to test their tribal messiah to see if he is treating them as real children or merely as witnessing candidates. There is a great deal of difficulty in the process of nurturing and restoring the children of the satanic realm to the heavenly realm. This is a process that should be accepted readily by parents.

Spiritual children may put their spiritual parents continuously through tests. We need to understand that this is a process of children accepting their spiritual parents as real parents. Some of these spiritual children may give us very hard times and leave in the end. However, this is the same process that Heavenly Parent had to experience with humanity and the same path that True Parents had to walk in order to restore and raise blessed families. In the end, this process should be expected, as it is a way of experiencing the sorrowful heart of Heavenly Parent and becoming the parent of the original Adam's family. Those who are in the position of parent will grow further and be placed on the same level of growth toward Heavenly Parent and True Parents whose heart we experience through this blessed process. We should remember that at the end of this path of tribulation there is a great reward. This reward hides itself and remains unseen until the very end, when we pass the test. Passing the test of one child will connect you to the larger group of which the child is a member. The providence of restoration is a providence of overcoming conditions. We now live in an age when we overcome those conditions. We can access the larger conditions that are in the background. That is why we should not be disappointed or discouraged when we are put through tests by our spiritual children. Rather we should keep Heavenly Parent and True Parents as our guiding lights and never give up. The tribulations are given to us by Heavenly Parent, our vertical parent, who wants to raise us into parents.

6.4 Parents' Love for Their Spiritual Children

There are a few parental characteristics that are vital in loving your spiritual children until the end.

First is enduring attention. The Blessing puts the spiritual parent and his spiritual children into a parent–child relationship. Therefore, they cannot treat each other like strangers after the Blessing. A parent and his children are to live together and share the joys of life together. A spiritual parent must give continuous attention to his spiritual children. The parent can use social media or text-messaging applications to convey the teachings of True Parents and establish a tradition of starting each day with heavenly messages. While doing so, he can ask them how they are doing. The parent will feel good, and the ones on the receiving end of the attention also will feel loved. However, a heavenly tribal messiah will still be forced to limit the time and attention given to his own children in order to build relationships with his spiritual children. This can be overcome by letting the direct children take part in his heavenly tribal messiah activities, which also will help them later to grow into the heirs of his works.

Second is investment of love. Some people are outgoing and generally like people. However, there are a lot of spiritual parents who are more focused on how many people they bring than on learning how to take care of them after they have joined. It is difficult to build a deep relationship unless you can gain a victory through investing love. Investment of love can begin from small things. Spiritual parents should utilize holidays to spend time with their direct and spiritual children. Occasions such as Christmas parties, celebrations for entering or graduation from school, or Blessing anniversaries can be used as well. The spiritual children will begin to feel loved as their spiritual parents continue to invest love.

Third is embracing, forgiving, and persevering. Spiritual children have been raised outside the heavenly realm, and therefore may end up disappointing their spiritual parents from time to time. In each instance of disappointment, the spiritual parent has to understand and embrace them and help them find their way back to the righteous tradition. This process of deviation and returning will continue for a long period of time. A spiritual parent has to embrace and forgive them each time and treat them as he would treat his own children. Giving new life to a spiritual child is immensely difficult, just as one has to endure a searing pain when giving birth to a child. We must love them and understand that they are on the path to growth.

> "Love and live for the sake of your spiritual children with the heart of a parent and in the shoes of a servant."

A Story of the Yoon Won-il and Ahn Dong-heon Family

My name is Ahn Dong-heon, and I was blessed in the 430 Couples Blessing. I have lived all my life as a missionary. Ever since I joined the church in 1964, I have dedicated my life to seeking new people, getting them to submit their registration form, and making sure they attend services at the church. I have never been lazy or regretted my life as a missionary. My head always was filled with thoughts of how to guide more people into the movement. It is impossible to face the challenges of life and keep giving without the foundation of love. I didn't know it meant that I invested love, but in hindsight, I never treated anyone halfheartedly. My spiritual children made me sad as a parent countless times. Sometimes it was so difficult that I almost wanted to abandon all of them. What I learned through investing my love is that everyone is different. I believe that one of the most important teachings in the Divine Principle is that every human being has a unique character. As they are all unique, it is difficult to love them if you remember every one of their faults and mistakes. There were many different cases of spiritual children. I would consider only a few of them to be successful; many of them grew distant. I lost 90 percent of my spiritual children, and only 10 percent remain today. This is a telling story of how much love we have to invest in order to restore the world. Each individual, each family is all very precious. It feels like these families are all that I have left in my life. I pledge to spend the rest of my life to educate my spiritual children so that they may remain as my tribe members.

◀ Members of the Navalta tribe listening to a Divine Principle lecture

Section 7 Educating Spiritual Children

7.1 The Status and Heart of Filial Piety as Spiritual Children

Yeh-hwa leading a Divine Principle seminar

As a filial child, the most important thing is maintaining the lineage inherited from the parent (purity) and having a heart of love (hyojeong: a heart of filial piety) toward the parent. The first and most important education for those who have entered God's realm through the Blessing is purity education. The second is hyojeong education, which teaches how to unite in heart and be ready to obey and follow the words of our original parents, the True Parents. It is important not to lose our new lineage. Learning new teachings through the Principle is ultimately part of the process of restoring one's lineage. Before beginning a Blessing ceremony, the direction that True Parents most often give to the participants is to not defile their lineage. Hence, the heart of appreciation for True Parents pushing them to live a life of chastity as young people and of fidelity toward their spouses is the filial heart that most eases their parents' hearts. A spiritual parent's responsibility is to support their spiritual children to fully maintain their qualification as filial children who offer acts of filial piety with loving hearts toward Heavenly Parent and True Parents.

After completing her three-year memorial period for the settlement of Cheon Il Guk following True Father's Seonghwa (Ascension), True Mother has been emphasizing hyojeong, which has a deeper meaning still. True Mother is showing the way of filial piety and of inheritance to all Cheon Il Guk's citizens. Everything was completed by the time True Father ascended, yet he should have been able to go to the spirit world on the foundation of at least one restored nation. However, we failed to complete the restoration of a nation before his Seonghwa. Therefore, True Mother personally offered jeongseong to Heavenly Parent for three years after his ascension and set a condition to free True Father in the spirit world. The foundation of True Mother's condition in front of Heavenly Parent as the True Parents became a foundation of hyojeong toward Heavenly Parent and the True Parents. Therefore, blessed families on earth should follow True Parents' example and fulfill their duty of filial piety to True Parents. This is necessary because we need to restore at least seven nations to provide a lasting foundation for True Parents to stand on. Thus, the responsibility of heavenly tribal messiahs is to pull out Satan's roots and establish hoondok family centers in their mobilization areas, in each small village neighborhood, town and city. Heavenly tribal messiahs should carry out activities to spread the Word to local residents and show them the fundamental path of life for humankind by teaching them about True Parents' life course.

People generally understand that filial piety means that the child, a subordinate, fulfills their duty of attending the parent, a superior, with undivided devotion. Yet the ancient manuscript Records on Acts of Filial Piety (Korean manuscript originally created in the Goryo Dynasty and was first published in 1415 by King Chungmok and revised in 1428) reveals that filial piety begins when parents worship and live for the sake of their children and teach them the way of life. Hence, hyojeong is the most important virtue for heavenly tribal messiahs to teach their spiritual children. Heavenly tribal messiahs should guide the blessed families in their tribe to lead their daily lives attending Reverend Sun Myung Moon and Dr. Hak Ja Han Moon as the True Parents of Humankind.

> "Practicing filial piety is
> providing education after the blessing."

7.2 The Strategy for Educating Spiritual Children

① Teach your spiritual children to maintain a basic life of faith. What that life of faith includes will vary according to the country where your tribe is located, but tribal messiahs who have held large-scale Blessing ceremonies should establish a location for an interreligious Sunday afternoon service that allows people of all faiths to attend freely. During the service, tribal messiahs can incorporate rituals such as offering different forms of religious prayer in front of Heavenly Parent. Yet we recommend that during the sermon the heavenly tribal messiah should be the center, testify to True Parents' words, and speak about true family values and peace movements. Those who have a small number of spiritual children should manage their tribe in the form of having hoondok services in a small group. In this case, it would be a good idea to offer interfaith services in a local church in cooperation with other nearby heavenly tribal messiahs. Heavenly tribal messiahs should educate their tribe members to pray for God's nation and to receive His righteousness. They should gradually educate them to make voluntary donations for the sake of God's nation and righteousness. Also, tribal messiahs should encourage them to serve as volunteer staff members for interfaith services and other projects of the tribe.

② Teach your spiritual children to study the Word and practice it. They should read the Word every day and make an effort to apply it to their lives. The Word is the central point of growing one's faith. Therefore, you should prepare a variety of True Parents' books so that your spiritual children can trust and accept the Word with an obedient mindset. Then they will be able to receive enlightenment and wisdom along with their growing faith. Furthermore, they will gain conviction in the Word and spread it themselves.

③ In the long run, focus on educating the family's children (spiritual second generation) more than the already married couple. There is a certain limit to the growth of an already married couple's faith, but their children have greater potential because they are purer than their parents. Thus, heavenly tribal messiahs need to invest more into educating their tribe members' children. It is appropriate to have intensive workshops at each level of training for people who are capable of becoming public leaders through Divine Principle education, purity education, and Blessing education. We need to prepare them to receive the Blessing in the future.

④ **Pass on the heavenly tribal messiah mission.** One's restored tribe is not meant to exist temporarily but must last forever. The tribe's second generation should spread the Word and have a sense of purpose to save the world. Centering on that purpose, they need to strive together as a united community to systematically grow and develop their tribe.

▼ A Blessing ceremony in Kim Sang-gyun and Etsuko Uda's tribe

The Story of Celestino and Raimelda Navalta's Daughter, Yeh-hwa

The second-generation daughter and only child of the Navalta family is Yeh-hwa, who is currently a high-school student. Her father, Pastor Navalta, is the official Divine Principle lecturer at the Philippine Headquarters. Mr. and Mrs. Navalta have led busy lives in public work, and they are active in educational efforts for their spiritual children in their mission country. Although Yeh-hwa did not receive her parents' love to the fullest, her appreciation and respect for her parents are stonger than most people's. While she did not have the opportunity to spend much time with her parents, as many people were always visiting their home due to her parents' public positions in the church, she understood her parents and quietly endured. Despite her young age, she has recently taken the responsibility of giving Divine Principle lectures to support her parents' heavenly tribal messiah activities. She usually gives lectures on the introduction to the

 Divine Principle and the Principle of Creation. She hopes to become an amazing Divine Principle lecturer like her father.

▼ Kim Sang-gyun and Etsuka Uda

Section 8 Leading the Local Society

8.1 Localization

While working to give the Blessing to 430 families, each time a heavenly tribal messiah brings a person he has met in his mobilization area to participate in the Blessing, a great number of connections can be formed through that person, and the family will come to have frequent interactions with them all. Then the family will grow attached to that locality, and thus their living environment is expanded. When the heavenly tribal messiah culture takes root in a locality and forms a tribal realm, localization takes place naturally. In the long run, the mobilization area becomes the hometown of the tribe, regardless of where the original hometown of the heavenly tribal messiah family may be. The heavenly tribal messiah is the person who was sent to a locality as a representative of Heavenly

Parent and True Parents, and as such must strive to fulfill the duty of being a parent to the locality. This means that in that region, he or she should become influential in all fields—religion, education, culture, politics and economy—and lead the tribe to become a mainstream force of influence in the area.

8.2 Transforming the Local Breakthrough Model into a Heavenly Tribal Messiah Center

The local breakthrough movement (*tongban gyeokpa* 통반격파) was begun in the 1980s, when True Parents declared the Home Church movement and asked members to set up grassroots organizations in every local neighborhood to carry out activities centered on our ideology. *Tongban gyeokpa* was a movement in which blessed families went to the most local neighborhoods, blocks, townships, districts, counties and cities in the society and lived with the local residents and educated them through True Parents' words and banished Satan by holding holy wine ceremonies. The tribal realm formed by a heavenly tribal messiah, on the other hand, is focused on setting up a framework for hoondok family centers, forming hoondok family church congregations. From the perspective of educating people, the two movements are similar, but the mission of the heavenly tribal messiah is more significant, for it involves connecting people to the lineage of Heavenly Parent through the Blessing ceremony and making them the children of Heavenly

◤ Kalasin home group Happy Day participants

Father. It means adopting a locality as one's hometown and attending Heavenly Parent and becoming enrooted at that place.

> True Parents' words: "In running a hoondok family center, the neighborhood and block branch leaders are the most important. The village branch leader comes next. On the day on which the village, neighborhood and block branch leaders unite with each other, everything is completed. For them to unite, they need to be settled in their area. True Parents are the branches, and you need to put down your roots. Only then can you grow worldwide. The first place the kingdom of heaven will take root, in all of history, is Korea." [*Chambumo Gyeong* 5-2-5-23]

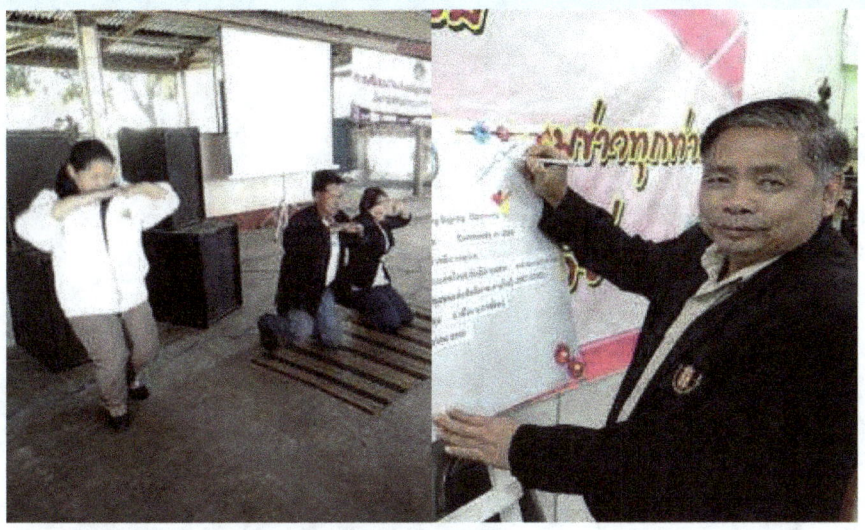

◣ Various activities in Kalasin home group Happy Day events

8.3 Expanding the Social Impact

Social impact refers to the degree to which an individual or a group influences the society to which they belong. It is very important for the tribe formed by a heavenly tribal messiah to influence the local society, in order to bring it closer to the heavenly standard and to Heavenly Parent. Through such influence, even a relatively small group of dedicated people is enabled to lead the local society, ultimately making national restoration, the mission given to us by True Parents, an achievable reality. To generate social impact and be able to maintain great influence in the locality with only a small number of group members, you need to join with other tribal messiah families in your mobilization area to carry out activities that can bring more people together.

The Experience of Kim Sang-gyun and Etsuko Uda's Family in Korea

After joining the church in Japan, I participated in the 6,000 Couples Blessing in 1982 and came to Korea to join my husband after finishing my three-year course of public work. Right away I began the work of collecting signatures for the Citizens' Federation for the Unification of North and South Korea and educating others in Jeongreung-dong, Seongbuk-gu. It was very difficult at first, but the local people began to take interest in a Korean mother-in-law and Japanese daughter-in-law working together in unity over a long period of time. I also developed good relationships with a number of local organizations, including women's organizations in Seongbuk-gu, such as Saemaul Women's Club, the Veterans Association, the National Alliance for the Reunification of Korea, the Living Right Movement and the Women's Union. I collected signatures from people in those groups, signifying their participation in the true love movement, and also performed Blessing ceremonies.

The direction of my work involved dedicating myself completely to gaining recognition from John the Baptist figures and residents of the local society. As a result of such activities over many years, in December

2008 I received a plaque of appreciation from the Women's Union for attending my parents-in-law with devotion and also for service to the society, and in 2013 I received a letter of commendation from the chief of Seongbuk-gu. After that, the direction of my work changed. Heavenly Parent has guided me to the point where I now am leading the local society and awarding others. I have risen to the position where I now present such awards as the True Family Movement Model Award, the Filial Daughter-in-Law Award, the True Family Award and the Fruitful Mother Award to the people who help create a healthy society through the true family movement, upon the recommendation of the women's organizations of Seongbuk-gu. In addition, I witnessed to 120 new families in this region, and so, together with my other spiritual children, I was able to perform the heavenly tribal messiah Blessing ceremony of 430 couples in Yu Cheon Gung. When you serve others and devote yourself unceasingly for a long time in a region, as I have done, you can rise to the position from which you can lead the local society. I personally experienced this amazing miracle, and even today I am doing my best to contribute to the providence with a joyful heart together with my spiritual children in the neighborhoods and blocks.

Mr. and Mrs. Kojima

◤ A tribal assembly at the Tokai church in Osaka

8.4 Leading the Local Governance

A heavenly tribal messiah tribe with connections to its local area comes to have a role in the governance of the area by participating in all matters, great and small. In other words, when the leading class of the locality has a certain problem, the leaders will communicate with one another centering on the heavenly tribal messiah couple, who in turn will offer their opinions directly and indirectly and thus come to stand in the position of the leader. This is based on their influence at the grassroots level of that local society. In short, they come to acquire political and financial power. When the number of such heavenly tribal messiahs increases nationwide, even the restoration of the nation becomes possible.

"National restoration is possible with only a few heavenly tribal messiahs."

(True Parents' words)

❝
8.5 Social Impact Management Strategy

① Create close-knit groups (home groups) in various parts of the local society. Organizations should be formed and expanded through individual connections. In your mission area, there should be no local leader you do not know about, and conversely there should be no citizen who does not know about you. However, in reality many local residents may refuse to show interest in activities of FFWPU because of prejudices stemming from certain religions. Therefore, you need to be wise enough to set a target audience and choose possible encounters and candidates in order to form connections with all of your targets.

② Take an interest in major issues of the local society and the trends of public opinion, and try to propose solutions from a Divine Principle point of view. The interests of residents differ from place to place. Therefore, at all times you must carefully analyze and reflect on the interests of the public and the problems of the community. You also should remember that, since most social problems stem from individualistic egoism, they cannot be fundamentally resolved. Therefore, it is advisable not to be swayed too much by the social issues of the time; instead, first emphasize to the public that they should work on resolving the fundamental problems, and then go on to enlighten the society through the teachings of the new Word.

③ Inaugurate branches of various providential organizations and projects. You should learn about each of the various providential projects and those in charge of them, and you should make an effort to introduce such projects as the pure love movement, the Peace Road, Tongil Moodo, WFWP, UPF and IAPP to your mission place, if possible. By introducing such providential projects, you will come to have many points of contact in which the public can show interest.

Regional Restoration in Kalasin, Thailand

Sangkom Netsopa and his wife were recognized on Foundation Day 2015 as the first couple in Kalasin Province to complete the heavenly tribal messiah mission. Between then and November 2017, seventeen couples have completed their missions. Each couple is in charge of one district. More and more blessed families from abroad are flocking to the region, having chosen it as their mission place. These blessed families are from either Korea, Japan, America and Europe. Home group leaders are being trained by couples who have completed the mission. Of course, these home group leaders are at various stages of growth. We have yet to have a home group leader who has completed the mission, but the number of home group leaders is rising steadily. We will be able to say that we have passed the real turning point in the providence when a home group leader can complete his or her mission. In addition, Kalasin is one of 100 provinces in Thailand. Most of the administrative officials and influential people in the local societies within Kalasin Province have received the Blessing, and they also are actively cooperating with FFWPU activities. Though they have received the Blessing, they need to fulfill their own duties as administrative officials in addition to carrying out activities for FFWPU, since most of them are working for the government. In FFWPU, there is no province like Kalasin, where so many people have received the Blessing, and it is very rare to find a place where most of the leading class have been blessed. However, the leading class needs to go beyond the confines of the Blessing activities and work hard to expand them into a new peace village movement centering on the values of FFWPU.

❋ Discussion Topics

1) In what stage are you stagnating at present? Discuss with others the problems that prevent you from moving forward.

2) If you have gone through any good experiences while passing through each stage, discuss them with others.

3) If there are any difficulties in your mission place, discuss ways by which you can resolve them.

This is the story of the Kojima family of Tokai Church in Nagoya Region, Japan. The summer of 2015 marked the 21st anniversary of their return to their hometown. All those years, they had been persecuted in Nagoya, which was both their hometown and home to many other members of the Kojima family, and they also had gone through various difficulties. However, in the end they won the recognition of their relatives and local residents and succeeded in breaking through at the grassroots level. To celebrate the 21st anniversary of their return to their hometown, they hosted a tribal gathering at the Tokai Church in the Osaka Region for their spiritual parents and relatives who had supported them during that time.

Mr. Kojima is the manager of the cooperative association and one of the leaders of the prefectural council. This region is home to many people in the Kojima tribe, and Mr. Kojima's parents were so well known locally, with many connections in local society, that everyone still remembers them. Mr. Kojima is building his reputation as a leader among the local residents by exercising his leadership in three directions: economic activi-

◤ A heavenly tribal messiah Blessing festival organized by Sultan Kudarat in Mindanao

ties through the cooperative association; political activities through the citizens' hall (community center); and educational activities through the video center and his own home. Since the local residents have complete faith in him, he was solicited by the Liberal Democratic Party, the current majority party, to run for city council. He is making efforts to achieve balanced development in his work in all three fields of politics, economics and education without leaning toward any one field in particular.

Of course, he has problems of his own. In Japan it is very difficult to bless even one couple. Mr. and Mrs. Kojima are currently working hard to complete 430 couples; as of today, they have blessed 210 couples. In addition, they also have to find a way to make this group of blessed couples, who have different dispositions, live in different regions and are at different levels in their life of faith, into one community. Nevertheless, they will work hard to the end and complete their mission without fail.

Introductory Questions

If you have several families of spiritual children, how do you plan to begin the work to complete your heavenly tribal messiah mission?

If you already have completed the 430 couples, how do you plan to guide them?

If you are a first-generation member, what do you think your heavenly tribal messiah activities will be like 20 years from now? Consider it from the viewpoint of history, the viewpoint of your children, and the viewpoint of your future descendants.

If you are a second-generation member, how are you going to inherit your parents' will? Are you planning to follow in their footsteps and walk the path of the heavenly tribal messiah?

Section 1 Spreading the Passion for Heavenly Tribal Messiah Activities

1.1 Spreading the Passion in the Tribe

There are many cases in which only the blessed members are actively engaged in activities, while their spiritual children remain idle followers. The messiah himself works very hard, but his spiritual children do not grow. The spiritual children will grow rapidly if they are led to participate actively in heavenly tribal messiah activities, in the same way that their spiritual parents received rebirth through receiving the Blessing. Not only the heavenly tribal messiah family, who stand at the head of the tribe, but also the newly blessed families should be passionate about heavenly tribal messiah activities. For this, they first should begin participating in the activities. Second, they should continue to be educated to make sure that they live according to the Principle. They will grow if these two things are done properly. They won't be able to experience what they learned in the Principle unless they participate in the activities. Avoiding participation will undermine their faith, and even a continued Principle education will not be able to change their lives. This is why we, the heavenly tribal messiahs, should not let the tribe members be mere followers or bystanders. We need to strike a balance between education and experience by guiding the tribe members to restore their own 430 families. By doing this, they will be able to practice what they learned and form their own tribe.

1.2 Expanding the Tribe by Raising the Sense of Calling

The willingness to share the responsibility of heavenly tribal messiah activities and the desire to expand the tribe define the quality of the members in the tribe. If a member receives training and then shows eagerness to participate in heavenly tribal messiah activities, that person's faith has good potential for growth. It would be in that person's interest to be given providential responsibilities.

> "We have to help the people (our spiritual children) to gain the same sense of responsibility that we have."

1.3 Precautions When Spreading the Passion

① **Preliminary research is a must in becoming a spiritual parent and, eventually, a heavenly tribal messiah.** You have to always be prepared, and you need an Abel figure whom you can visit and talk to if something unexpected happens. In other words, you have to maintain a relationship with your spiritual parent, a heavenly tribal messiah, or a friend who has progressed further in their activities, and ask them questions as things unfold before you.

② **If you see one of your tribe members showing growth in faith, it will be good to share a portion of your responsibility with that person.** This is especially true as a group of 430 families may have been brought in small groups, each led by their own leader who is in the position of John the Baptist. Since each group was guided by a different leader, the members show different speeds of growth in faith. The individual members will have varying degrees of faith, even if they are cared for and educated together. Because of this, the leader of that group needs to monitor the growth progress of his members.

③ **Invest extra care in the family who act without any guidance.** Blessing activities need to be carried out with the careful guidance of the church or its pastor. However, some members may neglect their relationship with the pastor and fail to report their activities. In such cases, these members should be guided to work together with their pastor who is in the position to represent

True Parents.

④ **We need to help the activities of our spiritual children who have their own spiritual children.** One of the reasons the members of a tribe work together is because they are in a family relationship. Giving unconditional support to each other leads to mutual growth. One of the best ways for a spiritual parent to help their spiritual child grow quickly is to share with the child a portion of the parent's previous responsibility. If the child stands in the parental position, his faith will grow more quickly.

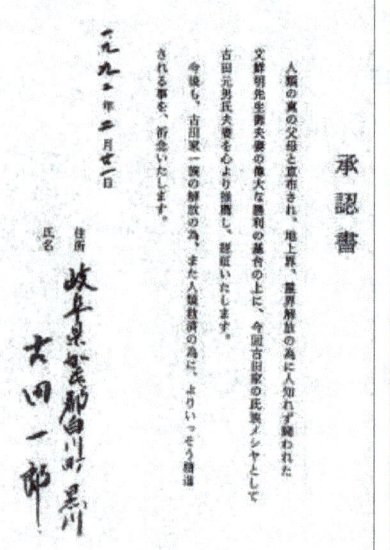 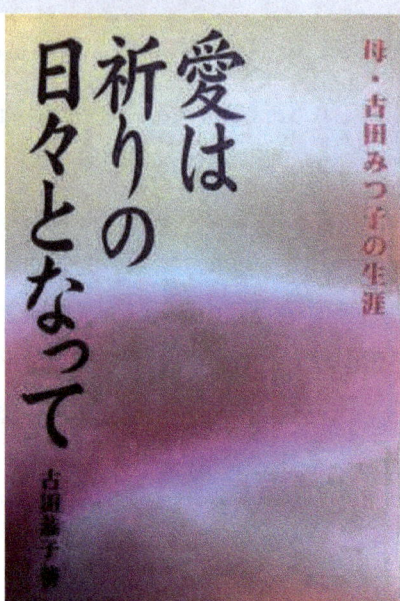 

▼ The Furuta tribe's plaque for 50 years in the church, published history and 50-year banner (from left)

The Expansion of Heavenly Tribal Messiah Activities in the Philippines

My name is Julius Malicdem, and I am the Cheon Il Guk special envoy to and the national leader of the Philippines. I want to give you a report regarding heavenly tribal messiah activities in the Philippines. The people of the Philippines have been working harder than any other people in the world to restore their nation and be good children of Heavenly Parent. In the Philippines, there are currently 147 families who have completed their heavenly tribal messiah activities. This was possible because all of the Filipino members have worked together in unity in order to complete their mission of heavenly tribal messiahship. Many families are still busy trying to complete their mission.

Ever since the Sultan Kudarat at the southern region of Mindanao, Philippines, completed his mission in 2012, heavenly tribal messiah activities have been spreading like wildfire across the nation. Though it came about gradually, the blessed members in the Philippines responded to Heaven's call to complete their heavenly tribal messiah activities, and they became very self-confident while doing it. A series of national-level Blessing ceremonies helped the members complete their missions. In summary, the Philippines Family Federation aided many of its members in completing their missions as heavenly tribal messiahs.

We believe that heavenly tribal messiah activities spread quickly in the Philippines because we first created a foundation for the Cain-type tribes. When we look at many of the success stories in Philippines, the heavenly tribal messiahs set their own mobilization areas, called barangay (villages), and focused their efforts on those areas. What are Cain- type tribes? The term "Cain-type tribe" refers to a group whose leader, who is not a member of the Family Federation, first receives the Blessing and then goes on to restore his own tribe. Many leaders of this kind, often referred to as John the Baptist figures, are working as public servants and are influential leaders of their communities. Our members' heavenly tribal messiah activities have borne fruit successfully thanks to the efforts of these John the Baptist figures. Community leaders and local government officials are being educated about our marriage Blessing and are encouraging others to receive the Blessing. Thanks to this, heavenly tribal messiah activities in many regions are finding success even more quickly. The Family Federation sends a few blessed members to Cain-type tribal Blessing ceremonies to form trinities or clusters with other Cain-type tribe members. These tribe members who received the Blessing are encouraged to help and support each other. The blessed members then educate these tribe members to bring them to the spiritual level where they themselves can become "true parents, true teachers, and true owners."

The next set of examples I'd like to give are when the members completed their heavenly tribal messiah activities while sharing each other's financial burden. Let me tell you a story of some members who came to the Philippines from abroad in order to complete their heavenly tribal messiah activities. A few blessed members have created a system in which they work with the Filipino members in a region to fulfill the standard of victory for their heavenly tribal messiah activities. These international members financially support their Filipino counterparts, and the Filipino members not only complete their heavenly tribal messiah activities in their own region but also help the members in their neighboring regions. They work together to victoriously complete their blessing of 430 couples and also create a cooperative system of managing the new members.

When we look at what has been accomplished so far, a strong spirit of teamwork and a clear vision for the heavenly tribal messiah activities have been vital in the success of our national restoration. The Filipino members have experienced a tremendous growth through the heavenly tribal messiah activities, which has been the engine that propelled this upward growth. Our system as a whole is growing as well. Members are categorized into those who are still working to complete their mission and those who are working as coordinators, mobilizers, and supporters. They have created a system through which they help and support each other through

Furuta Tribal Creed

We are following in the footsteps of the ancestor of our tribe, Mitsuko Furuta, who joined the Holy Spirit Association for the Unification of World Christianity in October 1965 and walked a path of fervent faith. On February 21, 1992, we declared that Motou and Kyoko Furuta were the tribal messiahs of the Furuta Tribe and were recognized by 120 members of our family, following which we received special recognition from True Parents as the first tribal messiah in Japan. To commemorate the 50th anniversary of the ancestor of the Furuta Tribe joining the church, 97 members of the tribe gathered for a special commemorative service on July 5, 2015, and offered our gratitude to True Parents.

1. The members of the Furuta Tribe shall believe in and attend the Messiah of all humanity, the True Parents of Heaven, Earth and Humankind, inheriting the traditions of their lives and studying their victorious words that have investigated and revealed all the problems on earth and in heaven that no others have solved throughout history, as expressed in the *Divine Principle, Cheon Seong Gyeong, Pyeong Hwa Gyeong* and *Chambumo Gyeong* as the instructions for life, and by living diligent lives of absolute faith.
2. We shall humbly practice the lifestyle of "living for the sake of others," which True Parents have suggested and demonstrated throughout their lives, and make it our goal to become persons possessing characters of love.
3. We shall ceaselessly seek to harmonize with others and put unwavering effort into serving not only the members of our tribe but also the other people with whom we are acquainted, our neighbors, those in need and, furthermore, the society and the nation with a spirit of mutual support.
4. We shall cooperate in maintaining and supporting the environment around us so that our descendants can properly inherit True Parents' teachings and way of life.
5. We shall carry out all of our activities in alignment with the realization of these purposes.

August 1, 2015
Heavenly Tribal Messiahs
Motou and Kyoko Furuta

their own distinctive roles. Going forward, the Family Federation will continue to manage the tribes systematically and give them support so that they can exert influence in their own communities.

▼ An exhibition of materials about True Parents

Section 2 Recording the Tribe's History

▼ A determination rally for 430 families and new-start gathering by the Aoyama tribe

2.1 Significance of History

The blessed family members are people prepared by Heavenly Parent. They joined the movement not by accident but by Heaven's design. They joined the Family Federation because of their ancestral background. Each blessed family has its own story. They also have great significance in that they participated in the providence in the same period of history as True Parents. However, the members of the Family Federation have not had the time to reflect on their footsteps because they always have been busy keeping up with the ongoing progress of the providence. All of their providential activities will be recorded and used as educational materials. Their actions will help them form their own tribes, serving as the basis upon which to educate their tribe members.

2.2 Historical Materials for Future Generations

Our tribes will be able to form strong communities if we pass our historical records to future generations. We have to always work together with the upcoming generation so that they will remember taking part in the heavenly tribal messiah activities. We have to help them maintain a record of their activities and share them with others.

We should not throw away the historical materials which were accrued while participating in the advancement of the providence in the same period with True Parents. We should develop a habit of organizing them neatly. One helpful activity is to turn these materials into a book, in such a form as your own autobiography. If not just one or two persons but all the members of the tribe develop a habit of keeping a historical record as events are held, they will not have to go through difficulties in the future trying to gather the materials all at once.

2.3 Types of Historical Materials

Collecting the following types of items will help to tell the story of the tribe's history.

① Awards: the awards that were given either by the church or directly by True Parents

② Commemorations: special commemorative occasions, for example, with True Parents or involving any historical providential moment

③ Official church events: published texts or photographs related to certain events

④ Origin of the tribe: items or places of value to the tribe, places such as a tribal center or church center where a Blessing ceremony or special event was held

⑤ Accomplishments of the tribe

⑥ Historical records of the individual members of the tribe

The Pride of Japan, the Furuta Tribe

The Furuta family is one of the prominent families in the Japanese church who served True Parents closely for a very long time. Mr. Motou Furuta is a second-generation member in faith and a senior church member in the Family Federation Japan. He has been in charge of the overall financial activities in Japan for many years. His contribution to the providence is great, and many members of his tribe joined the church and became blessed members. Currently there are four generations of members in the Furuta tribe. Many Furutas became church public servants, and, thanks to this, they are now a well-known, very prominent tribe in the church. They held a tribal assembly in 2015 at which their tribal vision was declared and even published a book that contains their historical footsteps. The Furuta tribe gathers once a year to hold a tribal meeting. When True Parents directed the blessed families to go back to their hometown and become tribal messiahs, the entire Furuta tribe moved back to their hometown and performed a ceremony to declare themselves tribal messiahs. Thanks to such efforts, True Parents gave them the title of the "First Tribal Messiah in Japan." The Furuta tribe, including their other spiritual children, altogether number 500 families. However, it is only recently that they started to properly guide their spiritual children who received the Blessing.

"When we started to guide them properly, we realized that the blessed members in my tribe were struggling with many problems, and some members even showed a reluctance in accepting us as their spiritual parents. I understood their feelings because, even though they received the Blessing through us, we hadn't communicated for a long time, so it was understandable that it was difficult to accept us as their spiritual parents. I realized that this is the difficult path of parents. This is the very path that True Parents had to walk! After experiencing the parental heart that True Parents had for us, my shoulders became heavy with a sense of responsibility. Now my wife and I are living each day while experiencing the desperate heart of True Parents. We haven taken our first step into the realm of True Parents' parental heart."

The heavenly tribal messiah mission is truly the path that all blessed members of this age must walk.

Section 3 Establishing a Tribal Vision

3.1 Significance of a Tribal Vision

The term "vision" has the following meanings:

- Focus or direction;
- A specific mission from Heavenly Parent given through a special revelation; or
- A "passion" or a "dream."

A person's potential can be realized and their goal achieved in the process of transferring their vision to others.

A vision (dream) is the beginning of leadership. Leadership can develop within us only when we start to dream. A dream is truly the central element that helps us understand more about leadership.

Then how is a vision born? A vision is born when the grace of Heavenly Parent inspires us and finds a dwelling place within ourselves in the form of passion. When a burning passion begins to dwell in our heart, a vision is born along with the sacrificial actions aimed at achieving it. We develop a vision, create a plan to achieve it, and begin to train ourselves in order to have the ability to carry out the plan. We then bring together the people who share that vision and help each other so that we can overcome the obstacles. Without a vision, a leader cannot be a leader in the truest sense. Without a vision, the only thing that a leader can become is a competent manager. However, vision has to do with more than just leadership. Vision requires a group of people who share it. A leader always dreams about his vision and prays for it to come true. His entire months are scheduled toward achieving his vision. Vision fires us up and makes us achieve great things.

3.2 Examples of Tribal Vision

The following are examples of a tribal vision statement and tribal creed:

"Family members are those who walk the road that leads to an identical destination."

◥ Soomboon Boonpetch giving a lecture to his tribe

3.3 Strategy in Designing a Tribal Vision

① A strategy to establish a tribal vision

First, a vision must be aligned with True Parents' ideal of Cheon Il Guk and also with the goals of the Family Federation. At the same time, a vision has to be written in a set of clear words and expressions that plainly define the tribe's core activities.

Second, it is good to create a draft version of the vision that incorporates the strengths of the heavenly tribal messiah and the common traits shared by other members of the tribe.

Third, the members of the tribe should get together and discuss the draft version of the vision. The discussion should focus on making sure the vision is achievable.

Fourth, after finishing the discussion and finalizing their vision,

▼ Heavenly tribal messiah activities by the Soomboon Boonpetch family

the tribe members should make the vision official. This helps them build a sense of responsibility and can serve as a link that binds together the members of the tribe.
② Plan for a "Vision Declaration Ceremony" that includes introducing a set of detailed steps that will lead to accomplishing the vision.
③ If possible, the heavenly tribal messiah should take the lead in writing down the tribal vision. It should be preserved in a permanent format so that it is not merely a temporary motto but one which will be passed down to the future generations. It might also be beneficial to develop family visions along with the tribal vision.

Tribal Vision Declaration Ceremony of the Aoyama Tribe

Mr. Aoyama, who works as a lecturer at a video outreach center, always had a keen interest in those who leave the movement. His own spiritual parent, who was a French missionary, left the Family Federation as well! He knew the stories of the many in Japan who have left the church. Such a circumstance led him to delve into the issue, and he always had a desire to guide those former members back to the movement. As a competent counselor, he has a knack for consoling others' hearts. His method of witnessing is to develop a deep relationship with others and move their hearts. Those who have left the movement often don't want to meet him in person, so he wrote many heartfelt letters to them. Their responses were cold at first, but Mr. Aoyama's efforts, which often continued onward after five or even eight years in some cases, warmed their hearts. His devotion in writing letters to those who have left the movement has guided many of them back into the church. This means that we can say that Mr. Aoyama is an expert in the matter of restoring past members. Hence, he has set his tribal vision to revolve around his passion for helping past members back into the movement. Many such people have their own deep stories. Mr. Aoyama worked toward resolving their sorrowful hearts. Thanks to this, Mr. Aoyama's tribe is one of the tightest communities in the Japanese movement. They support each other wholeheartedly.

Section 4 Organizing the Tribe

4.1 The Significance of Organization

The 430 couples in a tribe have a friendly relationship with each other and share a common sense of belonging. However, such a group is hard to maintain unless there is a proper system built into it. We use the term "tribe" to describe them, but what links them together is not bloodline. Rather, they are united based on their common faith. They each have their own previous relationships and cultures, so it is difficult to create a cohesive tribal community. That is why much effort should be made to create a culture of heart centering on the Family Federation culture.

4.2 Selecting Leader Figures

The heavenly tribal messiah couple alone can do only so much. As the number of new blessed families in the tribe increases, so does the workload of the heavenly tribal messiah couple. The partner families that formed a trinity at the initial formation stage of the tribe also will have their work cut out for them. That is why we must always look carefully for any candidates who have the potential to serve as leaders. The success rate for a tribal community increases as the number of those who can take responsibility increases as well. The time it takes to turn a new member from a trainee to a leader-figure core member needs to be shortened. Heavenly tribal messiah activities can be successful in the long run only if the members work together and help each other. This is because the newly blessed members have to be trained in faith before the inspiration they received from the Blessing becomes faint. In many cases, this short but golden window of opportunity goes unused and is wasted. This is why we have to work together with our direct offspring or Abel-type spiritual children.

We have to increase the number of talented members within the tribe, going from three to 12, and to 36, and let them play minor management roles that can help us maximize our influence over the tribe. These middle managers first have to go through a seven-day workshop and then receive training twice a week. In these sessions they should be educated on how to lead hoondokhae in the family, how to create a home group, how to give a ten-minute Divine

Principle lecture, and how to live based on their tribal vision.

4.3 Organization on Multiple Fronts

Heavenly tribal messiahs have to manage their tribal blessed members through a hookdok family center. At the same time, they have to take care of their spiritual children who may live all over the country. This means heavenly tribal messiahs have to work on multiple fronts. A tribal hoondok family center performs the role of guiding the members in the community in their everyday lives of faith. Such a center cannot take care of spiritual children who live outside that community circle, so a system needs to be devised with the capability to take care of these spiritual children. That is why, no matter how far such Abel-type children may live from the tribal center, they should use their vacation time from school or work to visit the tribal center and receive training. Financial support also should be given to the spiritual children to help them visit and connect to the tribal hoondok family center. Additionally, periodical meetings and sharing of information should take place, fostering a sense of belonging within the spiritual children, although they may be separated from the tribe physically. Heavenly tribes are encouraged to operate their own online group, using smartphone messaging applications, through which they can announce their tribal activities, receive feedback on those activities, and help the members understand what is going on.

4.4 Types of Tribal Organizations and Activities

A heavenly tribe consists of the following three types of groups. The first consists of core members who act as leaders and received the Blessing as already married couples. These members are also in charge of public relations in the tribe. They are the John the Baptist figures who have been prepared by Heavenly Parent for a long time. They are rooted deeply in their community and know the community inside out. They help their heavenly tribal messiah manage the entire group by leading the subgroup or the home group leaders.

The second group consists of the direct children or the Abel-type spiritual children. They could be our direct second-generation children, our siblings or relatives who received the Blessing, or the already-married couples who received the Blessing at a young age after coming into contact with the Family Federation's messages. As they are the core blessed members of the movement, they can be counted on to participate in heavenly tribal messiah activities with eagerness. They can assist the activities of the heavenly tribal messiah by sharing what is happening in the hoondok family center and helping other members understand what is going on.

The third group consists of the members in our region who are our neighbors or in our tribe who received the Blessing. They require further training in the basic teachings of the Family Federation. Those among this group who show a willingness to participate in the management of the tribe can be selected and brought forward as mid-level managers. They can serve as a home group leader.

Some of the people in the first group may play this role as well. These leaders can look after their own tribe members and start building their own foundations to become heavenly tribal messiahs.

① External group led by a John the Baptist core member (members who received the Blessing as already married couples who can manage and mobilize the members whom they brought to the tribe and also take care of public affairs)
② Disciple-level group centering on Abel-type spiritual children (young people in blessed families who can take care of paperwork, organization management, education, the management of second-generation members, and preparing the environment)
③ Leaders who manage the tribe, raising them as participants in heavenly tribal messiah activities (those who show potential within the tribe, those who received a special calling, or those who are extremely eager to participate)

"Abel and Cain must unite."

4.5 Precautions When Forming an Organization

① Responsibilities should be given only to the members who have developed an ability to digest the teachings they receive, those who have shown truthfulness and a potential for leadership.

Obviously they also should agree with our messages. The leadership role should not be given lightly to those who may have participated in our events a few times or seem to be intelligent but have a limited understanding of the Principle and have a self-centered character. Ideal candidates are those who are willing to learn and those with a sense of ownership who let their actions speak louder than their words.

② Secondly, those who have received some training should be given minor leadership roles at first. In this way they can be assimilated and be further trained in offering jeongseong to Heavenly Parent, living a hoondok-centered life, and giving Divine Principle lectures.

③ Direct offspring (second- and third-generation members) should be given responsibilities as well. While helping their parents who are acting as heavenly tribal messiahs, they can build relationships with other tribe members based on trust. Later they can develop a list of other second-generation members within the tribe; this list can be used in training and educating them to become leaders. If the tribal messiah's direct children are of sufficient age, they should be trained by helping their parents who have become heavenly tribal messiahs. Through this course they will gain modesty, humility, and the ability to convey messages based on the Divine Principle.

A Shining Example of Home Group Leader: the Soomboon Boonpetch Family

My name is Soomboon Boonpetch, and my wife is Kolnee Boonpetch. I am the former head of a district hospital in the Baan Pao region located in Thailand's Buriram Province. I worked a long time as the chairman who guided 12 villages within the Baan Pao region, and I am currently serving as a vice chairman.

Before joining the Family Federation, I had a dream in which light began to shine from the East over my country, Thailand, which was filled with evil spirits. The world in which we live is a place where everyone pursues happiness but none is able to achieve it, only shedding tears and moaning in pain while on the path. Right after I joined the Family Federation, I vowed to participate in every activity that the movement had in store for me. I began to believe that True Parents are no doubt the brightest light in the world. I was so inspired by their teachings, so I began to spread their messages across my region. I became a member of the Family Federation after receiving the Blessing and completing the three-day ceremony in 2013. I visited Korea in 2014 and saw True Parents for the first time at Cheon Jeong Gung. I received so much grace from True Parents at that time, and its memory still makes me happy.

It's difficult to describe all the gratitude and respect I have for Heavenly Parent and True Parents. Other blessed members in the village of which I am in charge are also living very happily while being thankful for the love and grace of True Parents. There are still many things that I have to learn from the leaders of the Family Federation, but I do what I can in my

◤ Lek Thaveetermasakul's family together with their tribe

capacity to fulfill my responsibilities. We are regularly holding home group meetings and worship services. We still have many improvements to make, but we are doing what we can to have our own one-day and two-day workshops to teach Divine Principle, True Parents' life course, the significance of the Blessing, the traditions of the blessed family, and how to lead one's own home group.

I often have spiritual experiences in my prayers. Once, the people in my region were suffering greatly because of a year-long drought. My wife and I offered a solemn prayer jeongseong to Heavenly Parent. After that, the prime minister of Thailand, Prayut Chan-o-cha, visited our region and promised financial support to alleviate the effects of the natural disaster. I was truly thankful. I offer my sincere gratitude to Heavenly Parent, who allowed this type of miracle to take place after I became a blessed family member.

Lek Thaveetermasakul's family receiving an award from True Parents as the first family to bless 430 couples as heavenly tribal messiahs

I love the people in my region, and I am willing to do anything for them. I now am striving to complete my mission of blessing 430 families, and I will make sure that all of them follow True Parents' guidance. In addition, I will support the young people in a way that allows them to have the right kind of moral values and have a successful life.

One hurdle that we have to face in doing home group activities is that it is difficult to gather the people, since this is a rural area. People all follow their distinct farming calendars, so I can't force them to come to events. However, home group activities are extremely important in my region. This is because we have to first get together in order to spread our movement's positive teachings and good traditions. I am really feeling that our community is becoming more and more one grand family. Thank you.

Section 5 Leadership and Tribal Ministry

5.1 Special Features of Tribal Leadership

Heavenly tribal messiahs have the responsibility to settle 430 families in their lives of faith. For this, they have to have a very parental heart and practice good leadership. They have to deal with two realms of children: the first being the realm of their direct children to whom they gave birth, and the second being their spiritual children who are like adopted children. They have to strike a balance between the two realms of children, the Cain-type and the Abel-type. The number of spiritual children usually far exceeds that of the direct children. It is of utmost importance to find the right balance between the two. True Parents, too, had to struggle to find the balance between their direct children (True Children) and the blessed members. The second generation of the True Family has walked the same course as well. Every child deserves love, and all the children should unite in harmony. It is not easy for the parents to make this happen. Things become even more complicated if the parents have to move beyond the family and operate on a tribal level. If a tribal realm is formed while its members are not fully mature in their faith, there will be too many individuals who require separate care. Because of this, only a good, well-thought-out plan can guide them.

Generally, tribal leadership refers to the leadership in a group in which people are connected by blood. However, a heavenly tribal messiah's tribe consists of not only blood relatives but also spiritual children. This feature may make the group more susceptible to internal conflicts between its members. Therefore, the tribal messiah must wield a great level of leadership if he or she is to bring harmony within his community. While managing his tribe, the tribal messiah should work to raise a number of mid-level leaders. The heavenly tribal messiah can then focus on managing the mid-level leaders, and these leaders can be given the responsibilities of looking after the spiritual children in the tribe. In addition, the heavenly tribal messiah should regularly organize group workshops, so that the tribe members can receive the care that the mid-level leaders' efforts lack. More importantly, a tribal hoondok center should be established as quickly as possible to host weekly worship services. Here the tribal messiah needs to mature the people's faith through sermons and holding leadership training for the mid-level leaders after each service. Moreover, education experts who are prepared by Heavenly Parent should be selected among the direct children or

Abel-type spiritual children who joined the movement long before. These people can be brought up as professional lecturers. A heavenly tribal messiah cannot give all the education that is necessary for the members of the tribe. Therefore, a number of lecturers should be raised on a variety of topics, and they can be dispatched on request to a regional home group to give lectures.

5.2 Husband and Wife's Parental Leadership

Sometimes a large group of spiritual children are restored all at once through a Blessing for married couples. In this case, the heavenly tribal messiah couple has to quickly step into the role of their parents. The longer it takes until spiritual training is provided for the new members, the harder it will become to form a proper parent–child relationship with them, because the inspiration they received at the Blessing quickly begins to fade. That is why it is more prudent to go through Blessings for 50 couples at a time, even though you already may have secured more candidates than that. If it is difficult to have separate ceremonies for each 50 couples, you should have them all blessed at once but work on them group by group to form a proper realm of disciples. At the same time, you have to focus on creating mid-level leaders. The more time that passes after the Blessing without a proper parental status being formed, the harder it will become to overcome relational difficulties. First, therefore, actively use the tools available to you, such as social media, to give them news on how you are doing, if you can't meet them in person. Second, there should be a training system in place by which the new members can come and participate after the initial 430-couple Blessing. As mentioned before, the mid-level leaders need to be raised and trained to manage a home group system, hold family hoondokhae, and give ten-minute Divine Principle lectures. A heavenly tribal messiah hoondok family center should be established for weekly interfaith worship services. Until such a venue can be established, local school buildings can be rented.

> "Become the parents of your tribe."

5.3 Elder Son-Type or Elder Daughter-Type Leadership in the Realm of Children

Once a 430-couple tribe is formed, it is imperative for the heavenly tribal messiah couple to quickly select a number of blessed members who can be entrusted to help with their work and be raised as heirs. These members will work in the position of the first sons or daughters of the tribe. Such elder son-type leadership is absolutely necessary—and not just to lessen the messiah couple's ministerial workload. One of the reasons most blessed members experience difficulties after holding a Blessing is that they have failed to raise blessed members who can take the position of the first son or daughter (heir). In addition, they often were unable to raise mid-level leaders who could help them. These people need to be capable of following the heavenly tribal messiah couple absolutely. There should not be any distance between them and the messiah couple. It is probably not an overstatement to say that people who can play the role of middle managers are absolutely critical to the successful formation of a tribe.

5.4 Special Features of Tribal Ministry

A harmonious relationship is required between direct ministry and indirect ministry. Locations such as Korea, Japan, and the United States, where faith communities already have settled down, may have formats that are different from what is outlined above. In other words, a blessed family who successfully completed their 430-couple tribe very often try to turn their new members into core members by integrating them into the Family Federation. In this case, the heavenly tribal messiah who formed the tribe needs a plan that will enable him to flexibly deal with indirect ministry. This is described in detail in a previous chapter. Ministers have to adapt to the leadership style of the age. They should move out of the singular, direct-ministry style and toward pioneering and expanding hoondok family centers. These centers should be guided to develop, stage by stage, and later become separate branch churches. This means that the heavenly tribal messiah has to report the official number of tribe members in the tribal hoondok center. Not only the tribal messiah but also his family members and the members of the church need to prepare to form an independent branch church. Before branching out, the heavenly tribal messiah, as the first step, has to perform indirect ministry within the Family Federation church. At the second stage, a place should be rented for the new hoondok family center. The members in small numbers can move back and forth between their church and the new center, but they have to train the tribe members who have not become the core members of their center through the methods of raising mid-level leaders: creating a home group, training about family hoondokhae, a weekly interfaith worship service, and a weekly meeting of mid-level leaders.

5.5 Precautions for Tribal Leaders

① **The couple needs to unite, show what it's like to be model parents for the tribe, and create a firm foundation for their status as the tribal parents.** Moreover, their direct children or heirs (the Abel-type spiritual children) should work together with their parents to show other members how to unite centering on the visions of True Parents and the tribe.

② **The parents should always have the heart to forgive and embrace tribe members.** Many tribal children will give you challenges before they accept you as their parents. At each step of the way, you have to be prepared to forgive and embrace them.

③ The heavenly tribal messiahs are the tribal parents, but they simply can't remember everyone in the tribe. Because of this, it is of critical importance to find spiritual children who can act as heirs or mid-level leaders.

An Example of Leadership by a Couple: Cheon Il Guk Special Envoy Lek Thaveetermsakul's Family

I served as the national leader of Thailand for nearly 20 years. When my duty finished in 2006, I decided to begin my heavenly tribal messiah mission. However, I had no idea how to begin. I only knew that I should make every preparation necessary. I believe that the husband and the wife have to be absolutely united. After praying deeply to Heaven on this issue, my wife and I made a solemn determination to dedicate ourselves to heavenly tribal messiah activities. We believed that Heaven's gate would open wide for us if we completely aligned ourselves with the Will of Heavenly Parent. In hindsight, I can see what a key role my wife played in the successful completion of the activities. I am truly grateful to my wife. The wife's role is very critical in the heavenly tribal messiah mission. I realized that the woman, who is in the motherly position for the family and for the tribe, must first be settled in firmly.

I want to express my sincere heart of gratitude to True Parents, who bestowed upon the heavenly tribal messiahs and blessed members a tremendous grace and blessing. It was beyond anything I could imagine. Heavenly Parent's guidance and protection and True Parents' victorious foundation have allowed us to complete the Blessings to form our tribe. We will continue to strive so that our tribe can serve as a model for other tribes.

Section 6 Creating an Environment

6.1 Hoondok Family Center (Hoondok Family Church)

A hoondok family center should be established within the heavenly tribal messiah's residence. Interfaith activities may bring people from all walks of life, so using the term "center" is preferable to "church." Names such as "Heavenly Tribal Messiah Hoondok Family Center," "True Family Culture Center," or "Hyojeong Culture Center" could be used, but in principle, the center should belong to the Family Federation for World Peace and Unification International.

**Family Federation for World Peace and Unification
– True Family Cultural Center –**

"Establish a house where Heavenly Parent can take charge."

6.2 The Elements of a Hoondok Family Center

The following rooms are the very least that are required in a center:

No.	Location	Significance
1	Prayer room	This is the holy place with True Parents' portrait, holy candles, and chairs where people come to pray or receive counseling.
2	Chapel (meeting room)	This is a relatively large space where worship services, workshops and other meetings can be held.
3	Office	This is the working space where the administrative work of the tribe is managed and where various items can be be stored.

6.3 Tribal Center

It is important to establish the place of origin of the tribe (hometown). The places that have been used for various providential activities, such as Blessing activities, life of faith, or other places of great providential importance, have a great significance for the members of the tribe. These places are full of memories. Churches may disappear if they move to a different location, but a tribe's heavenly tribal messiah hoondok family center is a place of great historical importance. A hoondok family center can be designated as a holy place if it has a long history of providential activities. This is why selling such a location should be discouraged. Even if a hoondok family center expands and becomes a large Family Federation church, the original smaller center can be used for other church events, such as church rituals, holidays, or other commemorative days.

6.4 Center Management Strategy

① **A center should have strictly divided spaces for living and ministry.** They always should be kept clean. In some cases, it might be difficult to separate these spaces entirely in the initial stages. In such a case, at least the prayer room, which is the holy place of the center, should always be kept clean and never used for personal activities. If some members take residence in a center, those members will have difficulties in terms of privacy or educating their children, because centers are always viewed as a public space. If personal life and ministry are mixed up, the minister's authority won't hold and visitors may feel uncomfortable. Because of this, public and private spaces should be separated strictly, and the members should learn to be respectful and courteous.

② **A prayer room, which serves as the holy place, is essential.** The holy place provides a space for prayer, and it plays a central role in the house's spiritual environment. This is where True Parents' portrait and holy candles are kept. All ministerial activities revolve around the holy place. The more jeongseong is offered to

Heavenly Parent in the prayer room, the more authority the center will be able to have in the region. Visitors to the center may be guided to recognize the prayer room as an important place and use it to offer jeongseong to Heavenly Parent. If this is established properly, the success of the center is guaranteed. Having a proper prayer room can be the first step in a successful education of life of faith.

③ **The utility of a space is more important than its convenience.** If the spiritual atmosphere of a certain space has been expanded through offering jeongseong to Heavenly Parent and True Parents, that place is filled with the history of heavenly works and good memories. A tribal ministry can have a higher chance of success if it has such a place filled with a heart of yearning for Heaven.

Section 7 Education System

7.1 The Significance of Education

Guests who have received the Blessing require a lot of education. The student is filled with gratitude and respect for the educator and ultimately comes to be a disciple. That is why, if possible, the heavenly tribal messiah should not stop at being just the person who introduced somebody to True Parents, but should personally educate their guests. Do not leave the education to be done by the pastor but oversee it yourself. This is the ideal way for the formation of a tribe and for the development of the hoondok family church. Your greatest investment of time and money should be for education. The core of a heavenly tribal messiah's duties, apart from Blessing activities, is ultimately to convey our teachings. Therefore, the basic core of heavenly tribal messiah activities is to design a curriculum for spiritual children, create education programs for them and run the programs. In the past, the education was left up to the pastor, but the era has come when blessed families are taking personal responsibility for the education of their guests.

7.2 Selecting a Place for Educational Programs

Selecting a place for the education to take place is very important. The following three things must be taken into consideration:

First, it is better if the area for education is separate from the living area, so the first task is to prepare a place for the education. If your living area is large, you can have the lecture room in your home. However, during the beginning stages, it is safer to first use a

Figure 4-4) Family Federation Korean Headquarters' True Parents' Words on Kakaotalk Messages

Family Federation church building in the region, if there is one, or a video center or any other space that you can use for free. Another option is to use a town center, administrative agency, school, other public facility or a coffee shop with a meeting area by reserving it each week and paying per use.

Second, it is best to select a place that is reverent and quiet. The further away it is from the living area of the guest, the better the result.

Third, you must place True Parents' picture at the front of the lecture room. A place without True Parents' picture cannot be said to be a sanctified place. We must attend True Parents' picture. Through the spiritual authority of True Parents, that place can become sanctified and cleansed and become a public place.

7.3 Stages of Education

This is the method for guiding guests whom we meet on a daily basis and educating them in stages.

① The Stage of Creating Bonds of Sympathy

First, bring guests to events held by NGOs that are connected to the providence, and have them get a feel for the activities we are doing. Second, apart from bringing them to events related to Family Federation, there is also the option to have mutual exchange and develop friendship through foreign-language study groups, sports, cultural activities, service projects and other diverse groups. Third, invite them to the tribe's hoondok center small group meeting, so they will have a positive impression of the activities of the Family Federation.

This is the first stage. It acts as the bridge to moving to the second stage, where they will learn the Divine Principle.

② Stage of Divine Principle Education

Begin to systematically teach them the first and second parts of the Divine Principle in depth. This means you go further than simply explaining one or two chapters in the Divine Principle, which is usually the goal for first-time guests. Working with them one on one, focus on studying the red and blue text of the first and second parts of the Divine Principle, and have your guest understand the Divine Principle.

③ Stage of Education about True Parents' Life Course and Thought

When guests study the Divine Principle, they become curious and ask questions about True Parents and whether they are the Messiah. It is very rare for someone to accept True Parents as the Messiah right away, simply by hearing the Divine Principle. Therefore, first have them read True Father's autobiography, *As a Peace Loving Global Citizen*, chapter by chapter, and then talk about it with them. At the next stage, many guests will search the Internet to find out more about the True Parents whom they have heard about in Family Federation. This is to try to get an objective view of the situation. However, this may bring about a lot of misunderstanding. Therefore, in the long run it is not enough for them to simply recognize True Parents as amazing people. It is only when we teach them in detail about True Parents' life course, on the foundation of the

Divine Principle, that they can establish their faith. Next, have them read the hoondok textbooks that were given by True Parents, and take time for questions and answers. If you can educate them to that stage, there will be a lot of growth.

④ Stage of Education of Traditions

Without education about traditions, guests who receive the Blessing have no idea how to use True Parents' picture, holy candle, holy salt, holy wine, etc., after the Blessing. There must be education after the Blessing. They should be taught the church holidays, rituals, etc., that Unificationists practice according to our tradition.

⑤ Stage of Spiritual Education

All the teaching that was done based on knowledge must now move toward internal spiritual education. Have them read True Parents' words on the spirit world, and teach them about fasting and a life of prayer. In particular, encourage them to participate in the workshops held at the CheongPyeong Training Center, and educate them so that they can liberate their ancestors and live a spiritual life.

⑥ Stage of Education about Self-Sacrifice

If you teach them only the knowledge of the Divine Principle and spiritual aspects without the stage of devotion and suffering, it will be difficult for them to understand Heavenly Parent and True Parents' hearts. It is important to have them experience fundraising and witnessing, as the senior families traditionally have done.

Through this process they can experience public training. They come to learn the ownership mindset and heart of a leader. After this process is over, have them make a commitment as core members of the local church, give them the opportunity to guide new members and give them responsibility.

⑦ Stage of Education of Life as a Blessed Family

This is not just the stage in which you teach them about the significance and value of the Blessing but also the stage in which you teach them in detail the practical principles that a blessed couple must experience as they live together. It is basic education on conjugal relations, children's education and other knowledge that is necessary for realizing an ideal family.

⑧ Stage of Practicing Heavenly Tribal Messiahship

All couples who receive the Blessing have the responsibility to fulfill their mission as heavenly tribal messiahs. You should use the heavenly tribal messiah textbooks to educate them on how to fulfill their mission as heavenly tribal messiahs. This book is part of a collection of five books that the international headquarters' Heavenly Tribal Messiah Academy has published for this purpose.

⑨ Stage of Leadership

Our ultimate goal in educating people is to raise up leaders who are necessary in realizing Cheon Il Guk. Heavenly tribal messiahs must help them go through much strengthening of capabilities, so that

The Family Pledge

1. Our family, the owner of Cheon Il Guk, pledges to seek our original homeland and build the Kingdom of God on earth and in heaven, the original ideal of creation, by centering on true love.

2. Our family, the owner of Cheon Il Guk, pledges to represent and become central to heaven and earth by attending the Heavenly Parent and True Parents; we pledge to perfect the dutiful family way of filial sons and daughters in our family, patriots in our nation, saints in the world, and divine sons and daughters in heaven and on earth, by centering on true love.

3. Our family, the owner of Cheon Il Guk, pledges to perfect the Four Great Realms of Heart, the Three Great Kingships and the Realm of the Royal Family, by centering on true love.

4. Our family, the owner of Cheon Il Guk, pledges to build the universal family encompassing heaven and earth, which is the Heavenly Parent's ideal of creation, and perfect the world of freedom, peace, unity and happiness, by centering on true love.

5. Our family, the owner of Cheon Il Guk, pledges to strive every day to advance the unification of the spirit world and the physical world as subject and object partners, by centering on true love.

6. Our family, the owner of Cheon Il Guk, pledges to become a family that moves heavenly fortune by embodying the Heavenly Parent and True Parents, and to perfect a family that conveys Heaven's blessing to our community, by centering on true love.

7. Our family, the owner of Cheon Il Guk, pledges, through living for the sake of others, to perfect the world based on the culture of heart, which is rooted in the original lineage, by centering on true love.

8. Our family, the owner of Cheon Il Guk, pledges, having entered the Era of Cheon Il Guk, to achieve the ideal of God and human beings united in love through absolute faith, absolute love and absolute obedience, and to perfect the realm of liberation and complete freedom in the Kingdom of God on earth and in heaven, by centering on true love.

they can develop into lecturers and leaders. In order to do this, they first must be raised up to become people who can be home group leaders, local leaders, center lecturers and heavenly tribal messiahs.

7.4 Method and Contents of Education

1) Divine Principle Education

The following is the recommended order for conducting a Divine Principle lecture program. The example in Figure 4-2 shows a program in which the message of the Divine Principle is delivered using various tools, making use of recent developments in technology.

Figure 4-2) Order of a Divine Principle Lecture Program (Example)

No.	Activity	Detailed contents
1	Opening songs	• One of the guests can be the MC and begin to sing holy songs to create a good atmosphere. • Other guests hear the holy songs and begin to make their way to the lecture room.
2	Report prayer	• The MC or one of the guests can give a simple report prayer.
3	Scripture reading	• The lecturer reads out a paragraph or a Bible verse that is part of the content for the day's Divine Principle lecture.
4	Video presentation	• Watch a video that is related to the lecture's topic and will create a good atmosphere. • If you do not have a video to show, you can also use a photo, newspaper article, case stories, etc.
5	Introduction	• At this point, the lecturer asks a question related to the topic.

6	Divine Principle reading (for one-on-one education)	• Emphasize True Father's directions to study the Divine Principle by reading it aloud, and have the guests read aloud the color-coded parts of the Divine Principle.
	Divine Principle lecture (for group education)	• Use the lecture presentation that is prepared to explain the topic. If there are other diagrams that you think will be effective, you can also use those images.
7	Additional explanation	• You may need to explain more, depending on the level of understanding of your guests. • You can use other videos or examples to make the lecture content more relatable.
8	Closing	• The lecturer summarizes the day's lesson. The lecturer announces when the next lecture is scheduled.

When you are holding Divine Principle workshops, please keep the following things in mind.

First, if it is possible, at dawn on the last day of the Divine Principle workshop, have the participants go to the holy ground or a secluded area near the education center, do a reading and offer a prayer of new beginning. Also, on the last night, it is good to have them do a holy candlelight prayer gathering and offer a prayer of repentance and new beginning.

Second, prepare videos that are related to each lecture topic to make the Divine Principle lecture more real and easier to relate to. Videos are very effective education tools. Lecturers should take the time to organize videos in advance.

Third, ultimately the content in the Divine Principle is not easy. If possible, it is good to make the schedule intensive to awaken their spiritual realization. If their living environment and the education get mixed, the possibility is lowered. If possible, do the education intensively over the course of three days. If they do not have the time, do it every evening for four hours over the course of a week, or use two weekends in a row. You also can do it over the course of four months or 16 weeks for two hours every week.

Fourth, the length of the lectures can be adjusted according to the color-coded parts in the Divine Principle. If there is not much time, give a lecture based on the red parts; if you have more time, use the blue and yellow parts as well.

Fifth, if they receive grace after the Divine Principle lecture, the nurturing process after the education is important. Establish a hoondok condition for a set period of time, and encourage them to do hoondokhae. Even after this period is over, have them inherit the tradition of hoondokhae by constantly assigning them hoondok material to read.

Sixth, if you think the guest has received enough education on the Divine Principle, educate them about True Parents' life course and the rituals and traditions of the Family Federation.

Figure 4-3) Three-Day Divine Principle Education Schedule (Sample)

Time	Day 1	Day 2	Day 3
08:30–09:30	Preface and Principle of Creation 1	Resurrection 1	Moses' Course 1
09:50–11:00	Principle of Creation 2	Resurrection 2	Moses' Course 2
11:20–12:30	Principle of Creation 3	Predestination, Christology	Jesus' course

12:30–13:30	Lunch	Lunch	Lunch
13:30–14:40	The Human Fall 1	Part II Introduction to Principle of Restoration	The Parallels between the Ages in the Providence of Restoration 1
15:00–16:10	The Human Fall 2	Adam's Family	The Parallels between the Ages in the Providence of Restoration 2
16:30–17:40	Eschatology	Noah's Family	The Period of Preparation for the Second Advent of the Messiah
17:40–19:00	Dinner	Dinner	Dinner
19:00–20:10	Heavenly Parent's Work of Salvation	Abraham's Family 1	The Second Advent
20:30–21:40	Video	Abraham's Family 2, Testimony	The Second Advent

(2) How to use the Education Textbooks and Social Media

You can use social media as a method of education. These days, nearly everyone owns a smartphone and uses it every minute of the day. It is not an exaggeration to say that much of that time is spent visiting social networking sites. You can use social media to send your guests a paragraph from True Parents' words every day, send them links to information about church events or news, or the church website. If you use Facebook Messenger to consistently send messages every day, they will have access to the church, which will support their life of faith. It is good for the headquarters in each nation to classify and provide messages so that members can use them long term for their guests through social media.

The following (Figure 4-4) is an example of message witnessing.

These are also a source for materials that you can use for your lectures. It is good to use all kinds of audiovisuals to make the material in the lecture more approachable and stimulate the visual and auditory senses.

3) Family Federation Rituals and Ceremonies

① Pledge Service

A *gyeongbae* (bow) is the way we greet Heavenly Parent and True Parents. The pledge service, which we hold at 5:00 a.m. on Sunday mornings, An Shi Il mornings and mornings of the eight major holy days, begins with a *gyeongbae*. It is good to do pledge service every day during the week as well, if you can. If it is difficult to do it every day, another option is to decide how many times a week you will do it and set a consistent schedule to create a tradition. From August 15, 2013, by the solar calendar, True Parents established a tradition of having hoondokhae daily at 6:00 a.m.

> We have gathered at 6:00 a.m. today. I am hoping that we can use time more efficiently to match our bodies' rhythm so that we can move forward to offer up 100 percent, 120 percent before God. In order to do that, I thought that I need to give you some vitality and energy, and that is why I told you to gather at 6:00 a.m. Did I do well? (Yes.) Are you grateful? (Yes.) It is so that we all can go

forward together. That is True Parents' love. Do you understand?
[True Mother, 2013.08.15]

In case your children are still young, you can be flexible in deciding the time of the family pledge service and hoondokhae, but whatever time you decide, you should be consistent with it. Whether it is in the morning or evening, stick to the time consistently and adjust when necessary, according to the age of your children. However, the time of the public pledge service cannot be changed.

The following is the way to offer a bow.

- First of all, maintain your line of sight at 45 degrees. Place your feet evenly together, leaving about 5 centimeters (almost 2 inches) between them. Your arms are at your side, and your hands are loosely open.
- Place both hands in a straight line with the right hand on top and bring them to your eyebrows.
- Your hands remain at eyebrow height, while you bend your right knee or bend both knees at the same time.
- Bend your back, place your hands onto the floor and bend so that your forehead very slightly touches your hands and your entire body is bent. (Be careful not to raise your bottom.)
- Wait for a brief moment (or get up in accordance with the MC's directions)
- When you get up, keep your hands on the floor and first raise your right leg or both legs at the same time.
- Once you are up, raise and place both hands to eyebrow height and then return to your original position: at attention with

your arms by your side.

- After the bow, lightly nod your head to show respect.

In case there are members with physical problems or a lack of space, they can bend from the hip and do a half-bow while standing, rather than a full bow.

The following (Figure 4-5) is the suggested order of a family pledge service.

Figure 4-5) Order of the Family Pledge Service (example)

No.	Led by MC	Detailed Content
1	Line up	Line up. (Normally the parents are not the MCs. Have the children take turns to be the MC. The parents may be the MC if the first child is still below elementary school age.)
2	Light the candle	The officiator lights the candle at the front of the room.
3	Silent prayer	Silent prayer (quiet your heart for 10 or 20 seconds.)
4	Offering of bow	Offer a bow to Heavenly Parent and True Parents.
5	Family Pledge	Recite the Family Pledge slowly while thinking of the meaning.
6	Offering of Bow	Husband and wife bow to each other, children bow to parents, and children bow to each other. Do the bows in that order.
7	Prayer	True Father's prayer (Read from a book of True Father's prayers. Reading should be done by a person who can bring inspiration through the reading.)
8	Hoondokhae	The MC guides everyone to read and discuss the words of True Parents.
9	True Parents' Words	The parents only briefly explain the difficult parts or main points. During the discussion time, there will be questions, so keep the explanations under five minutes.

No.	Led by MC	Detailed Content
10	Discussion	Have the children talk about what they felt from the hoondokhae and what they would like to put into practice. During this time, the parents should just listen. Do not nag or lecture them. Have the children express their own opinions and ask questions. The parents talk only when answering the questions asked by the children. At the very end, the parents can summarize the discussions, but do not make it long. Instead spend a lot of time in praising your children for their motivation to put this into practice and for being honest about their thoughts and feelings.
No.	Led by MC	Detailed Content
11	Prayer of gratitude	Family members can stand in a circle, holding hands, while one person offers a prayer.
12	Put out candle	The officiator (parent) puts out the candle.
13	Closing	The officiator (parent) declares that the service has been completed.

② Family Pledge

In the family pledge, families resolve to do their best to fulfill their mission and duty as a family centered on Heavenly Parent and True Parents. It is a confession of faith for Family Federation members. It is a standard and guideline for our life of faith, so it is always good for members to recite the family pledge. The family pledge normally is recited during family prayer meetings, public meetings, the first day of the month, holy day pledge services, etc. The family pledge is a declaration of the blessed families that Satan cannot attack this family because it has no ties to the world of Satan. The tradition of the family pledge is a tool that establishes Godism, breaks down all kinds of difficulties and helps us bring victory.

The family pledge was established on May 1, 1994, and announced publicly on May 2, 1994, at 8:45 a.m. to a group of world leaders gathered at the official residence in Hannam-dong, Seoul. From then on, all members and blessed families worldwide began to recite the family pledge. There is a difference in significance between "My Pledge," which was recited at pledge service before May 2, 1994, and the family pledge. The family pledge is to be the standard and guideline for the daily life of blessed families and members. It is a pledge to find the ideal family that was the origin of the ideal of creation. The family has to become the substantial manifestation of the pledge.

③ Prayer

In the Family Federation, prayer is reporting, and the Heavenly Parent of heaven and earth is not an abstract existence but a substantial existence and the living parent of humankind. Therefore, prayer is similar to when a child reports to his or her parents. It is a conversation or exchange in which the corporeal child reports substantially to an incorporeal parent.

Individual prayer is a time of spiritual exchange and reporting that connects and strengthens the parent–child relationship between Heavenly Parent and me. It is a time to repent for the past, to find out Heavenly Parent's wish for me, and to connect to the heart of filial piety. Public prayer is a time to repent and determine to get rid of the Fall and return to our original position through the restoration of the relationship between Heavenly Parent and human beings. When carrying out activities, Blessed families, who have been called first by Heavenly Parent, should focus their determination on finding His children that are still lost and comforting His sorrow and pain.

We pray in order to transcend our own strength and borrow the strength of Heavenly Parent and the spirit world. That is why we should not pray centering on ourselves but on the salvation of humankind from Heavenly Parent's perspective. We should pray concerning our actions and transformation in order to achieve that goal. We should pray about Heavenly Parent's task that we can do centering on where we are standing, the people we are connected to and the environment. Only then can great works happen.

Prayer is the act of reporting to Heavenly Parent. Blessed central families have no relation with the fallen world. They have come to stand in the position where they are connected to God's world of heart before Adam and Eve fell. This means they are standing in the place of the unfallen family of Adam that was completed when God's ideal of creation was realized. Therefore, they stand in that position with that qualification and report by praying on their behalf. The path for the perfected family of Adam is to report every day and work toward realizing the ideal world.

The following are some suggestions for offering prayer.

When you pray, first pray for Heavenly Parent, the Origin and Creator of the universe, then for the spirit world and the cosmos, and then for the public figures and members worldwide who are working hard for the world providence. After that, you can pray for your country, spiritual children, your tribe, your family and the task that you must accomplish.

People who are just starting out in their life of faith must go through the above stages and pray for their family and relatives to be saved. If they pray for world issues from the beginning, it may be very burdensome. In the beginning, they will pray for the people closest to them—their parents and their beloved children and spouse—to be saved. After that period has passed and they have grown, the content of their prayer will change. If we take the content of people's prayers as an indicator, we can see that as they become more anchored in their faith, the method and content of their prayer develop to include more public topics.

Today we are in the era when we pray in the name of the blessed central families. Today, whoever is a blessed family can offer up prayer in their name. We have gone through the eras when we prayed in Jesus' name, then True Parents' name; and today we pray in the name of our blessed family. These days, we do prayer reports. If we do not do prayer reports, we cannot receive any of God's rights of ownership. In order to receive part of God's right of ownership, we must become representative families of God's nation.

✣ How to end a prayer

On March 20, 2013, at a banquet held at Cheon Jeong Gung, True Mother mentioned the meaning of "creating the environment" and, in this era of Cheon Il Guk opened by Heavenly Parent, directed a new way for the True Grandchildren, and also all the Seonghwa children and students worldwide, to end their prayers:

"I report this in my name, _____, a third (second, fourth, etc.) generation from a blessed family. Aju!" However, first-generation members can pray in their own name: "In the name of _____. Aju!"

Document number: Int'l HQ No. 234

"Aju" means the best position. The *ju* character in "aju" means owner (主) and reside (住). It means, "Become the owner of heaven and earth, then stand in the position where you will be in the very end." "Ah, I have become the owner of the original hometown, so I must go home and live there!" When we say "home" here, we are referring to the place where Heavenly Parent resides. It is the place where the eternal true couple, True Parents, achieve the realm of oneness and where Heavenly Parent's internal heart can reside. "Aju" means "my blessed family has returned and is standing in the position of the original family of Adam."

The following texts explain about the four Cheon Il Guk holy items.

④ Cheon Il Guk Holy Wine

The marriage Blessing of the Family Federation for World Peace and Unification is not a simple, typical religious ceremony. It is a change of lineage ceremony through which a person's lineage changes from that of Satan to God's. The holy wine used in Blessing ceremonies has been upgraded and renewed according to the providential progress until now.

Traditional Holy Wine: The traditional holy wine, which changes the blood lineage of fallen humans, began to be used after True Parents' Holy Wedding in 1960. The traditional holy wine also contains the meaning of rebirth through the eradication of the original sin. True Father explained that the traditional holy wine was the term of contract made between God, Satan and True Parents.

Cheon Il Guk Holy Wine: The Cheon Il Guk holy wine was made and stored by True Parents on October 23, 1999, in East Garden. On that day, True Parents issued the Proclamation of the Liberation Day for the Blessing of the Entire Cosmos, through which they proclaimed the unity of the four great realms of heart, the liberation of children, couples and the liberated realm of the Parents of Heaven and Earth. The Cheon Il Guk holy wine was distributed to each regional president on August 20, 2003, after the Holy Marriage Blessing Ceremony of the Parents of Heaven and Earth Opening the Gate of Cheon Il Guk on February 6, 2003. This was used at the Cheon Il Guk Registration Blessing Ceremony of True Revolution of the Heart and True Liberation and Release in 2004 and at the Cosmic Blessing Ceremony by True Parents on October 14, 2009.

Cheon Il Guk Foundation Day Holy Wine: At the 40-day memorial service of True Father's ascension, which was conducted in BonHyang Won on 9.11 by the heavenly calendar in 2012 (October 25), True Mother said the following: "When True Father was still alive, he instructed that holy wine for the Foundation Day of Cheon Il Guk be made and stored at CheongPyeong. This is the holy wine that was newly made." She asked that all Unificationists participate in the Cheon Il Guk Foundation Day to cleanse their bodies and minds through the Cheon Il Guk Foundation Day holy wine, and then distributed the holy wine to all regional presidents.

Cheon Il Guk Special Holy Wine (distributed on 3.16 by the HC in the fourth year of Cheon Il Guk, April 22, 2016 by the solar calendar): This special holy wine was made after True Parents instructed that a holy wine be prepared to bequeath at the 56th anniversary of True Parents' Holy Wedding after the third anniversary of Foundation Day.

Comprehensive Special Grace: All families participating in the Special Holy Wine Ceremony for the Four-Year Course of Hope for Vision 2020 will be able to receive a special grace that will cleanse them from all problems, including unprincipled ones that cannot be resolved. This special grace will be given on the foundation that all participants have completely repented for their past faith and lives. This is a comprehensive grace bestowed on us by True Parents from the cosmic level of the Cheon Il Guk Era to enable all families to be reborn as new—or "reborn"—blessed families with all the attributes of a blessed family.

The holy wine that was distributed on the 16th day of the third month in the fourth year of Cheon Il Guk is the holy wine that can be used in the field today. This holy wine, which is one of the Cheon Il Guk Holy Items that were distributed to the Cheon Il Guk citizens, is allowed to be used during the Blessing ceremony. All other types of holy wines in the church need to be discarded. Blessed members must go through the holy wine ceremony if they have not participated in a holy wine ceremony using this holy wine. All blessed families and second-generation Unificationists are to drink this holy wine with renewed awakening and determination to forgive, love and unite with one another in accordance with True Parents' words.

The following is the method for multiplying holy wine. Undiluted holy wine, holy salt, normal wine, and a mixing container should be prepared. The ceremony should take place in a sanctified place such as the chapel room or the prayer room. If the circumstance dictates that a church cannot be used, then it should be done in a room with True Parents' portrait where blessed members offer jeongseong to Heavenly Parent. The church pastor first multiplies the holy wine and divides it among the members. Next, blessed families themselves can multiply it and use it.

- Sanctification: Sanctify the purchased wine with holy salt.
- Prayer: Prayer for the multiplication of the holy wine
- Mixture: Mix the undiluted holy wine and the wine you purchased at a 1:4 ratio (one part, original holy wine; four parts purchased wine.)
- Completion Prayer: Prayer for having completed the multiplication of the holy wine

When making a large amount of holy wine, regard the multiplied holy wine as the undiluted holy wine, and multiply it again in the same manner.

⑤ Cheon Il Guk Holy Salt

The tradition of holy salt began after True Parents' Holy Wedding. True Parents made the first holy salt on the day of their Holy Wedding, 3.16 (lunar) in 1960, and used it to sanctify every side of the church before the actual ceremony. After the Holy Wedding, True Parents instructed that this holy salt be distributed to all Unificationists worldwide. This marked the beginning of the tradition of a life of sanctification through the holy salt.

Holy salt is needed to separate from Satan. On the victorious foundation of True Parents' Holy Wedding, True Parents made holy salt, using the salt Heavenly Parent used to exterminate evil, as a means to separate from Satan and to sanctify and bring everything that had fallen into Satan's dominion, including humans, creation and the environment, back to God's side. Holy salt also can sanctify and separate good and evil. Salt typically helps maintain the cleanness and wholeness of things. In the same manner, holy salt separates good and evil and has a sanctifying function that helps people maintain a wholesome life. All people of faith should conduct a basic type of sanctification ritual. This is a basic sanctifying ritual which all Unificationists should practice to separate from Satan in their lives, which can be invaded easily by Satan. Furthermore, this is also a separation ritual to distinguish what belongs to Heaven. Holy salt is a condition that enables creation to newly exist and to belong to Heaven. Hence, True Parents mentioned that this holy salt won't be necessary at all in an entirely restored world.

Unlike the holy salt that had been used previously, this holy salt was initiated through emphasis on rebirth, through a rebirth ceremony held on August 16, 2003, that will enable all Unificationists to make a new start. The Cheon Jeong Wang Gung holy salt, which was bequeathed to all regional presidents on June 13, 2006, has since been used instead of the original one. True Parents, furthermore, created and gave us the Cheon Il Guk holy salt. After True Father's holy ascension, True Parents ushered in a new era based on the foundation of sincere memorial jeongseong offered centered on BonHyang Won. Marking the beginning of a different era, True Parents bestowed on us the Cheon Il Guk holy salt on 3.16 by the heavenly calendar, 2016 (April 22).

❋ The Significance of the Cheon Il Guk Holy Salt

(a) Used to support the practice of a life of strictly dividing good and evil to wholly become Heavenly Parent's true child.

(b) To separate good and evil, which can be compared to Heavenly Parent and Satan, to pursue the determination to lead a pure life of faith, to attend Heavenly Parent as the sole standard of life, and to live as Heavenly Parent's child.

(c) Life of faith in the Cheon Il Guk era itself is a sanctified life; hence, it is a life of separation between good and evil.

(d) Salt symbolizes separation between good and evil, purification of things, and possesses a sanctifying function.

About using Cheon Il Guk Holy Salt

1) Starting from 3.16 on the Heavenly Calendar, 2016 (April 22), the basic prayer to offer when sanctifying an item with holy salt is "In the name of the True Parents of Heaven, Earth and Humankind and in my name, _____, owner of Cheon Il Guk, I sanctify this." The holy salt is to be sprinkled in a cross-direction (from the north to the south, from the east to the west).
2) All goods purchased by members, such as groceries, clothing, furniture, car, etc., should be purified with holy salt.
3) A gift received from a friend of a Unificationist should be sanctified with holy salt. A Unificationst may also wish to use holy salt to sanctify a gift received from another Unificationist, unless that person specifies it had already been done.
4) When conducting a three-day ceremony or dedication ceremony, the holy salt is used to sanctify the venue or room.
5) When sanctifying a room, stand in the center of the room facing north. After saying the basic prayer, toss a small quantity of the salt toward the north, then to the south, east and west. From the center of the room, spread the holy salt in a clockwise circle as a condition to cover the entire room.
6) When purchasing or renting a building or land, do the preceding step from the center place. As for the remaining rooms, as in the case of a building, open the doors to other rooms and sprinkle the holy salt three times in the room symbolically.
7) When sanctifying land, walk around the property (its full perimeter, if possible) sprinkling small amounts of holy salt on the ground as you walk. If the land is too big and it is difficult to holy

salt the entire place, move to the center of the land and sanctify it in the same manner in which a room or place is sanctified.

8) In principle, a sanctified object should not be given away to the satanic world. However, if for unavoidable reasons, a sanctified object needs to be sold or donated, offer a prayer so that the object remains sanctified only during the time it was used by your family.

9) When eating food in a restaurant or a friend's place, one can sanctify the food with holy salt; however, if the atmosphere does not allow it, lightly blow three times on the food instead of using holy salt. In the same manner, when sanctifying an object in the absence of holy salt, do so by blowing on it three times.

10) After participating in a funeral, you should holy salt yourself to completely cleanse yourself, spiritually, from everything connected to death in the satanic world. This sanctification should be done before entering the church or your home. You do not need to sanctify yourself if you have attended the Seonghwa (ascension) ceremony of a Unificationist.

The following (Figure 4-6) explains the multiplication of holy salt. The church pastor first multiplies holy salt and divides it among members. After that, blessed families themselves can multiply it and use it.

Figure 4-6) Holy Salt Multiplication Ceremony Order

No.	Procedure	Details
1	Prepare Holy Salt	• Prepare some holy salt that will be the seed.
2	Sanctification of the Premises	• Sanctify the place in which the ceremony is to take place.
3	Sanctification of the New Salt	• Purchase some new salt and sanctify it with the holy salt.

No.	Procedure	Details
4	Multiplication	• Make seven equal piles of new salt as well as a pile with an equal amount of "seed" holy salt. If just a few grains of this "seed" holy salt are available, the seven piles should also consist of only a few grains each. Multiply only this small amount at first, and go through the same procedure a second time in order to make a greater quantity.
5	Report Prayer	• The report prayer should follow these lines: "I multiply this holy salt in the name of the True Parents of Heaven, Earth and Humankind and my name,_____, owner of Cheon Il Guk."
6	Mixing of Salt (Order Is Important)	• Divide the seed holy salt pile, and strew it on each of the seven piles of new salt.
7		• Mix the seed holy salt and new salt in each pile.
8		• Mix all the piles together.
9	Prayer of Gratitude	• Offer a prayer of gratitude.

⑥ Cheon Il Guk Holy Candles

❇ Origin and Significance of Cheon Il Guk Candles

Birth Candles: *Chilseong* candles, made up of seven candles, began to be used from Ye Jin Moon's birth (12.11 by the lunar calendar, 1960). These candles are used as a condition to create a holy environment during the birth of Heavenly Parent's child.

Shimjeong Candle: (Inherited on Jan 5,1966) This candle contains the determination to comfort Heavenly Parent's sad heart, which was caused by the Fall of His human children, and the determination to become Heavenly Parent's true sons and daughters who will achieve His Will.

Aecheon Candle: (Inherited on May 20, 1984) This candle symbolizes that True Father and True Mother are one and signifies True Parents' true love.

Tongil Candle: This candle was passed down to us on the foundation of the 120-day condition True Mother offered with her children from September 5, 1995, to January 2, 1996. This candle encompasses the unified qualities of the Birth Candle, *Shimjeong* Candle, and *Aecheon* Candle.

Cheon Jeong Gung Candle: This candle was passed down to regional presidents at the entrance into Cheon Jeong Gung and Coronation Ceremony on June 13, 2006.

Establishment of Cheon Il Guk Candle: On 1.2 by the heavenly calendar in 2012, True Parents bequeathed this candle to all blessed families at the Cheon Bok Ceremony conducted in the Cheon Bok Gung in commemoration of True Parents' 93rd birthday, golden anniversary, and 70th birthday. On this day, True Father said, "All of humanity must attend the heavenly family and lead lives of one lineage, one tradition and one resemblance. Centered on this candlelight, we must light everything to ensure that the light in the church, country and world does not die out."

Cheon Il Guk Holy Candle: On 3.16 by the heavenly calendar in the fourth year of Cheon Il Guk, True Parents ushered in a new age on the foundation of sincere memorial jeongseong centered on BonHyang Won that was offered after True Father's universal ascension. This holy candle has been bestowed to us to use in this new age.

The following tells when to use the Cheon Il Guk Holy Candle. When we light this holy candle, Heavenly Parent can reside with us and can work through us. This holy candle can be used at any time when offering jeongseong, individually or in a group, for the fulfillment of Heavenly Parent's Will.

- When offering special conditions to receive the Blessing
- When conducting the three-day ceremony
- When giving birth to a child (one can use one or seven candles in this case)
- When conducting the dedication ceremony of a blessed child
- When celebrating the 40th day, 103rd day and other birthdays
- When there is a serious undertaking in the family
- When doing a set prayer condition for a common goal set by the church
- When doing hoondokhae (scripture study) or holding a worship service in church or in the family
- When doing pledge service on *Anshi-il*, holy days, etc.
- When carrying out activities for the establishment of the substantial Cheon Il Guk

A holy candle must be lit with a holy match or a holy lighter. When extinguishing the flame of a holy candle, do not blow it out with your mouth. Instead, extinguish it using two of your fingers or a candle-extinguishing tool. All existing holy candles' qualities are encompassed within the Cheon Il Guk Holy Candle, bequeathed to us on 3.16 by the heavenly calendar, 2016 (April 22). As of this date, we are to use only the Cheon Il Guk Holy Candle.

The following (Figure 4-7) explains how to multiply the Cheon Il Guk Holy Candle.

Figure 4-7) Holy Candle Multiplication Method and Order (Example)

No.	Procedure	Details
1	Sanctification	• Purchase three new candles and sanctify them with holy salt. The new candle must be white or pale ivory in color, and must be at least 5 inches long.
2	Place	• Prepare a candle holder or plate on which to put the seed holy candle.
3	Candle Placement	• The seed holy candle, placed on the candle holder, must be put in Heavenly Parent's position, and the newly purchased three candles are to be put in Adam's, Eve's, and the child's position in the form of the four-position foundation.
4	Report Prayer	• To begin the multiplication, offer a prayer along the lines of "I multiply this holy candle in the name of the True Parents of Heaven, Earth and Humankind, and my name,_____, owner of Cheon Il Guk."
5	Inheritance	• Light the seed holy candle with holy matches. • Hold the seed holy candle with both hands (the right hand should go above and the left hand should support the candle from underneath) and light the Adam, Eve, and child candles in that order. Once that is done, the seed holy candle must be returned to its original position (Heavenly Parent's position).
6	Prayer of Gratitude	• Offer the concluding prayer while the candles are still lit.

One can also multiply the holy candle on a one-to-one basis.

Figure 4-12) Altar for Childbirth Prayer (Example)

The following (Figure 4-8) explains how to multiply the Cheon Il Guk Holy Matches.

Figure 4-8) Holy Matches Multiplication Method and Order (Example)

No.	Procedure	Details
1	Sanctification of Matches	Purchase three (or one) new boxes of matches, and sanctify them with holy salt.
2	Matches Placement	Place the seed holy matches in Heavenly Parent's position and the purchased three boxes in the Adam, Eve and child positions, as in the four-position foundation.
3	Report Prayer	Offer a prayer of multiplication along the lines of: "In the name of the True Parents of Heaven, Earth and Humankind, I would like to multiply the holy matches."
4	Inheritance	Take the seed holy match and put it above the matches in the Adam, Eve and child's position, in that order, and then return it to its original position (Heavenly Parent's position).

| 5 | Prayer of Gratitude | Offer a brief concluding prayer. |

⑦ Cheon Il Guk Holy Soil

Origin and Significance:

1) The holy soil was re-created through the entrance into Cheon Jeong Gung and the Coronation Ceremony. True Parents conducted the "Wishing for the Era of Peace and Tranquility of Cheon Il Guk and Citizens' Pledge Ceremony" in the front garden of Cheon Jeong Gung on June 6, 2006. Through this ceremony, light, the oceans, land, plants, animals and humans could be re-created. On this day, representatives of the 12 regions offered holy soil and holy water to True Parents. This holy soil and holy water were then separately mixed with soil and water from Cheon Jeong Gung. The holy soil, re-created in this manner, was then bequeathed to the regional presidents, who were instructed to bury it within the holy ground of each nation.

2) The holy earth is from the grounds of Cheon Jeong Palace, from the BonHyang Won (the original homeland). In commemoration of the 56th anniversary of True Parents' Holy Wedding, True Parents bequeathed the holy soil from BonHyang Won Cheon Jeong Gung to all regions with the hope that the multiplication of the substantial Cheon Il Guk holy soil, perfected at the time of the Cheon Il Guk Foundation Day, can open the way for the substantial Cheon Il Guk to expand to each region and nation.

3) Heavenly Parent created Adam by forming him from dust from

Figure 4-14) Dedication Ceremony Altar (Example)

the ground and breathing life into him. Thereafter, Heavenly Parent called Adam His body. Had Adam not fallen, Heavenly Parent would have dwelled within his body and both would have reached complete unity. Hence, the Holy Soil is a symbol of our re-creation to a state prior to Satan's invasion; it also symbolizes our restoration to the state of Heavenly Parent's body. Moreover, the expanded concept of body – tabernacle – temple – heavenly nation found in the Old Testament is also included in the holy soil. To conclude, the holy soil is a symbol for the development beginning with me, and moving out to include my family and the church, and expanding all the way to Cheon Il Guk.

Each regional headquarters, national headquarters and church

Figure 4-15) 103rd Day Celebration Ceremony Altar and Offering Table (Example)

must preserve the seed Cheon Il Guk holy soil, multiply it and bury it within the holy ground in each nation and church. Blessed families should keep the holy soil and use it during the Weonjeon (burial) ceremony, which is part of the Seonghwa ceremony.

The following (Figure 4-9) explains the order of the multiplication ceremony. The holy soil cannot be multiplied on an individual or family level. The church pastor is in charge of multiplying the holy soil used in the church and dividing it among members.

Figure 4-9) Holy Soil Multiplication Method and Order (Example)

No.	Procedure	Details

Figure 4-16) Scene from a coming-of-age ceremony held in the CheongPyeong Heaven and Earth Training Center

1	Preparation	• Prepare a quantity of holy soil (the original or seed holy soil).
2	Sanctification of the Premises	• Clean the place where you will multiply the holy soil.
3	Sanctification of the Soil	• Bring a quantity of holy soil from a holy site and sanctify it with holy salt.
4	Preparation of the Soil	• Make seven equal piles of the new earth (desert sand soil cover) as well as a pile with an equal amount of "seed" holy soil. • If there is only a tiny amount of holy soil, first make seven piles of the same quantity. • Multiply only this small amount at first, and go through the same procedure a second time in order to make a greater amount of the holy soil.
5	Report Prayer	• The report prayer should be along the lines of: "I multiply this holy soil in the name of the True Parents of Heaven, Earth and Humankind and my name,_____, owner of Cheon Il Guk."

6	Mixing (Order Is Important)	• Next, mix the soils in the following order." ① Divide the seed holy soil pile and strew it on each of the seven piles of the new earth. ② Mix the seed holy soil and the new earth in each pile. ③ Mix all the piles together.
7	Prayer of Gratitude	• Offer a prayer of gratitude.

What is especially important is how these holy items are kept in the family. Holy wine can't be used if it gets too old; holy salt may deteriorate or become contaminated; and holy candles may burn completely to the bottom. In these cases, throw them away, after offering a prayer to Heavenly Parent, and procure new ones instead of reusing them. For example, you can dispose of the holy candles or holy salt that can't be used after offering a prayer to Heavenly Parent and report what purposes these items served in the past. Your prayer can be: "I cease the functions of these holy items in the name of the True Parents of Heaven, Earth, and Humankind." You can use the holy items that are still in a usable condition by performing multiplication ceremonies.

⑧ Offering

An offering is made to establish the condition of jeongseong for us to go before Heavenly Parent. The offering is not done for Heavenly Parent but for ourselves. Through the offering, we can establish the condition to come closer to Heavenly Parent.

For tithing, when we offer one part, it establishes the condition of having offered the remaining nine parts to Heavenly Parent as well.

It means that by offering one tenth of our material possessions, we are offering up the whole. We do not offer everything to Heavenly Parent, but by offering one part with jeongseong, the remaining nine parts also can be accepted as holy things. In this way, those who live while tithing will never go to ruin.

The following paragraphs explain the way to prepare the offering.

First, we must offer the untouched and unchanging, pure and original thing. The offering is made in place of ourselves, so we must offer the best. We should not give an offering from the money that remains after we have used it. Heavenly Parent cannot accept that kind of money.

Second, we must offer something for which we have offered the most jeongseong. We should put it in the deepest place in our box and prepare it by offering sincere jeongseong. True Parents said that those who offer their tithe with sincere jeongseong will never die of starvation. Their descendants will not lack in material things. The offering is made in place of our life. Therefore, we must offer up the most precious thing. True Parents have said that we should carry it on ourselves for at least three days, sanctify it and then offer it.

⑨ Sunday Service

Sunday service is a time to offer ourselves and our week to Heavenly Parent. At that time, we should report our past to Heavenly Parent and atone for it. Sunday service is a day of formal reunion between Heavenly Parent and ourselves. Through the message from the pulpit, we become aware of the direction of the providence led by

Figure 4-17) Blessing Preparation and Participation
The following chart demonstrates the process of preparing for and participating in the Blessing ceremony.

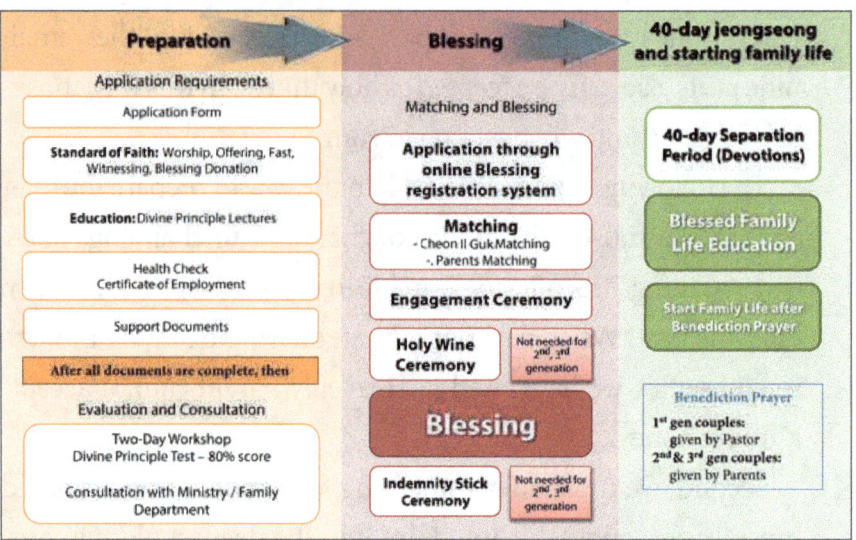

Heavenly Parent and True Parents and receive the direction in which we must go. It is a time to receive spiritual nutrients. Therefore, we must go after having prepared the soil of our heart, so that the seed of the word can be planted. Then, based on the message that we receive from Heavenly Parent, we must practice it and nurture it in our daily life. That is why Sunday service is a time to offer praise and glory to Heavenly Parent. It is a time when we should offer our gratitude to Heavenly Parent. Through that, we can fill our original mind with the love of Heavenly Parent.

Our attitude when attending Sunday service is important. First, when we come to Sunday service, we should do so on a foundation of having offered jeongseong. We shouldn't come to the church and

> ### Blessing Vows
>
> 1. Do you, as a mature man and woman who are to consummate Heavenly Parent's ideal of creation, pledge in front of Heavenly Parent and True Parents to become an eternal husband and wife?
>
> 2. Do you pledge to become true parents, raise your children to live up to the Will of Heavenly Parent, and educate them to become responsible leaders in front of the entire Unification Family, all humankind, and Heavenly Parent?
>
> 3. Do you pledge that, centered upon the True Parents of Heaven, Earth and Humankind, you will inherit the tradition of living for the sake of others and pass this proud tradition down to your descendants and the future generations of humankind?
>
> 4. Do you pledge that, centering upon the ideal of creation, you will inherit the Wlll of Heavenly Parent and True Parents, love the people of the world as Heavenly Parent and True Parents do, and ultimately consummate an ideal family which is the building block of the Kingdom of God on earth and in heaven?

pray. We should pray first, then go to Sunday service and offer even more earnest prayer. Jeongseong can be accumulated in a place that is opposite to the environment that secular people desire and the desires that they pursue. Second, when we come to Sunday service, we should not come without preparing. We should offer jeongseong with our whole heart. The more jeongseong we offer, the more Heavenly Parent will protect us.

⑩ Hoondokhae

Figure 4-18) Seonghwa Ceremony Process (Example)

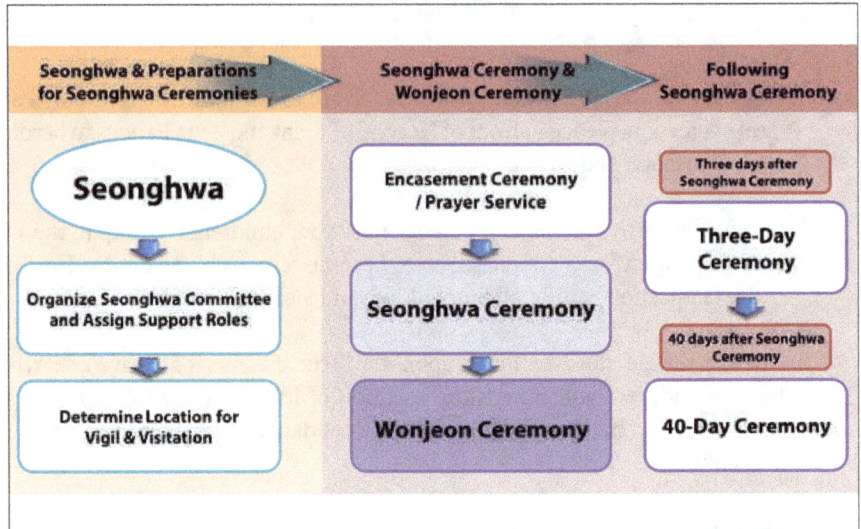

Hoondokhae is important because it is the substantial manifestation of a child (including spiritual children) resembling their parents, just as the parent resembles Heavenly Parent. Second, it is a time when the members of the tribe can learn the word and life of faith through the parents, centering on hoondokhae. Third, it is important because it is a time for the children to establish their faith value system and identity. Hoondokhae is for the parents and children, siblings (including spiritual children), family and tribe members. Through this time, they can establish the three great kingships and the four great realms of heart. It is especially meaningful because it provides the time for the family to attend Heavenly Parent and for the parents and children (spiritual children) to communicate. For individual hoondokhae, it is good to decide on a time and do it at the same time every day. Hoondokhae should be done daily in the family and at least once a week (for 40 minutes) in the tribe.

The hoondokhae meeting can be conducted as shown in the following (Figure 4-10).

Figure 4-10) Order for Hoondokhae (Example)

No.	Activity (Led by MC)	Detailed Content
1	Lighting of the Candle	Light the candle on the prepared altar.
2	Offering a Bow	Offer a bow before the picture of True Parents on the prepared altar.
3	Family Pledge	Recite the family pledge.
4	Prayer Report	The officiator, MC or one of the participants offers a representative prayer.
5	Hoondok Reading	Do the hoondok reading. The officiator selects words from the three Cheon Il Guk holy scriptures that are appropriate for the participants and the providential environment.
6	Questions and Answers	If there are any participants who do not understand some part of the reading, they can ask the officiator about it.
7	Group Discussion	Have an interactive discussion on the topic. Ask a few people to comment on what they felt and how their perspective should change. Then they can declare their determination from having received strength from the word (in larger groups, it can be done by table).
8	Presentation	Each person talks about their inspirations from the day's reading and what they would like to put into practice, as well as how the family should change (three minutes each).
9	Singing and Benediction	Sing a few holy songs and have the officiator offer the benediction.
10	Offering of Bow and Closing	Offer a bow to True Parents.

Here we will explain about the Family Federation religious ceremonies. The religious ceremonies of the Family Federation are conducted inside the family, so they can be called family ceremonies.

Figure 4-11) Significance of the Family Federation's Family Ceremonies

Ceremony	Spiritual Objectives
Childbirth Prayer	• Offering gratitude for the blessing of a child bestowed upon the family by Heavenly Parent • Offering a pledge that you will raise the children in accordance with the Will of Heavenly Parent • Receiving education at the same time for the parental role regarding the prenatal education, childbearing and rearing
Baby Dedication Ceremony	• Can define the missions regarding the raising of the children in a way that befits a blessed family
103rd Day Ceremony	• Family members and relatives get together to offer their gratitude to Heaven and congratulate the family in accordance with the tradition of the True Family.
Coming-of-Age Ceremony	• Ceremony for the children of the blessed family to inherit their parents' faith and make it their own • Congratulate the children who turned or are turning 18, give them the sense of responsibility for absolute sex, and prepare them for the Blessing. • The children's parents help their children have a firm internal foundation for the Blessing.
Seonghwa Ceremony	• A ceremony of prayer and blessing to congratulate the life of the deceased on Earth, centering on Heavenly Parent and True Parents, and to wish the deceased well for his or her life in the spiritual world • Console the family of the deceased through the ceremony

⑪ Childbirth Prayer

Our first childbirth prayer took place on January 27, 1961, when the first True Child was born. During this ceremony, the family members celebrate the birth of a new life and pray for True Parents' blessing and protection for the newborn. Required items for the ceremony are: a birth candle or seven holy candles, Cheon Jeong Gung candle, matches, candle holder for seven candles, holy salt, and True Parents' portrait. The husband offers a prayer to Heavenly Parent about ten minutes before and after the baby is delivered. The Family Federation discourages the practice of birth control and abortion in principle. Boys can be circumcised, if the parents want it. However, each region may have its own policy, and the families may have to follow their respective regional or national headquarters' guidelines.

⑫ Baby Dedication Ceremony

The following explains the baby dedication ceremony.

The baby dedication ceremony started on February 2, 1961, with the dedication of the first True Child. This ceremony has the significance of dedicating the child to Heavenly Parent, pledging to raise the child as a heavenly child and a citizen of Cheon Il Guk, and offering the heart of gratitude for being entrusted with the responsibility. The ceremony should take place on the eighth day (or day 21 or 40) of the child's birth. What is required: a banner (Dedication Ceremony of …..), True Parents' portrait, a sanctified place, an offering table, and a Cheon Jeong Gung candle. In principle, the parents of the newborn must carry out the dedication ceremony. The following (Figure 4-13) explains the order of the ceremony.

Figure 4-13) Dedication Ceremony Order (Example)

No.	Procedure by the Head of the Ceremony	Details

1	Lighting the Holy Candle	The parents stand facing the altar and light the holy candle.
2	Silent Prayer	The parents hold the infant together and pray in silence.
3	Dedication	The parents kneel on the floor and raise the child slightly upward to dedicate the child to Heavenly Parent.
4	*Gyeongbae*	The parents place the child in front of the altar and perform one *gyeongbae* (full bow).
5	Family Pledge	Everyone recites the family pledge together.
6	Representative Prayer	Offer a prayer to ask Heavenly Parent to accept the child, to pledge to raise the child properly, to promise to give everything to the child in raising him, and to ask Heavenly Parent to allow the child to inherit a heavenly character
7	Closing	Put out the candle, and quietly offer a standing bow.

⑬ 103rd Day Ceremony

103 days represents the 100 days plus three days since a child is born on Earth after becoming Heavenly Parent's child. Centering no the number four, the 103rd day ceremony exists to celebrate this point of settlement and new beginning, and to offer gratitude to Heavenly Parent for this blessing. The ceremony is held on the 104th day after the birth. What is required: a banner (103rd Day Ceremony for _____ name _____), True Parents' portrait, a sanctified place, offering table, holy gowns, a Cheon Jeong Gung candle. This ceremony can be conducted in the same way as the dedication ceremony as outlined in (Figure 4-13).

⑭ Coming-of-Age Ceremony

True Parents taught us to "hold a coming-of-age ceremony at this place for anyone who is above 18." This direction was given on November 12, 2004 (10.1 by the lunar calendar) when True Parents were visiting the visiting the facilities for learning traditional propriety and culture during the dedication ceremony of the CheongShim Youth Training Center. A coming-of-age ceremony is a ceremony in which the young participants who have turned 18 and satisfied the Blessing standard mark their transition into adulthood and pledge that they will fulfill their individual portion of responsibility. This is their first stage in realizing Heavenly Parent's three great blessings for humankind: being fruitful, multiplying, and having dominion over the earth. Additionally, this is also the ceremony in which they pledge to become Heavenly Parent's true sons and daughters.

The second-generation members automatically inherited the original, sinless pure lineage of Heavenly Parent from their first-generation member parents. Still, they did not join the movement of their own accord, but merely followed their parents' path of faith. This ceremony provides an opportunity for the children who have turned 18 to pledge that they will attend Heavenly Parent and True Parents by their own free will. In other words, this is the ceremony in which the young participants understand that they have the responsibility to perfect their character and become the leaders who can advance the Providence in Heavenly Parent's stead. Second, this is a ceremony in which the participants with the pure original mind

Figure 4-22) Family Federation for World Peace and Unification Cheon Il Guk National Anthem

and body prepare to meet their true spouse. The coming-of-age ceremony is performed once a year in August at the CheongPyeong Training Center or a place designated by each nation's national

Figure 4-23) Family Federation for World Peace and Unification

headquarters. The participants should be the children of a blessed family, above the age of 18 by the Korean way of counting, who are not yet married.

Children who have grown to be 18 should prepare to leave their parents' home, determine to embark on a personal journey of faith as a perfected individual, and fulfill the requirements to receive the Blessing. Through the coming-of-age ceremony, the blessed children of the Family Federation pledge to fulfill their duties and responsibilities as members of the faith community, transforming into adults. After the end of the ceremony, they will have a sense of their own responsibility. In addition, they also gain the condition to be blessed under the authority of True Parents at any time.

⑮ Blessing Ceremony

The following is a description of the significance of the Blessing.

First, through the Blessing we can sever our satanic lineage and return to Heavenly Parent through True Parents. If True Parents had appeared in the garden of Eden centering on Heavenly Parent, they would have passed on their Blessing, on behalf of Heavenly Parent, to all generations to come. True Parents' faith in Heavenly Parent allows them to inherit everything from Heavenly Parent, and we inherit everything from True Parents. By inheriting everything from them, the sons and daughters who are born within the eternal realm of victory are elevated to the status of sons and daughters of Heavenly Parent.

Second, the Blessing allows us to resemble Heavenly Parent, who is a being of dual characteristics, with each characteristic in complete harmony with the other. Those complementary characteristics are manifested separately on earth as man and woman. This means that if one man and one woman can unite in mind and body, they can resemble the whole of Heavenly Parent's original characteristics.

Third, through the Blessing we can inherit Heavenly Parent's love. In addition, we can inherit Heavenly Parent's authority of re-creation. The joy that Heavenly Parent felt after creating Adam and Eve can be experienced again through marriage. Next is the realm of direct dominion. We can experience all these wonderful blessings through receiving the Blessing upon the foundation of perfection. That is why a marriage Blessing ceremony is where original love manifests, where the couple is bestowed with the ideal

◤ A group of members from Lee Gye-hyeong and Kang Deok-rye's tribe visiting the Paju weonjeon

authority of creation, and where they can unite as one in mind and body as subject and object partners to receive God's authority of dominion.

Fourth, the Blessing allows us to create a world of peace in its truest sense. If we all become one global family through cross-cultural marriage Blessings, there will not be any hatred left on Earth. Through receiving the Blessing, we can show to the world that cross-cultural marriage transcends the barriers of nation, race, language, culture, and traditions, and that it is the ultimate method of realizing the ideal world of peace.

A husband and a wife who are to receive the Blessing must have the following solemn mindsets.

First, those who are to receive the Blessing must be ready to love only their spouse. If a person has other thoughts, he or she is hurting the spouse. A couple should become the mother and the father in heart to the other. They need to form a family that will inspire the people of the world to say, "I want to make a family just like yours."

Second, those who are to receive the Blessing need to train themselves to eliminate selfish thoughts. They are not allowed to have a selfish heart as they prepare to marry. They have to align their heart with the heart of Heavenly Parent and True Parents. They then can receive the Blessing and inherit everything from their parents. They give to each other the kind of love that is perfected in their own family, the kind of parental love they have received from their parents, and inherit everything. This is the meaning of the Blessing. From there, you can develop your individual character.

☐ Seonghwa Ceremony

The first Seonghwa ceremony was held January 8, 1984, after Heung-jin nim ascended to heaven. From that day, True Parents gave the blessing to blessed members whereby their funeral would be called the Seunghwa ceremony. Then on November 9, 2011, by the solar calendar, True Father heard the news of the passing of David Sang-cheol Kim. True Father then told us, through the Cosmic Assembly for the Proclamation of the Firm Settlement of the True Parents of Heaven, Earth, and Humankind and the Substantial Word of God, that, after the settlement of True Parents in the land of Korea which is God's homeland, the funeral of a blessed family member would now be referred to as the Seonghwa ceremony.

Figure 4-19) Seonghwa Ceremony Procedure

No.	Procedure	Significance
1	Seonghwa	Usually referred to as "passing," the Seonghwa is where people watch over a family member who is about to take the last breath on Earth. Other family members should clean the house and dress the soon-to-pass in the cleanest of his or her favorite clothes.
2	Dressing	This is the process of cleaning the holy body of the one who has passed (Seonghwa). The body is then dressed in burial clothes and wrapped in ceremonial shrouds.
3	Ipjeon Ceremony	Ceremony of placing the holy body of the deceased into the "wooden palace" (casket).
4	Seonghwa Ceremony	Ceremony in which the family members and relatives gather to celebrate the life of the deceased and offer prayers and other jeongseong for the soul of the deceased who will ascend to heaven.
5	Weonjeon Ceremony	The holy body is firmly settled into the ground at its heavenly resting place during this ceremony.
6	3-Day Ceremony	On the third day after the Seonghwa Ceremony, the family members visit the weonjeon place and offer a service together with other close relatives. It is good to prepare a simple food table for this occasion.
7	40-Day Ceremony	On the 40th day after the Seonghwa Ceremony, members of the family visit the weonjeon place and offer a service to commemorate the period of rebirth. The procedure for this service is identical to that of the 3-Day Ceremony.

☐ Cheon Il Guk Anniversaries

All events large and small that took place within the life of True Parents are of great providential and historical significance. Cheon Il Guk anniversaries are the days when we commemorate and congratulate the victories gained by True Parents as they worked tirelessly in their lifetime to follow Heavenly Parent's providential course.

There are eleven major Cheon Il Guk anniversaries. These are the most important events that should be commemorated by the blessed members who live in the age of Cheon Il Guk. They include True

Parents' Holy Wedding, which is the anniversary of the day when True Father and True Mother became the ancestors of humankind and opened the gateway for fallen humanity to be saved. After the Holy Wedding, True Parents overcame numerous challenges and obstacles. They completed the Era Before the Coming of Heaven, finally opened the Era After the Coming of Heaven and the Foundation Day. After completing his mission on Earth, True Father returned to Heavenly Parent's side in 2012, on 7.17 by the heavenly calendar.

The lives of True Parents have established a set of values and ideals that are upheld by Cheon Il Guk and serve as important traditions through which we can build our own individual and communal identity as the children of True Parents. As we live in the age of Cheon Il Guk, we should continuously pledge to live the kind of life that befits those values and ideals.

Figure 4-20) Important Cheon Il Guk Anniversaries

Anniversary	Significance
True Heavenly Parent's Day	We offer our gratitude for all of Heavenly Parent's efforts and pledge to live within the realm of Heavenly Parent's direct dominion. (1.1 HC)
True Parents' Birthday	We offer our gratitude to Heavenly Parent for sending True Parents to us. (1.6 HC)
Cheon Il Guk Foundation Day	This day marks the beginning of the age of Cheon Il Guk. This is the age when heaven and earth were cleansed of all stains of the Fall and restored. (1.13 HC)
True Parents' Day	We are reminded of the value of True Parents and strive ourselves to become a true parent and a true child. (3.1 HC)
Anniversary	Significance

True Parents' Holy Wedding	On this day, Rev. Sun Myung Moon and Dr. Hak Ja Han Moon, the True Parents of humankind, manifested as True Parents for the first time in the history of humankind through the Marriage Supper of the Lamb. We celebrate this day to commemorate the beginning of human salvation and rebirth. (4.11 HC)
Day of All True Things	We try to embody the requirements to be the true owners of all things. (5.1 HC)
7.1 *Jeol* / Day of God's Proclamation for the Eternity of Blessing	We understand the value of True Parents, and strive to protect our absolute sex. (July 1)
7.8 *Jeol* / Declaration of the Realm of the Cosmic Sabbath for the Parents of Heaven and Earth	We offer our gratitude and congratulations for the declaration of the Realm of the Cosmic Sabbath. We pledge to attend Heavenly Parent at each step of the way. (7.7 HC)
Foundation Day for the Unified Nation of Heaven and Earth	We understand the nature of Cheon Il Guk and join the effort to establish the substantial Cheon Il Guk. (Oct. 3)
True Children's Day	We understand our role as true children of Heavenly Parent and pledge to fulfill the requirements of that role. (10.1 HC)
Anniversary of True Father's Seonghwa	This is the day True Father completed the providence on earth and departed to heaven where Heavenly Parent resides. This is the day we commemorate the preciousness and the glory of True Father, who offered his entire life for human salvation. (7.17 HC)

The holidays and anniversaries of the Family Federation are the days when we commemorate the missions accomplished on earth by True Parents. The 35th Parents' Day, in 1994, was a particularly important day as it was the day when "true" was added to the names of several of the holidays. All of the members of the Family Federation should spend seven days offering jeongseong to Heavenly Father around each holiday: three days before the day, the day itself, and three days after the day. This is to inherit the heart of Heavenly Parent and True Parents. The three days before each anniversary, especially, need to be spent with a pure heart. Members should refrain from any outbursts of anger and not focus on secular business during these days. Family members should unite and offer jeongseong together with a pure heart.

(4) Cheon Il Guk Symbols

The following (Figure 4-21) explains the symbols of Cheon Il Guk, which all citizens of Cheon Il Guk should remember.

Figure 4-21) Cheon Il Guk Symbols

Symbol	Details
	National bird: Crane. The crane symbolizes the preciousness of true love and true life, mutual reciprocation, and the principle of the universe.
	National flower: Rose (masculine). The rose symbolizes a firm determination and the masculinity within a true family that lives in accordance with True Parents' teachings.
	National flower: Lily (feminine). The lily's petals symbolize the purification of the world, the bud symbolizes purity, and the stem symbolizes the spirit of noble service and sacrifice. Lilies represent purity.
Symbol	Details

National flag: Unification Church Symbol.
The Unification Church symbol was designed by True Parents in January 1965 inside the former Cheongpa-dong Headquarters church.
1) Red symbolizes power, energy, activity White: purity and holiness
2) It symbolizes that the universe is formed around Heavenly Parent.
3) Square: Four-position foundation
4) The center circle: Heavenly Parent
5) The arrow marks: Give and Receive

Next is the Cheon Il Guk National Anthem. The following explains the purpose and the background of the Cheon Il Guk national anthem.

The Foundation Day of Cheon Il Guk is the beginning and the origin of the substantial Cheon Il Guk. Holy song no. 1, Blessing of Glory (no. 3 in the Korean Holy Songbook), was used as the Cheon Il Guk national anthem after the Entrance into Cheon Jeong Gung and Coronation of the King and Queen of Peace in 2006. Then on the occasion of Foundation Day, True Mother ordered the creation of a new national anthem with lyrics that are befitting of the age of Cheon Il Guk and encompass the ideas of Cheon Il Guk's sovereignty, people, and territory. The Cheon Il Guk national anthem was created to help people naturally discover Cheon Il Guk's vision, praise the True Parents of Heaven, Earth, and Humankind, and wish for the eternal peace and prosperity of Cheon Il Guk.

With regard to the development of the new anthem, True Parents directed that the song's tune and lyrics should praise Heavenly Parent and the True Parents of Heaven, Earth, and Humankind and wish for the hopes and vision of Cheon Il Guk to fill the entire world and the cosmos. Following this direction, the new national anthem was created to contain the Cheon Il Guk symbols, which are the rose, lily, crane, and the national flag. The Cheon Il Guk national anthem is built on the powerful and energetic tune of holy song no. 3, New Song of Inspiration (no. 2 in the Korean Holy Songbook). The original melody of the holy song was maintained, while the lyrics were changed to better describe the Cheon Il Guk vision for freedom, peace, unification, and happiness.

The following texts explain the Family Federation Symbol.

The Family Federation symbol is the visual and conceptual symbol that depicts the idea and philosophy of the "true family centered on Heavenly Parent." The symbol shows that "the true family is centered on Heavenly Parent and true love is the origin of true universe." In other words, it depicts the unity of three generations of a family centered on true love under the sun that symbolizes Heavenly Parent. The entirety of the symbol signifies the four great realms of heart and the three generations of kingship. The reciprocating circle around the realm of true family symbolizes "heaven and earth (the cosmos) that are eternally unified centering on true families."

7.5 Guidelines on Educating Members

① The heavenly tribal messiah couple first must embody what they teach. Those who are receiving the education should be drawn to naturally respect the lecturer, seeing how he lives a principled life. The parents first must be educators.

② A tribe must raise its own set of lecturers. Often it is difficult to invite a professional to give a lecture. That is why it is advisable to select a few of the tribe members and train them as lecturers.

③ Preparations should be made so that lectures can be given anytime, anywhere.

④ A systematic and sequential education should be given to the blessed members of the tribe, so that the entire tribe can be educated in the future.

⑤ An external professional should be invited to give lectures on the topics that cannot be handled by the tribe members.

The Lee Gye-hyeong and Kang Deok-rye Family's Focus on Educating the Second Generation

We have focused on educating the second- and third-generation members of the blessed families. These include various special events, such as bicycle trips on Yoido Island on Children's Day and parties during the Christmas holiday season. We also visited the Paju Weonjeon with them on the Day of the Victory of Love. We have shared our hearts with them on special occasions, such as school graduations and coming-of-age ceremonies. For the ones who already have received the Blessing, we have supported their families with engagement ceremonies, Blessing celebrations, baby showers, 103rd-day ceremonies, first-birthday celebrations and other important milestones.

Since True Father's Seonghwa in 2012, we have determined to raise the second- and third-generation members in accordance with Heaven's Will. On the first anniversary of Father's Seonghwa, we held an eight-day workshop for blessed children in Gochang, which was attended by 80 second- and third-generation members. To mark the second anniversary of the Seonghwa, we made a pilgrimage together, following the path taken by True Parents. For the third anniversary, we gathered 33 second- and third-generation members and did a 14-day tour of providential sites in the United States, including the Twin Peaks holy ground, Shimjeong Garden, Lake Tahoe, Young-jin nim's temporary weonjeon in Reno, Las Vegas, Cheon Hwa Gung, the Grand Canyon and Sedona. For the fourth anniversary, we visited places in Korea that were significant to True Parents and the providence, so that we might inherit their hearts.

For the first year, we focused on educating them for the Blessing. We held engagement ceremonies for two second-generation couples and arranged for three of our second-generation couples to be support staff for the fifth anniversary Seonghwa Festival.

Figure 4-24)

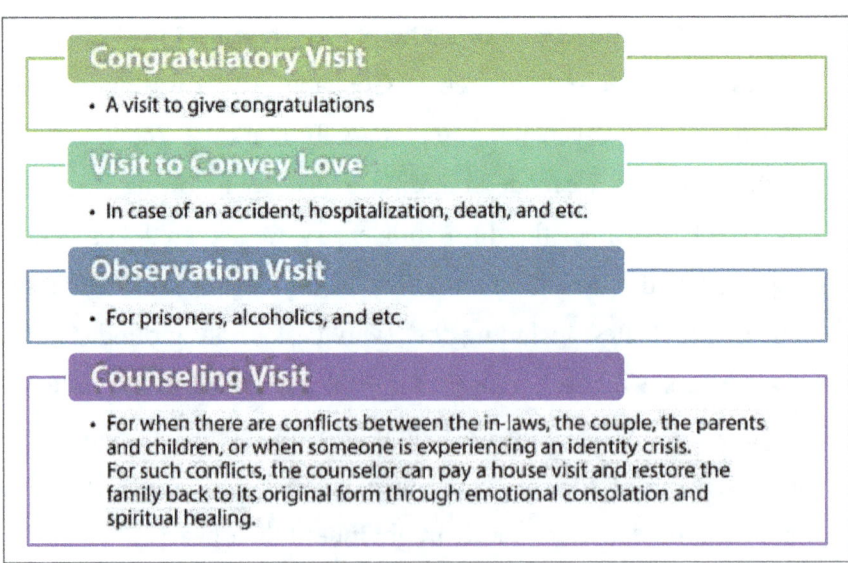

Congratulatory Visit
- A visit to give congratulations

Visit to Convey Love
- In case of an accident, hospitalization, death, and etc.

Observation Visit
- For prisoners, alcoholics, and etc.

Counseling Visit
- For when there are conflicts between the in-laws, the couple, the parents and children, or when someone is experiencing an identity crisis. For such conflicts, the counselor can pay a house visit and restore the family back to its original form through emotional consolation and spiritual healing.

Section 8 Pastoral Visits and Counseling

8.1 The Significance of Counseling

In a counseling session, one person counsels a person or a group of people on any issues or problems that they might have in their lives. What is counseling? Counseling does not mean telling people what to do or what not to do. The basic function that counseling should offer is to calm the person's mind and find a solution for any entanglement within the person's relationships, whether it be between a husband and a wife, within a family, or with other people in general. In other words, the counselor needs to help the person find a solution for their trouble and effectively counter any negativity he has in life. A heavenly tribal messiah is in the parental position, making his position as a counselor special. Unlike other general counselors, the tribal messiah already has a friendly relationship with the person who wants counseling, and he already knows some details about the person's life. In addition, the tribal messiah and the person have a close bond of heart.

A heavenly tribal messiah has at his disposal spiritual resources such as prayer and hoondokhae. Using these tools, the tribal messiah can exert a great influence on the person's fundamental life problems. He has to be able to instill in the person the right set of values and answer the questions the person may have regarding sin, forgiveness, or guilt. The tribal messiah also has to be able to help families that experience problems. A heavenly tribal messiah needs to actively utilize this kind of pastoral counseling.

8.2 The Counselor's Philosophy

First, a heavenly tribal messiah needs to be open and sensitive to the religious traditions of the person receiving the counseling. In many cases, those who already may have received the Blessing still find themselves in conflict with their former religious tradition. Therefore, a tribal messiah should respect the person's religious tradition and feel at ease, even though that tradition's practices are different from those of our movement. Moreover, he must understand the person's religious experiences and common religious features, and have an overall attitude of unity and integration. In other words, he should focus more on the common features of the two religions, not their differences, and help the person understand that the Family

Federation's Divine Principle is the more comprehensive and inclusive teaching.

Second, a tribal messiah should avoid focusing on ideological differences or arguing about dogmas. Even if it comes to a conclusion, a religious argument is bound to leave a mark on the person's heart. If it doesn't come to any conclusion, then the previously existing religious conflict is only worsened. Because of this, religious arguments should always focus on similarities, not on differences.

Third, a pastoral counselor needs to possess expert skills in dealing with religious experiences. He needs to form a counseling relationship with the person being counseled and use both verbal and non-verbal communication effectively. This can help the counselor interpret the person's religious experiences and help such experiences make sense and be integrated harmoniously with his life. In this way, the counselor also can modify his ministerial methods or processes.

8.3 The Attitude of a Counselor

As a counselor, you are not there as a teacher, but to help the people you counsel to find their way. Therefore, when counseling, you should not try to hastily provide an answer. It is important to be courteous to people, taking care to call them by the name or title that will make them the most comfortable. Do not try to fill their mind with religious contents. If the heavenly tribal messiah comes on too strong and tries to impose his religious points of view, the people being counseled may feel overburdened, because they are not prepared to deal with that. Another important thing is to keep any promises you make with them. A secret must remain absolutely a secret.

When counseling, you need to be a good listener. Always listen attentively. In many cases, people can find the answer themselves, if you just help them to talk through the problem. Ask questions that can help them to find the answer, rather than giving advice, teaching them, preaching or giving directions.

Sometimes counseling sessions can become very long. Make sure you continue to pay attention and show interest. Offer empathetic comments when you can, and compliment them on things they have done well.

Congratulate them on obstacles they have overcome. Ask questions that will help lead them to find the answer. One mistake many counselors make is cutting people off in mid-sentence, so try to avoid this. When people look for counseling, it is often when their heart is troubled. In such a state, it is common to repeat the same message a number of times. If they stray too far from the point, ask questions to help them get back on track. Take care to speak to them in a conversational style that will make them most comfortable.

In any counseling session, ultimately you should lead the person being counseled to Heavenly Parent and True Parents. Make sure that, when he leaves the center, he has hope and determination to solve the problem he is facing. Help him find the courage to be part of the community and to overcome his obstacle through prayers and jeongseong.

8.4 Techniques of Counseling

1) A counselor should always be focused on the problem being described. A counseling session is a very important time of reporting, A counselor should do everything in his power to help people solve the problems that are plaguing them.
2) The counselor should make sure people feel free to express whatever they want to. This means the counselor must guarantee privacy regarding what has been said.
3) The person who is there to receive counseling should do most of the talking, while the counselor spends most of his time listening attentively.
4) Instead of diving too deeply into one issue, a counselor should ask questions that focus on the solution.
   Example: "I see that you've experienced ...... What thoughts were in your mind at that time? If one of your friends found himself in the same situation, what would you tell that person to do first?"
5) Help them understand why the person who created the problem acted the way he or she did.
   Example: "Why do you think your wife acted the way she did? What do you think was going through her mind at the time? Do you think there was something you could have done to help the

situation before your wife did what she did? Okay, if you were to go back to that situation, what would you want to do differently?"

6) If the person who is there for counseling can't find the solution to the problem, the counselor can ask if there was a similar situation in the past.

Example: "I see, that's what has happened to you. It must have been very difficult. But you persevered and endured. For this, you have my tremendous respect. I want to applaud your efforts. Have you ever experienced a similar problem in the past? Or do you know any of your friends who experienced a similar problem? I see. Then let's come back to the issue at hand. Okay, what do you think you need to do now, when you look at this problem from the perspective of the solution that you have found? This is a better solution than what you did last time. What are you planning to do after this meeting? That's good. Listening to your solution also gives me energy. You are a very clever person. You know how to come up with solutions. Let us pray together."

In a counseling session, delving deeply into a solution may lead the focus away from the problem at hand. Simply ask questions as to why the visitor got into the current problem. Next, allow the visitor to reflect on his past experiences that were similar to the current one, and encourage him to think about how he pulled himself out of difficulties in the past.

8.5 Precautions When Counseling

① **If possible, a holy place (the prayer room with True Parents' portrait) should be used for counseling sessions.** However, if the person will be more comfortable in another place, any room that has been specially sanctified can be used for counseling, even though it doesn't have a portrait.

② **Offer a reporting prayer to Heavenly Parent before beginning each counseling session.** The counselor has to decide what spiritual resources he will use. This decision can take into consideration the nature of the person's problem. The counselor should pray throughout his day. He also should pray before beginning a counseling session. It is good to pray again after the counseling is over (reporting).

③ **A counselor should counsel from the viewpoint of Heavenly Parent.** When counseling from a religious point of view, you are trying to connect a person to Heavenly Parent and True Parents, and from a life-of-faith point of view, you are seeking to solve his problem.

④ **Listen attentively and empathize.** If the counselor listens attentively, people will have an opportunity to express their feelings, which may help to untangle the knots in their heart. If this happens, they will feel that their heart has become lighter. (Listen and empathize.) Pray for each person's family to overcome the problem.

⑤ **Do not jump to conclusions regarding the problem.** Church leaders tend to talk a lot. However, the problem is that this habit is being applied to their counseling sessions as well. The counselor should ask prudent questions, so that people can find the answers within themselves, which will lead to a quick resolution of the problem. There are many cases in which a person finds his own solution if the counselor, even if he is not a trained expert, just sits there and listens attentively. This will help a person to find a solution by himself.

⑥ Observe carefully. A good counselor gains a lot of insight on people just by observing very carefully. With this knowledge, the counselor should focus on the source of the problem. Additionally, if the counselor asks questions like, "What kind of problem would you like to solve through today's counseling session?" it will help the counselor understand what kind of mental state the person is in and what he wants to solve through this session. This can help the counselor understand what questions to ask and ultimately shorten the overall counseling time.

⑦ The details of the counseling should never be revealed to anyone. The conversation should remain secret, not even shared between a husband and a wife. If you promise secrecy, you have to keep that secret to the end. In other words, the details of a counseling session should never be revealed without the person's consent. This also means the details of a counseling session should not be used as an example in an educational session. A great counselor never tells anyone about what he learned through his counseling sessions (non-disclosure of private information).

8.6 Significance of Pastoral Visits

To Heavenly Parent, each human life holds the same value as the universe. Heavenly Parent wishes for everyone to be saved and become a person who has reached full maturity. Heavenly Parent's love for His children provides the greatest motivation for a pastoral visit.

Pastoral visits are different from regular visits. A normal visit involves people getting together to spend time together and discuss everyday issues. In a pastoral home visit, the visiting pastor stands in the position of Heavenly Father's messenger who is visiting the house to console, to care for and to help heal his flock through prayer and counseling. The tribal messiah who is visiting in the role of a pastor must listen to what the other person wants to say and provide whatever support he can that may lead to a resolution. Through such actions, the tribal messiah may help the person feel grateful for the love of Heavenly Parent and True Parents. Through this, the member's faith can grow to another level.

8.7 Attitude for Pastoral Visits

① An attitude of trying to guide Heaven's children
② An attitude of deeply loving a soul
③ An attitude of encouraging spiritual growth

④ Heavenly Parent's presence and love visiting the family

Note: Reasons people may prefer to decline a pastoral visit to their home:

- It's hard to prepare foods and snacks.
- Too much energy has to be spent on cleaning the house.
- There is a tradition of handing an envelope with "gratitude" money in it to the visiting minister.
- The minister talks only about the importance of tithing or the religious activities in his church, rather than showing interest in the family being visited.

8.8 Types and Methods of Pastoral Visits

The following (Figure 4-24) shows different types of pastoral visits. Heavenly tribal messiahs engage in ministerial activities by visiting blessed members in a variety of different circumstances.

8.9 Procedures and Instructions for Pastoral Visits

The procedure for a pastoral visit is as follows: Welcome → Chat → Hoondokhae → Meal → Farewell. Also, the heavenly tribal messiah should bring a gift for the family he is visiting.

The hoondok service in a house visit should be a simple, minimal service. The heavenly tribal messiah should not try to give too much through his message. Instead, the family worship service provides a good opportunity to give a message that is tailored to the family members. The tribal messiah should carefully select his message so that it can benefit the family and prepare them to experience Heavenly Parent's heart.

It is good for the tribal messiah to keep a record of his visits. These records are similar to the medical records kept by doctors, and they can serve as an important set of tools for his ministry. Therefore, it is helpful to keep a detailed record of the personal situation, conditions, or any future developments regarding the members of the family he visited. These materials can help the minister in the future by giving insights to his past activities. Not only that, they can be used in determining the level of training each tribe member has received.

Figure 4-25) Example of a Counseling Card 1: Basic information about visitor Front Page

Husband's Name			Wife's Name		
Nationality			Nationality		
National ID No.			National ID No.		
Date of Birth		Husband (Passport Photo)	Date of Birth		Wife (Passport Photo)
Date of joining Family Federation			Date of joining Family Federation		
Spiritual Parent			Spiritual Parent		
Occupation	Home) Mobile)		Occupation	Home) Mobile)	

Licenses or Certifications		Date of Ascension			Licenses or Certifications		Date of Ascension		
Divine Principle Education	3-Day, 7-day, 21-day, 40-day				Divine Principle Education	3-Day, 7-day, 21-day, 40-day			
Current Address					Current Address				
E-mail					E-mail				
Names of Children	M/F	National ID No	Generation	Blessing Status (In Details)	Names of Children	M/F	National ID No	Generation	Blessing Status (In Details)
		-	1st 2nd 3rd				-	1st 2nd 3rd	
		-	1st 2nd 3rd				-	1st 2nd 3rd	
		-	1st 2nd 3rd				-	1st 2nd 3rd	
Work Experience					Work Experience				

Figure 4-26) Example of a Counseling Card 2: Faith Information Back Page

Couple Counseling Grade	A. B. C. D	Reason for Coming to Church	Parents' encouragements. Moving. Rejoining. Guided. Other
Worship Participation	Regular. Irregular. Only the day service. Only the evening services. Only the Wednesday services. Rarely participate		
Church Education	• Finished Elementary-grade Education Finished • New-member Education • Finished Divine Principle Education (1-Day, 2-day, 3-day, 7-day, 21-day, 40-day, other) • Finished Long-distance Education Level of Education		
Level of Education	• Graduated from elementary school • Graduated from middle school • Didn't graduate middle school • Graduated from high school • Didn't graduate from high school • Graduated community college • Graduated University (Major:) • Graduate School (Major:)		
Talents	Musical Instrument ( ). Choir. Painting. Drama. Arranging flowers. Calligraphy. Sports ( ) Other ( )		
Ability	Educational social activity. Management. Research. Volunteer service. Missionary. Book. Audiovisual. Other ( )		
Church Position Experience	Elder__Years. Deaconness__Years. Deacon__Years. Region Head__Years. Church Leader__Years. Church Board__Years.	Donation	Tithing. Monthly Donation. Gratitude. Holiday

Special Note	When		Date	
	Where		Period	
Current Core Issue			Anticipated Solution	Solution Record counseling methods, counseling period, and a stage-by-stage road map.
Month / Day	No. ( )	Counseling Technique (Method)		Future management and next counseling date	
		Counseling Details			
Month / Day	No. ( )	Counseling Technique (Method)		Future management and next counseling date	
		Counseling Details			

The following are a few guidelines for when a heavenly tribal messiah visits the home of one of his tribal families.

First, everyone has a unique story, and so do the members of the family whom the tribal messiah is visiting. Therefore, he should focus on listening to their stories. Listen attentively and allow the family to make a report to the heavenly tribal messiah.

Second, in a friendly and compassionate manner, the heavenly tribal messiah should talk about the issues that are central in spiritual growth.

Third, the heavenly tribal messiah should do more than just understand the members' situations. His efforts should raise the faith of the family members, so he may have to exert effort in guiding the members to the right path.

Fourth, the heavenly tribal messiah who is visiting a home represents his church. Thus, he should bring a message of faith, hope, and love on behalf of the living community.

Fifth, a pastoral visit should be an opportunity for the family members to experience Heavenly Parent, commune with the Holy Spirit, and listen to the teachings of True Parents.

Sixth, the ultimate purpose of a pastoral visit is to connect the family members to Heavenly Parent. It should help them restore their faith if it's lost, strengthen it if it's weak, love True Parents, serve their community, and nurture their spirit.

New tribe members who have been living a life of faith for only a short period still have doubts in their heart. Therefore, efforts should be made to visit such members often, so that their heart can settle down. Visit them often to befriend them. Teach them their roles as church members. Introduce them to the many organizations operated by the Family Federation, and let them find themselves a home within the movement.

8.10 Precautions for Pastoral Visits

① **Pastoral visits can take place outside the house as well.** Some families may want a pastoral visit with their minister—just not in their house. In that case, the tribal messiah couple could meet the family at a coffee shop or a quiet restaurant. The tribal messiah couple should pay for their own meal in principle, but they could accept the offer if the other couple strongly insists on paying for the meal. The new modern lifestyle has made it difficult for family members to prepare the foods and clean the house in preparation for a house visit. Therefore, a growing number of people are less comfortable with someone visiting their home.

② After arriving at the house, first visit the prayer room where True Parents' portrait can be found and offer a *gyeongbae* (full bow). When visiting a home, the heavenly tribal messiah should first pay respect in the place where its family members offer jeongseong to Heavenly Parent. This is a expression of respect for the family and the expression of gratitude for Heavenly Parent and all of their ancestors in the spirit world for protecting the family. (Location)

③ If it is the first pastoral house visit by a tribal messiah, sanctify the house with holy salt. If the family still has not settled down as a blessed family, the family can be sanctified through a sanctification ceremony. After this, the minister can select a room to serve as their prayer room, and he can provide them with a set of basic guidelines regarding the faith and traditions of the movement so that the head of the family can begin their own family ministry.

④ Put the visited family at the center of the worship service or hoondokhae. The tribal messiah should elevate the status of the family's husband and wife so that they can lead their family ministry. He or she can teach them the methods in detail so that they can be at the center of the family worship service and not just remain as bystanders. One of the important functions of pastoral visits is creating new hoondok family churches.

⑤ When visiting a family with an issue, only the tribal messiah couple should attend and not bring anyone else along. Any visit to a family with an issue should focus on maintaining their privacy and resolving the issue. Therefore, it is best if the tribal messiah couple alone attend. In this case, it is preferable for the tribal messiah couple to pay the visit together, rather than having a one-on-one counseling session. Here, some counseling tools can be utilized to assess the level of the problem.

8.11 Various Counseling Tools

The following tools can be used by a heavenly tribal messiah who is visiting the home of one of his tribe members. (Figure 4-27) is a survey on marriage satisfaction. This survey can be used to assess the marriage satisfaction of a couple, which can provide useful insight into the couple's situation and serve as a basis for generating a solution.

Figure 4-27) Marriage Satisfaction Program - Mark from 1 (do not agree) to 5 (strongly agree).

	Details					
1	I know what my spouse wants from me in our marriage.					
2	My spouse makes efforts to make me feel comfortable.					
3	I have many worries regarding our marriage.					
4	If I had to marry again, I would not marry a person similar to my spouse.					
5	I can always trust my spouse.					
6	My life would have been very empty had I not married.					
7	My current marriage puts a great number of constraints on me.					
8	I feel that I am bored with my marriage.					
9	I know what my spouse's married life is like.					
	My marriage has negative impacts on my health.					

I feel angry and frustrated because of the things that happen in my marriage.			
I think I have the adequate ability to properly manage this marriage.			
I hope that my current marriage continues for eternity.			
I think I will be even more satisfied with my marriage as time goes on.			
I am tired of trying to make this marriage work.			
I think my marriage is as happy as I had anticipated.			
My marriage gives me more satisfaction than anything else in my life.			
My marriage is becoming harder as years go by.			
My spouse often makes me angry.			
My spouse gives me plenty of opportunity to express myself.			
My marriage so far is a success.			
My spouse treats me as an equal.			
I want to pursue things other than my marriage that enrich and give value to my life.			
My spouse encourages me to do my best.			
I feel that my marriage has been oppressing my character.			
The future of my marriage is hopeful.			
Details			
I have a sincere interest in my spouse.			
I have a good relationship with my spouse.			
I am afraid of losing my spouse through divorce.			
My spouse takes my free time away unfairly.			
My spouse does not treat me fairly.			
My marriage helps me to achieve the goals that I had set before the marriage.			
My spouse puts efforts into improving our relationship.			
My spouse and I experience difficulties because we have different hobbies.			
Both of us like each other's ways of showing affection.			
Unsatisfying sex life is acting as an obstacle in my marriage.			

My spouse and I have the same opinion in terms of which actions are right and appropriate.				
My spouse and I do not share the same philosophy in life.				
My spouse and I have a few hobbies that we enjoy doing together.				
I sometimes wish I had not married my spouse.				
I am certainly unhappy with my current marriage.				
I want to engage in sexual relations with my spouse with a joyful heart.				
My spouse does not respect me much.				
It is difficult to trust my spouse.				
My spouse usually knows what I think or feel.				
My spouse does not listen to the things I say.				
I often engage in a joyful conversion with my spouse.				
I am certainly satisfied with my marriage.				

The following (Figure 4-28) is a table that helps analyze a conflicted marriage relationship. A couple can fill this table out together to assess their conflict level. This can provide a useful insight into the couple's situation and serve as a basis for generating a solution.

Figure 4-28) Healthy Method of Quarreling between a Married Couple

1) It should be non-violent.
2) It should only take place in a designated place. Only fight within a room designated for the purpose.
3) Do not fight in front of you children.
4) Do not make your quarrels draw out for long.
5) Admitting your faults can help restore your marriage life.
6) It is absolutely forbidden to compare your family with other families.
7) Do not insult your spouse's character.
8) Do not care about who wins or loses.
9) Do not revisit the same issue over and over again.
10) Try to see things from your spouse's point of view.

Question 1. Assessing from the couple's quarrels, what kind of problems do you think you have?
Question 2. How do you score against the 10 do's and don't's? (Draw a circle to the ones that you are successful

with, and mark with a X on the ones you are not.)

	Questions	Answers
1	Not using violence	
2	Fighting only in the designated place.	
3	Not fighting in front of you children.	
4	Not drawing out your fights.	
5	Admitting your faults.	
6	Not comparing with others.	
7	Not insulting one's character.	
8	Not revisiting the same issue.	
9	Not caring about who wins.	
	Trying to stand in each other's shoes.	

The following (Figure 4-29) is a survey regarding the potential to improve a couple's relationship. This survey may help assess how likely it is that the conflicts between the couple can be resolved. It could provide useful insights into the couple's current situation and serve as a basis for generating a solution.

Figure 4-29) Ability to Improve a Couple's Relationship

※ **Affection**
1 = Never, 2 = Sometimes, 3 = Often, 4 = Very Often, 5 = Always

※ **Companionship**
1 = Never, 2 = Sometimes, 3 = Often, 4 = Very Often, 5 = Always

※ **Caring**
1 = Never, 2 = Sometimes, 3 = Often, 4 = Very Often, 5 = Always

9	I support my spouse in completing urgent tasks by helping out with the	1	2	3	4	5

Score (me) _____
Score (spouse) _____

※ Evaluate your scores for each category
10–20 points or less: no ability to improve marital relations
21–30 points: low ability to improve marital relations
31–40 points: normal ability to improve marital relations
41–50 points: good ability to improve marital relations (Divide the Caring score by 2.)

(Figure 4-30) below is a survey to evaluate the anger index of marital relations. This survey can be used to analyze the current situation by measuring the possibility of anger between spouses and used as data to seek appropriate alternatives.

Figure 4-30) Anger and Conflict

※ **Review the following statements and mark "Yes" or "No."**

No.	My anger level	

1	I often find myself tense even when I don't want to be.
2	I criticize others easily.
3	I stop a conversation or dealing with a person altogether if that person starts to feel unpleasant.
4	I feel pain in my heart when my family or friends fail to understand my desire.
5	I feel discouraged when I find out that someone else is happier than me.
6	When facing an important event, I worry too much about how to handle it.
7	Sometimes I start walking to another direction to avoid someone I don't like.
8	When having a discussion about a sensitive topic, I try to convince other people while raising my voice.
9	I can accept people who admit their shortcomings, but sometimes I have difficulties accepting people who won't admit their faults.
10	I really don't want to listen to any dissenting opinion when I explain about the reason I feel angry.
11	I don't easily forget the people who have wronged me.
12	When there is a misunderstanding, I immediately start thinking of counterarguments.
13	When I feel disappointed, I want to be alone in a quiet place.
14	I am very aggressive with anything that is related to a business, or even a game.
15	I fight emotionally when I see something unfair.
16	I know that it is wrong to blame others for my mistakes, but I still criticize them anyway.
17	When someone criticizes me publicly, I start thinking of how I can get out of that situation.
18	I sometimes frame others without considering the negative impacts my action will have on that person's reputation.
No.	My anger level
19	I act normally even when I am disappointed.
20	Making sarcastic jokes is something I am good at.
21	When someone is expressing their frustration towards me, my mind easily fall into conflicts.
22	I am known to ignore other people's desires, or be apathetic.
23	If I am given a position of authority, I will carry out my tasks very coldly and one-directionally.

◥ Members of Rupsingh Bhandari's tribe who participated in a heavenly tribal messiah Blessing

When anger arises between couples, it is because the desire to be loved is not satisfied, the desire to influence the spouse is not satisfied, or it feels like your spouse is trying to control you. The thing that causes the anger is the incorrect values systems and ineffective thought systems that surround us. In the end, the source of the anger is within us.

The following table (Figure 4-31) shows how to cope with conflicts among couples. Please consider what kind of efforts each person needs to make to solve marital conflicts.

How does your couple cope with conflicts? After marking your responses, compare your answers with your spouse's.

Figure 4-31) How to Deal with Marital Conflict

Method of Coping	Husband	Wife
Avoid the issue without solving it		
Winning and being victorious		
Adapting and giving in		
Negotiation and compromise		
Set mutual goals for mutual victory		

Here are some approaches for coping with marital conflict.

First: avoiding the conflict without dealing with it. This does not solve anything. There is a good chance problems will accumulate and lead to feelings of hostility due to helplessness.

Second: winning by defeating your spouse. This method is often used by people with "only child syndrome" who are concerned only with their own needs. This often is accompanied by a tendency to violence.

Third: adapting to what your spouse wants. People who are afraid of losing their spouse often use this approach, giving up on what they want themselves. This can lead to frustration from making unconditional concessions, and unequal positions in the marriage.

Fourth: negotiation and compromise. This is not the ideal way to solve a conflict, because both sides lose something.

Fifth: finding a way to achieve each other's goals and win both. This is the most effective solution. When this is successful, both partners can accept each other with joy by speaking the truth in love. This requires understanding our differences and respecting each other.

Section 9 Forming Disciple Groups

9.1 Stage-by-Stage Multiplication of Spiritual Children and Development of Parental Heart.

Just as True Parents blessed families by stages, moving from three couples to 12, then 36, 72, 124, 210, and 430 couples, we need to help the 430 tribal families to take root in the faith, stage by stage, and raise them as core members of the Family Federation. Expanding the realm of blessed members will help us experience the same joy that True Parents felt when they did the same. Getting people to receive the Blessing is the easy part. It is getting them to firmly settle down in the faith that is difficult. This is more difficult than bearing and rearing a child.

> "Experience True Parent's heart stage by stage."

9.2 Significance of Each Stage

It is advisable to form disciple groups stage by stage after their Blessing.

No.	Name						
3	Ok Se-jin	Kim Won-chang	Oh Kyeong-hwan				
12				Yim Won-shil	Lee Ok-hyeon	Cheon Jin-su	Kang In-su
36							
72							
124							
210							
430							

9.3 Precautions When Arranging Your Spiritual Children into Disciple Groups

① **Guide them to become disciples stage by stage without skipping any stages, if possible.** The groups of spiritual children that follow the heavenly tribal messiah should grow systematically while maintaining a solid relationship with each other. For this to happen, the tribal messiah needs to train and raise them as disciples stage by stage. He first should form a deep relationship with the first three families and gradually expand this foundation. Just as True Parents educated and restored blessed members step by step, heavenly tribal messiahs who follow True Parents' footsteps should also build their spiritual children's faith in stages, even if they receiving the Blessing right away.

② Guide the children through love, however difficult it may be. Spiritual children sometimes forget their child status after they work with the heavenly tribal messiah for a long time. In that case, the messiah should first form a firm parent–child relationship with them, based on faith, and always maintain the spiritual standard. If the vertical standard, which is the spiritual standard, disappears, leaving only the horizontal standard, it could cause the spiritual children to feel hurt and become distant.

③ Make leaders out of the children who have attained an adequate level of growth. It is good to practice the leadership of empowerment in which you give a portion of your responsibilities to your children who have attained a certain level of growth. This is helpful to your spiritual children's future growth, as it is to your completing your heavenly tribal messiah mission. The spiritual children who are brought up by their spiritual parents to a higher level of growth will always remember that with gratitude. However, spiritual children who are always treated as children and not given any responsibility will resent it and grow distant from their spiritual parents.

Section 10 Outreach

10.1 The Significance of Outreach

Leading a tribe is similar to the work involved in leading a church as a minister. External activities are necessary if the tribal community is to be rooted firmly in the community in which it is located. In other words, you have to engage in diplomacy. A tribe that focuses too much on internal activities will lose balance and become closed and exclusive, losing its influence over the community and its foundation. It is of absolute importance that a tribe engage in activities for the benefit of the society and create a friendly relationship with the community and its other organizations.

"Practice in your own community the vision of interdependence, mutual prosperity and universally shared values."

10.2 Methods of Outreach

First, establish a branch officer of a providential organization. The most advisable way is to create a Family Federation chapter. There are other providential organizations that could be used for this purpose, such as UPF, WFWP, YFWP, CARP, and the Martial Arts Federation. One of the tribe members can have the responsibility of managing a regional branch office.

Second, the above organizations can be connected to the issues that are unique to the community.

Third, perform the role of the manager of a public organization. If there is an opening in a local public organization, the messiah should actively fill that position so that he can be a recognized leader in the community.

Fourth, become actively involved in the projects that are carried out by non-profit organizations that are supported by the central government, local government, the city, the province, or the county. Welfare projects carried out by national budget, prevention projects that are considered to be of some importance by the government, or other various projects supported by the national budget can be evaluated, and the best ones chosen for active participation by the tribe. Then a tribe member who has a talent in that field can take a key role in such a project.

10.3 Precautions When Carrying Out Outreach Activities

① Encourage a tribe member to act as the head of a branch office of a providential organization. Providential organizations such as WFWP, YFWP, UPF, and CARP are non-profit organizations that seek to gain new members and expand by establishing branch offices. These providential organizations will welcome the efforts of heavenly tribal messiahs who seek to establish branch offices in this region. Carefully observe the tribe members to see who can bear the responsibility of managing a branch office. Expanding the tribe's sphere of influence by giving tribe members responsibilities and establishing a set of relationships with public organizations certainly will benefit the tribe's development.

② Find a unique outreach method that is right for the tribe. Find a challenge that the community is facing, and create a group dedicated to solving that challenge. The tribe members can fill some of the seats of such a group, so various different types of groups can be formed. It could be something simple, such as cleaning the streets, or a bigger, more sophisticated project. A tribe should not hesitate in discovering good projects and taking part in them.

③ Form friendly relationships with the leaders of the community and the people who are likely to show interest in your activities. Forming a 430-family tribe already equates to establishing an organization of a significant size. The size of the tribe should then expand through external activities. Communicate especially with the leaders of the local community to increase the scope and quality of influence. In addition, the tribal messiah needs to develop methods of actively engaging with other groups or communities that can be done as a group through a certain system. In the end, national restoration comes down to how much influence the 430-family tribes can exert in their respective communities. That is why we need to increase the scope of activities and the levels of society with which we deal.

④ **Form friendly relationships with the local media, and use them to frequently spread the tribe's news.** Despite the popularity of social media, in many communities the local media outlets still have a considerable influence. The importance of media cannot be overstated. Efforts should be made to have the tribe's activities be introduced in the local newspapers.

The Heavenly Tribal Messiah Who Skillfully Used Media

My name is Rupsingh Bhandari, and I am the president of CARP in Nepal. I have been walking the path of church public servant in CARP since I joined the movement in 2000. I went back to my home city, Kathmandu, after I was selected as one of the 12 families in Nepal who were given the responsibility of completing their heavenly tribal messiah activities. I faced great financial difficulties, but I carried on with an obedient heart. My wife and I had no foundation and nobody to help us. Still, we spent most of our time in meeting people and educating them about the Divine Principle. Then the number of people who were moved by our total devotion grew, and they started to help us.

My efforts were especially focused on inviting people from the local media to participate in our programs. I believed that it would greatly help to spread the news of our marriage Blessing event if press members learned our movement's teachings. I felt this would be a good strategy for the formation of the foundation for an external environment.

Fortunately, the press members who participated in our events wrote favorable articles. They published articles with positive titles such as "430 Couples to Promise Never to Part" and "People Who Promise to Form Healthy Families" and included pictures. Their articles had a surprisingly positive influence on my community. The people of other religions and I had had small conflicts every now and then, but after those articles, people realized that family is more important than religion. The positive reviews by the media provided an opportunity for the people who previously

Suda tribe members at a UPF event

rejected our message to turn around and take part in our programs. They also gave a clear answer to those who had been confused about our message before. People who were lukewarm about our activities before started to come to our Blessing ceremonies by their own volition. This series of events brought many changes in my way of thinking. The power of mass media was truly amazing.

I gave much thought to how to manage the tribe I had formed. Now I am working with broadcasting companies such as PeaceTV to create a live-streaming system through which I can hold worship services that can be viewed by the people of other communities simultaneously. Mass media are a vital component in the success of heavenly tribal messiah work, and we should create a model by which the local community, the government, and the media are integrated into the success of our activities.

◤ The Suda family

Section 11 Business and Finance

11.1 Significance of the Finances of the Hoondok Family Church and Tribe

No activity will be possible without a financial foundation (such as managing organizations and educating members). A source of finance must be established. The budget that is dedicated to managing a tribe is a public fund. In addition, the budget allotted for tribal activities is also a public fund. These funds can play a critical role in the success of the tribe, so they must be managed very carefully. For all activities, a public fund account should be created so that, if necessary, all of the transaction records can be disclosed to the public. Also, there should be a regular report to the nation's Family Federation. As religious activities are held with the foundation of an organizational body as well, the challenge of financial transparency will continue to exist. A church cannot carry out an activity successfully unless there is financial backing. That is why an adequate level of financial resources is required for a hoondok family church or a tribe to perform its duties.

The biggest financial problem, of course, is the lack of financial resources. This may lead to the leader's loss of authority, threaten the basic lives of the heavenly tribal messiah's family, and even damage the tribe members' faith. This is even truer for a heavenly tribal messiah, because he is in the position of pioneering a new church. There will never be enough money before his church begins to grow and its members start to make donations. This is truly one of the most serious problems. That is why the issue of financial resources has to be resolved for the tribe of a heavenly tribal messiah to be established and to flourish. However, risky moves, such as forming multiple businesses, getting into a multilevel pyramid scheme, or making speculative stock investments, should be avoided at all costs. One of the most basic principles of a religion's growth is to expand through spiritual revival that leads to the introduction of new members who make donations. Therefore, a heavenly tribal messiah should pray for the success of his members' businesses so that their success leads to the enrichment of the church's treasury. At the initial formation stage, however, a church should promote independence through active financial support from Abel-type spiritual children or by finding patrons.

Some heavenly tribal messiahs are reluctant to educate their new tribe members about donating. However, it should be remembered that donating is one of the duties of the Cheon Il Guk people, and the path for blessed members to receive heavenly fortune and the grace of expanding their financial foundation. Any church whose minister talks reluctantly about donating is likely to experience financial difficulties. Such an attitude should not be allowed to affect the growth of the tribe members and their receiving Heaven's blessing. If the heavenly tribal messiah worries about the spiritual children's faith, he should be bold and educate the members about making a habit of tithing.

11.2 Types of Financial Sources

There are different types of financial sources, such as regular contributions, membership fees (tithing), gifts, donations, fundraising and more. One of these methods needs to be applied to the church if it is to manage hoondok family centers, which require a great deal of money. When it comes to the donation that is similar to a membership fee, each church or region may have its own culture or policy. Therefore, the donation policy should be applied to fit the individual region's policies and regulations.

The following is a list of the types of donation.

First is tithing. Tithing has the longest history among the types of donation that are recorded in the Bible. Some believe that tithing is meant to increase the church's profit or enrich the ministers. However, its true purpose is to return the things of the earth to Heavenly Parent. In its original form, members have to donate their entire income before receiving it back. Today, however, only one-tenth of the income is donated to set a condition that the other nine-tenths also were given.

Second is the weekly donation. This is clearly advocated in the Bible, as found in Deuteronomy 16:16, 17 and 1 Corinthians 16:2, detailing the day and the method of donation. The weekly worship service donation should be considered and made first; any other donations (tithing, gratitude donations, etc.,) can also then be offered at that time.

Third is the gratitude donation. This is the donation you give to express your gratitude for successes in the past and the present, for your family and children, protection of the providence, and the guidance of Heavenly Parent and True Parents. Gratitude donations should be given as often as possible. They should be given whenever

Figure 4-33) Korean Heavenly Tribal Messiah Activity Report Form

신종메 완료자 월별 보고서(종족관리용)
Monthly Report for HTM Victor (for Tribal Administration)

부부사진 HTM Couple photo	대륙/ Region:		나라/ Nation:	
	대륙 신종메 원장/ Regional HTM Director:			
	주체/ Husband:			
	대상/ Wife:			
	신종메 활동 보고자/ HTM Reporter:			
	보고 날짜/ Date:			

1. 신종메 완료자 종족 구성원 수/ Structure of HTM Victor's Tribe

총 종족 가정수 Total Tribe Members	새 식구 Supporters	재적식구 Registered Members	일반식구 Associate Members	정 식구 Regular Members	미혼 축복대상자 Single Blessing candidates

2. 신종메 완료자 종족원 신앙생활 내용/ Life of Faith of HTM Victor's Tribal Members

헌금 생활자 Donating Members	월 평균 예배 참석자 Monthly Participants in Sunday Service	신종메 교육 및 수련/ HTM Education & Workshops	
		신종메 종족 모임 HTM Tribal Meetings	센터 수 Number of Centers
		Number _____	Centers _____

3. 신종메 활동 내용/ HTM activity contents

(1) 교육(훈독회, 원리수련 등)/ Education (HDH meeting, DP seminars, etc.)
1.
2.
3.

(2) 지역사회 연대 및 VIP 교류(정치, 경제, 문화분야 등)
Cooperative events with VIP's in the community (political, financial, cultural, etc.)
1.
2.
3.

**신종메 활동 관련 행사 사진과 간략 설명/ Please share HTM activity news and photos

there is an event for which to be grateful, such as a birth in the family, 100-day celebration, first birthday, regular birthday, 70th birthday, entering a school, academic advancement, graduation, new employment, promotion, opening a new business, expanding the business, purchasing a new house, moving to a new house, purchasing a car, leaving the hospital after hospitalization, receiving answers to your prayer, after the minister's house visit, seasonal events, revival events, and more.

Fourth are special donation, which are given on church holidays and other special occasions. The purpose of this donation can be determined based on the historical, cultural, or social context. There have been numerous instances of special donations throughout the history of the providence. The members of the movement can partake in True Parents' course on a conditional basis by connecting people to Heavenly Parent through witnessing and offering earthly things through donation. Most special donations are determined with True Parents' approval. Sometimes the Family Federation of each nation decides to collect a special donation for various purposes. A special donation can be collected in some cases when the church requires funds for a construction project or a purchase of supplies, or if it lacks financial resources in general.

11.3 Financial Stability

The successful management of finance is one of the key elements in

Figure 4-34) Heavenly Tribal Messiah Tribal Genealogy Sample

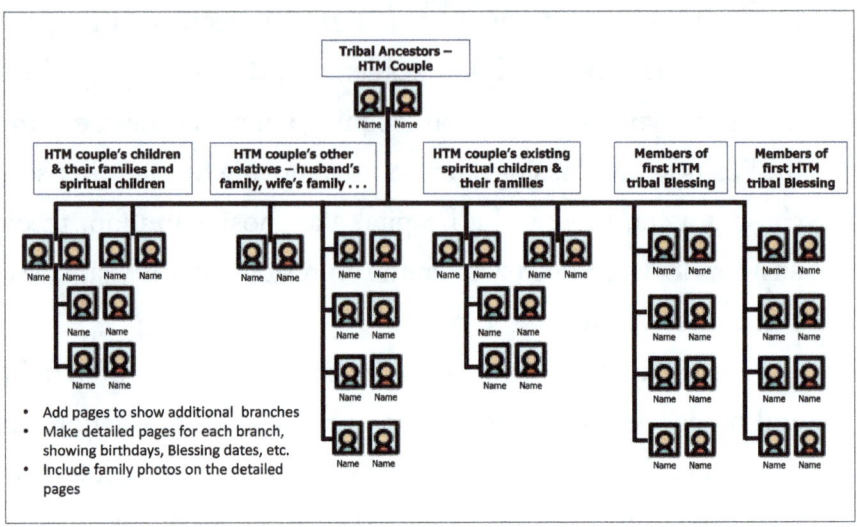

the success of heavenly tribal messiah activities. It is not an overstatement to say that the entirety of the success of a tribe depends on how well they manage their funds. Figure 4-32 introduces some of the managerial key points that are generally practiced in the world and can be helpful to the planning and spending of money.

Figure 4-32) Financial Analysis for Heavenly Tribal Messiahs

No.	Index Name	Explanation
1	Donation ratio compared to household income	Donations are given for the finance of the group but also symbolize the family being engrafted to Heaven's financial realm. A family that donates more receives more financial protection from Heavenly Parent. In addition, the group's financial situation will become stable.

2	Ratio of the regular fee by those in a tribe (tithing, etc.)	Tithing builds the financial basis of the group. In a non-profit organization, membership fees are the bedrock of its finance. The higher the rate of people who tithe, the more stable the financial situation of the group can become, and less volatility is expected because of low dependency on other income sources.
3	Structure of budget income (membership fee + donation + business income ratio)	The priority between regular membership fees (tithing), special membership fees (gratitude donation and other donations) and income through business activities should be: the regular membership fees first, special fees second, and business income third. The regular membership fees are the most important of the three. The special donations can help provide an insight into the ability to mobilize funds, and business income can give an insight into the group's economic realm and business potential.
4	Budget expenditure structure (ratio between management + training expenses)	Management expenditure is a fixed expense. It is good to minimize it. The more expenses are allotted for activities or training, the more growth potential the group has. Management expenses of most groups at their initial formation stage are high, but they gradually decrease, and at the same time the training expenses tend to increase.

Heavenly tribal messiahs usually have to spend most of their time in nurturing the tribe members' faith and building firm external relationships. Because of this, it is good for them to select someone who will be in charge of financial matters. It is difficult to talk to outside people regarding the group's financial management, but it is nonetheless a very important issue. That is why the tribal messiah has to consult with the families who have become disciples, in regard to financial matters. Review the above key points and share the financial situation of the group with other members. In addition, continuous efforts to secure more budget should always be made. The members with whom you share financial information should be considered part of the leadership team with responsibility for the group.

"Work together to restore earthly things."

11.4 Financial Management Strategy

① **Designate a financial manager among the tribe members.** As the size of the tribe grows, its budget also will increase. After some time has passed, keeping track of the financial records will be tough. That is why a financial expert or someone among the tribe members with experience should be found and be given the responsibility of managing financial matters. The responsibility for financial management should be given to someone who is wise and excels in faith. Unlike the financial matters of the outside world, those of a hoondok center are a collection of donations to Heavenly Parent. The financial resources will be able to expand and be protected from evil spirits only if someone of good faith is charged with handling the finances. Anyone who uses his position to strengthen his authority or someone who is not interested in investing in the center's expansion or training should not be given this responsibility. Such a person, no matter how much expertise he has, may end up blocking heavenly fortune from coming to the church. Someone who is extremely poor also should not be a candidate. This is because he sees the center from his limited scope. The best candidate is someone who has expertise, receives a lot of grace from Heavenly Parent, and is capable of managing the center from Heavenly Parent's perspective.

② **Create a bank account for the tribe's public funds, and report to the church.** No matter how large a donation is received, it will be useless if it is handled improperly. Just as the donations and offerings collected in the Old Testament Age did not leave the church treasury, those of this age also should be kept in a secure public funds account so that they may be separated from other funds and be spent through a set of procedures. In addition, the priority when it comes to the management of public funds is stability. Therefore, using such funds to make investments is discouraged.

③ **A regular amount of donations (tithing or monthly fee) should be given regularly (monthly or quarterly) to the church.** Regular tithing or monthly donations to the church should be made as part of a life of reporting.

④ **Public funds should be managed strictly.** When making a payment out of the public funds, it should be done in a way that is not wasteful. That is why receipts always should be given or received when public funds are involved. A report should always be made to the central figure without fail before making any expenditure from the public funds. The financial manager should always take special care so that Heavenly Parent's funds are never lost due to miscalculation, that Heavenly Parent's resources are not used wastefully or irresponsibly, that they are never use for personal purchases, never lent to anybody, and never used for personal business expenditures, even for a short time. Separating the bank deposit accounting and cash accounting is a good idea to prevent these problems. The ledger for the public funds bank account should not have any discrepancy with the bank account transaction record, and it should be reported to the minister at least once a month for an audit. The ledger for cash should be kept in a safe, and the cash collected from donations should be deposited to the bank account every Monday morning.

⑤ Conserve management expenses and prioritize investments in training. Office management expenses, transportation expenses, meals and living expenses should be kept to a minimum. Otherwise, there will be less money to be invested in church activities. The detrimental effect this will have on the financial management of the church will only increase over time.

The Hideo and Joyce Suda Family from England

My name is Joyce Suda. I was born into a Catholic family, and participated in the 1,275 Couples Blessing. I currently live in London, England. My husband and I are carrying out unique activities in our region. We hold gatherings twice a month for elderly citizens. We give massages, yoga or meditation classes, during which time we convey the teachings of Divine Principle and guide them toward receiving the Blessing. Like any other blessed members, we had our own worries about how to raise enough funds for our activities. We tried to solve this issue by asking for a small donation from the participants each time we held our gatherings. What we were amazed by was that we were not financially ready to do this, but God provided through miracles. He knew exactly what we needed and prepared them for us. I have been holding many events so far without much financial foundation, believing that Heaven will provide. I firmly believe in the importance of tithing and giving holiday donations in order to separate earthly things from the satanic realm and return them to Heaven. I am able to understand where I stand and create a greater providential vision only when I first create a condition through which Heaven's work can be manifested on earth. I also believe that, with Heaven's guidance, I can surpass my own limitations. Moreover, I am most certain that material blessings will materialize in order to manifest God's providence. I am still amazed at how we were able to raise the funds necessary to complete our heavenly tribal messiah activities. My husband and I are working very hard, and we firmly believe that the reason we are able to get the small necessary income for our family is because we made donations sincerely.

Section 12 Caring for Tribal Families

12.1 Tribe Management and Care

The heavenly tribal messiah who has completed his tribe by giving the Blessing to 430 couples now has the mission of helping these newly blessed couples to develop their faith through his continued ministerial activities. This cannot be achieved overnight. That is why there needs to be a system of care that can be helpful in guiding the process of nurturing people's faith. The heavenly tribal messiah has the mission of helping his tribal family members to develop their faith so that they themselves may one day also begin their own activities and fulfill their responsibility as heavenly tribal messiahs. In other words, heavenly tribal messiahs must stand in the position of parents to the tribe members and invest everything they have for their children. They have the responsibility to guide the tribe members to go through the three stages of growth to become Cheon Il Guk citizens. However, the already married couples who received the Blessing are slightly different. They require a lot longer time in faith training, and their quality of faith is bound to be relatively lower due to their long experience in the secular world.

Fulfilling the Heavenly Tribal Messiah
Responsibility for the Already Married Blessed Family
Blessing completed ⇨ Faith matures and perfected ⇨ Fulfilling Responsibility as Citizens of Cheon Il Guk

As blessed members, they need to learn about the Divine Principle, faith, and their responsibilities and missions. The tribe is of a considerable size, so as soon as possible, it is important to set up a system for keeping track of and caring for the tribe members. Caring for a tribe cannot be done solely by the heavenly tribal messiah couple. There should be at least three or 12 families during the initial stage who can help the messiah couple. Later on, more families who have become disciples should lend their hands in order for the tribe to be cared for effectively. It will be impossible for the heavenly tribal messiah couple to cared for the entire tribe by themselves without a disciple family.

There may be the following difficulties if the tribe is not cared for properly:

First, the tribe members will scatter without implementing a system for active participation. Heavenly Tribes are doing non-profit activities. The success of a non-profit organization depends on the number of active participants.

Second, low participation will lead to the dissipation of the tribe's identity and continuity. The tribe cannot be sustained without diligent care.

Third, the tribe's network cannot grow without proper management. The largest network an individual can handle is between ten to twenty people. It is very difficult to train the people in your network alone, if the network gets larger than this. That is why we need a proper networking system in order to manage the education process.

12.2 Management Tools

There are three types of management tools that can be used by a heavenly tribal messiah, to keep track of how many people are in the tribe, how many are active, and a brief summary of each person's situation.

First, preparing a report each month helps you keep track of how many members are active, and the profile information of each tribe member is usually kept using Microsoft Excel or Access. True Parents will establish the CheonBo Won genealogy center in the CheongPyeong Training Center. CheonBo Won is a place where the records of people who greatly contributed to the providence will be kept. One of the conditions to be inducted into CheonBo Won will be the completion of 430-couple heavenly tribal messiah activities. Anyone who completes these activities will be remembered not only through the records kept by his tribe members but also through the records that are kept in CheonBo Won.

Second, the records you keep should include an album that contains everyone's pictures. One of the strengths of a tribal album is that it can be used when offering jeongseong. It is easy to look through; it can be used as a management tool and as memorabilia. It is portable and you can make it artistic. Its drawback is that it gets more difficult to maintain as it ages, and it's difficult to update the information, unlike with a computer. That is why you could start your records with a physical album, but it is better to keep the records in both album and digital forms.

Third is the family tree, which describes the familial relationship of the blessed members of the tribe. A family tree is significant in that it can prepare the future registration of the 430 tribal family members. A tribal leader has to know who is in the tribe and manage and care for them properly.

True Parents set the goal of the heavenly tribal messiah providence as restoring 430 families. This is not a small number, and it is impossible for a couple to manage and care for all of them alone. That is why those who have completed the heavenly tribal messiah mission need systematic and effective ways of keeping track of and caring for their tribe. True Parents invested a lot of love and attention in the individual blessed members. In the same way, we have to invest love in our tribe members. The only effective way to do so is to use the power of science or, more accurately, information and communication technology.

> "Love each family with all your heart.
> To love, you must be attentive.
> Being attentive means that you know the ins and outs of each family."

12.3 Guidelines on Managing and Caring for Tribe Members

① **Don't try to collect the list of blessed members alone.** Find a person who can help you. There are many cases in which the members do activities alone. However, it is good to distribute the tasks and responsibilities, especially when we look ahead to the future. That is why the responsibilities should be divided at the formation stage of the tribe, difficult though it may be. In particular, a person of responsibility should be determined first; this person should be consulted in order to manage and care for the blessed members of the tribe.

② **Personal information should be handled with care and attention in accordance with the law.** Take care that personal information is not viewed by anyone who is not authorized. Even a church public official should not view a member's personal information without a good reason. The files containing such confidential information should be locked with a password, so that they are unreadable if copied without authorization. Great care should be given to the process of acquiring personal information. People are usually sensitive about handing over personal details. Some countries require special approval of the provider of the personal information. Those who carry out their activities should be familiar with these legal requirements.

③ Pay special attention to those who are reluctant to give their personal information. There will be those who are extremely reluctant to give their details. Their reasons might be that they don't trust other people easily, or that they have little interest in our movement. They are likely to have very little desire to participate in our movement, or to join future church events. They also may show a negative response when they are asked to participate. Since managing and caring for such people requires extra care, it is a good idea to divide them into a separate group, and treat them specially.

Tribal management and care system of Mrs. Kyoko Furuta

In the quest to complete my heavenly tribal messiah activities, I first started by finding my spiritual children who had scattered and by listening to their stories. I first divided my tribe members into generations, and started to manage their personal profiles using Microsoft Excel. I've made many spiritual children over the years, but I was not able to look after them because I was too busy with church work. Now, however, I have been calling them over the phone as part of completing my heavenly tribal messiah work. I was heartbroken when I thought back to all the days I was not able to spend with my spiritual children. Collecting their data served as the beginning point of restoring our relationship. There were many difficulties. In many cases, I was contacting them after a long absence in order to collect their data. I feel that creating a set of data and updating the data from time to time itself can create a very moving story. Paying attention to my spiritual children gave me newfound love for them. I used my computer to create an album and a family tree. I think I was the one who benefited the most from this activity. I felt that Heavenly Parent was with me, every step of the way. I felt that it was not I who was doing it, but Heavenly Parent.

✳ Discussion Topics

1) If you are a first-generation member, what would you do to ensure that the future generations of your spiritual children maintain their parents' faith?

2) If you are a second-generation member, what would you do to inherit and lead your parents' tribe?

3) What are the similarities and differences between your life course and that of True Parents?

Appendix 1   Revised International Standard for a Completed Heavenly Tribal Messiah Mission and Minimum Requirements to Receive Certification as Heavenly Tribal Messiah Victors

The following contents contain the international standard for a completed heavenly tribal mission as announced through official memo 2014-25, revised with amendments proclaimed on the anniversary of Foundation Day in 2018, and further revised at the victory celebration following the 2018 Youngnam Hopeful March Forward Rally for Heavenly Korea on 4.13 by the heavenly calendar (May 27, 2018), at which time, with True Parents' blessing, a "vertical standard" was added to the international standard for a completed heavenly tribal messiah mission.

This summary includes both the International Standard for a Completed Heavenly Tribal Messiah Mission, which is the final stage of a heavenly tribal messiah's work, as prescribed by the International Headquarters. It also includes the minimum standard required to become conditionally certified as a Heavenly Tribal Messiah Victor who is on the way to reaching the Standard for a Completed Heavenly Tribal Messiah Mission.

1. International Standard for a Completed Heavenly Tribal Messiah Mission

A. Carrying out one's duties as a Cheon Il Guk Citizen
B. Vertically blessing eight lines (husband's and wife's sides) of 430 generations of ancestors.
C. Horizontally forming a tribe of at least 430 couples through three generations.
D. Completing the Blessing of 430 couples horizontally and 430 generations of ancestors vertically, and having all tribe members maintain their faith

2. Overview of the International Standard

Category		Specific Content
A. Duties as a Citizen		Undertaking the duties of a Cheon Il Guk citizen as described in Article 21 of the Cheon Il Guk Constitution
	B-1) 430 Generations of Ancestors	**[B1-a]** Blessing 430 generations of ancestors from all eight lines of the family including four lines on the husband's side (father's lineage, mother's lineage, paternal grandmother's lineage) and maternal grandmother's lineage) and four lines on the wife's side (father's lineage, mother's lineage, paternal grandmother's lineage)
	B-2) Conditions for Ancestor Liberation	**[B2-a]** Participating in the two-day seminar
		[B2-b] Paying the registration fee and donation
		[B2-c] Offering a condition (50 bows for 21 days)
	B-3) Conditions for Ancestor Blessing	**[B3-a]** 100 days of devotions following the liberation of ancestors
		[B3-b] Participating in the 2-day workshop for the Ancestor Blessing Ceremony
	B-4) Life of Faith	**[B4-a]** Holding a welcoming worship service on the 40th day following the Ancestor Blessing Ceremony

C-1) Formation of 430 Couples	**[C1-a]** 1st Gen: Blessed couple leading a hoondok family group (heavenly tribal messiah couple)		
	[C1-b] 2nd Gen: ① Spiritual children couples ② Children and their spouses		
	[C1-c] 3rd Gen: ① Spiritual grandchildren couples ② Grandchildren and their spouses		
C-2) Witnessing			
C-3) Completion of the Blessing	**[C3-a]** Blessing Application Form		
	[C3-b] Education	[C3-b-①] Divine Principle	
		[C3-b-②] True Parents' Life Courses	
		[C3-b-③] Meaning and Value of the Blessing	
	[C3-c] Blessing Donation		
	[C3-d] Change of Blood Lineage		
C-4) Life of Faith	**[C4-a]** Tithing		
	[C4-b] Participation in Worship Service		

3. Explanation of Each Category of the International Standard for a Completed Heavenly Tribal Messiah Mission

A. Standards for the undertaking of duties as a Cheon Il Guk citizen: These include carrying out all duties of a Cheon Il Guk citizen (Article 21 of the Cheon Il Guk Constitution) as stated in the Cheon Il Guk Constitution.

1) Citizens of Cheon Il Guk must not lose the pure lineage of Heaven.
2) Citizens of Cheon Il Guk must not violate one another's heart or their human rights.

3) Citizens of Cheon Il Guk must not misuse public funds.
4) Citizens of Cheon Il Guk should read, practice, disseminate and educate through True Parents' words.
5) Citizens of Cheon Il Guk should serve as leaders of hoondok family groups and tribal messiahs for the sake of the substantial establishment and completion of Cheon Il Guk.

※ The detailed process of blessing 430 generations of ancestors is to be conducted according to the standards provided by the Cheongpyeong Heaven and Earth Training Center.

C-1. Standards for the Formation of 430 couples: The following standards must be kept when forming a forming a tribe of at least 430 couples through three generations.

1) 1st Generation (Head of Tribe): A blessed couple who are qualified hoondok family leaders as prescribed by the Cheon Il Guk laws and Constitution.
2) 2nd Generation
   - Spiritual children couples: Blessed couples formed from the spiritual children to whom the above-mentioned 1st generation blessed couple has witnessed
   - Children and their spouses: Blessed couples formed by the children born from the above 1st generation blessed couple
3) 3rd Generation
   - Spiritual grandchildren: Blessed couples formed from those to whom the above-mentioned spiritual children have witnessed

- **Spiritual children of your children:** Blessed couples formed from those to whom the children of the above-mentioned 1st generation blessed couple have witnessed.

C-2. Witnessing Standard: The following witnessing standard must be met under the guidance of the regional group chair appointed by True Parents and the national church headquarters (Cheon Il Guk Constitution Article 81 – referred to as the national headquarters):

1) Membership Registration Form: Newly witnessed people must sign and submit a membership registration form provided by their national headquarters or regional group chair, and resolve to begin their life of faith as citizens of Cheon Il Guk (Cheon Il Guk Constitution Article 19).

2) Beginning of Faith: They should meet the standard for beginning a life of faith as required by their national headquarters and regional group chair.

C-3. Standards for a Completed Blessing: Newly blessed couples must meet the standard of having completed their Blessing under the guidance of their regional group chair and national headquarters.

1) Blessing Application Form: Couples sign a Blessing application form provided by the regional group chair or national headquarters

2) Education

- Divine Principle Education: Understanding God (Cheon Il Guk Constitution Article 1) and the relationship between God and

humankind (Cheon Il Guk Constitution Article 2) through basic Divine Principle lectures
- True Parents' Life Courses: Understanding True Parents (Cheon Il Guk Constitution Article 4) through lectures on True Parents' life courses
- The meaning and value of the Blessing: Learning the value and importance of the change of lineage, and resolving to be reborn as a couple (Article 26) by eradicating the original sin through the Marriage Blessing officiated by the True Parents, the Saviors and Messiahs of humanity

3) Blessing Donation: Offering a Blessing Donation to True Parents as stipulated in the International Standard

4) Change of Blood Lineage
- Holy Wine Ceremony: Knowing the meaning and value of the Holy Wine Ceremony and participating in the ceremony
- Blessing Prayer: Only True Parents have the authority (Article 7) to give the Blessing Prayer. However, in the case of a single person Blessing or married couples Blessing, regional group chairs who have been entrusted with the authority to give the Blessing Prayer by True Parents or active church leaders who have been appointed by a national headquarters, can give the Blessing Prayer.
- Indemnity Stick Ceremony: The indemnity stick ceremony is conducted in an event presided over by a public church officer.
- 40-Day Separation: Couples are to remain sexually abstinent for 40 days

- **Three-Day Ceremony:** Conducting the three-day ceremony in accordance with True Parents' tradition

C-4. Standard for a Life of Faith: Practice a life of faith of a citizen of Cheon Il Guk through the basic practices of tithing, offering donations and participating in worship services

1) Life of Donation: Tithing at least twice every three months to the affiliated church of the tribe members or to the church attended by the head of the tribe member's hoondok family group (Article 20)
2) Participation in Worship Services: At least six times in each three-month period attend worship services in the church where the tribe member is registered or attend hoondok family group meetings

4. Guidelines on the Certification of Heavenly Tribal Messiah Victors

The International Standard for a Completed Heavenly Tribal Messiah Mission is the final stage prescribed by the International Headquarters described in the preceding pages. This final stage includes (vertically) blessing 430 generations of our ancestors, (horizontally) having all 430 couples within the HTM tribe complete all seven conditions (education, Blessing donation, Holy Wine Ceremony, Blessing Prayer, Indemnity Stick, 40-Day Separation, Three-Day

Ceremony), tribe members growing into regular members, and attending the Registration Blessing Ceremony.

Here is the minimum standard required to become conditionally certified as a Heavenly Tribal Messiah Victor. The conditions are as follows: Vertically blessing all 430 generations of ancestors, horizontally securing 430 couples as a HTM tribe, and having at least 43 couples out of the 430 couples that have completed all seven conditions. This is on the premise that the remaining 387 couples in the tribe will complete the seven conditions over time.

※ For now, the vertical standard for conditional certification as Heavenly Tribal Messiah Victors will be given to couples that have blessed 210 or more generations of ancestors from all eight lines. However, in keeping with progress made in the ancestor Blessing Ceremony being held the Cheongpyeong Heaven and Earth Training Center, the standard will gradually be raised until it reaches 430 generations, the final number required.

FFWPU International Headquarters will conditionally certify those couples as Heavenly Tribal Messiah Victors if they carry out the requirements for each category as described above.

5. Administrative Matters

A. Couples that complete the requirements to be conditionally certified as Heavenly Tribal Victors must be confirmed by their national leader, regional president and regional group chair (Signature is required.)

1) In order to be certified, the family must submit

① a receipt showing payment of the Blessing Donation

② and a list the names for all of the 430 couples in their tribe.

B. A report of the Heavenly Tribal Messiah Victors who have received the final signature of the Regional Group Chair should be submitted to the International Headquarters every month. The submitted documents will be evaluated and the numbers calculated. The names of these couples will be reported to True Parents, who will in turn present awards to these couples every year on Foundation Day.

Appendix 2 Heavenly Tribal Messiah Activities Checklist

The questions in this appendix have been developed based on the knowledge gained from interviews with those who have completed their heavenly tribal messiah mission. Each question is related to heavenly tribal messiah activities, and the higher your score, the higher your chance of completing your mission. Please use this information to reflect on and increase the efficiency of your activities.

Instructions

Choose the answer that most closely matches your situation. There is no right answer. Please respond honestly, based on your current feelings and past experiences.

1. What does your family think of heavenly tribal messiah activities?

① I am the only person who is interested, and it's difficult to get support from other family members.

② They are interested, but they are too busy to lend a hand due to their study or work.

③ They talk about the activities and show concern from time to time, but it's hard for them to actually participate.

④ They fully support my activities; it's difficult for all of us to participate.

⑤ Our family members are offering jeongseong together. Each of us has our own portion of responsibility defined. We discuss the difficulties of the activities through meetings and prayer sessions, and we make important decisions together.

2. Is the church you belong to engaged in heavenly tribal messiah activities?

① My church does not have any interest in the activities. It's riddled with internal problems, and it's not the right atmosphere to talk about the activities.

② My church is now awakening to the call, and there seems to be some discussion on how to start.

③ My church is relatively engaged with the activities, but the members are still unable to take ownership.

④ My church is united around the minister. The members work hard and get a lot of results. However, there has not been anyone who completed the mission yet.

⑤ My church is engaged with the activities with the minister's full support and the members taking ownership. The members are fully engaged in the activities on a daily basis.

3. **Does the minister of your church support the members' heavenly tribal messiah activities?**
   ① He is not interested and currently not prepared to take the lead.
   ② He is focused on something else that is meant to grow the church.
   ③ He gives his attention and support, which are helpful, but he is often busy with other church activities.
   ④ The activities are strongly connected to the minister's support and guidance.
   ⑤ The minister has already completed his activities, and his accomplishment serves as a good model for me.

4. **How much do you know about the people who have completed their heavenly tribal messiah activities?**
   ① I don't know them, and I don't care.
   ② I know them, but I don't have a deep relationship with them.
   ③ I envy them for their accomplishments.
   ④ I frequently contact them, and we discuss our interests.
   ⑤ I have a very cooperative and friendly relationship with some of those who completed their activities.

5. **Does your hoondok family center have plenty of materials to support your activities, such as pamphlets, print-outs, True Parents' teachings, Blessing guidebooks, True Father's autobiography and video materials, among others?**
   ① I've never used such materials.

② It is impossible to get such materials in my region. I have to create my own.
③ My center does not have any materials, so I have to get them from the National Headquarters whenever I need them.
④ I have the materials that will be needed for upcoming events.
⑤ I have most of the materials that I need in doing my activities, and they can be used at any time.

6. How is your family offering jeongseong to Heavenly Parent?
① We are not offering any jeongseong.
② I am the only one offering jeongseong.
③ My spouse and I offer jeongseong together.
④ The entire family is offering jeongseong.
⑤ All of the members of my tribe (the direct descendants and the spiritual children) are offering jeongseong at the same time of the day.

7. Do the people around you know about your heavenly tribal messiah activities?
① The people around me don't know what I'm doing.
② I'm working hard, but the people around me do not notice.
③ We are working hard together, so my individual work does not receive the spotlight that much.
④ My family and the church members know my activities well.
⑤ I proclaimed my activities to the public through a proclamation ceremony, and my neighbors know what I do because of my hoondok family church (home group) activities.

8. How are you gathering potential Blessing candidates?

① I have almost nobody to participate in a Blessing ceremony.

② I am contacting only close acquaintances.

③ I am making door-to-door visits in order to find candidates.

④ I am recruiting from my spiritual children's acquaintances.

⑤ I have a group of leaders who are helping me. My relationships with them are leading me to find Blessing candidates.

9. How are you explaining about the Blessing?

① I explain about the Blessing to candidates on a one-on-one basis.

② I meet the candidates together with other members and explain to them about the Blessing.

③ I bring the candidates to the church, and the minister or the person in charge of Blessing education gives them information.

④ I gather candidates and hold meetings to explain to them about the Blessing.

⑤ I educate the candidates and select those who are qualified to receive the Blessing.

10. How are you guiding the candidates to receive the Blessing?

① I only guide them to participate in church events. They don't know the details.

② It's already too much just to guide the new candidates to Blessing ceremonies.

③ My purpose is to make them submit an application, participate in a Blessing ceremony, and become a blessed family member.

④ It is important until the Blessing ceremony, but it is difficult to manage them afterward.

⑤ My candidates perfectly follow all the points of the Blessing procedure: the Holy Wine ceremony, the indemnity stick ceremony, the 40-day separation, and the three-day ceremony.

11. How are you engaging with your spiritual children after the Blessing?
① I can't handle them all by myself, so the church has to be responsible for them.
② I want to give more attention to my spiritual children, but it is such a big task and I don't know what to do.
③ I am very interested in my spiritual children, and I care for them, but I can't visit them often.
④ I try to love them and embrace them as much as possible, even if it means I have to sacrifice time.
⑤ They are my children in the end. I believe that I have to be responsible for them for their entire life.

12. How do you educate your spiritual children after the Blessing?
① I am unable to guide them at all.
② I make pastoral visits.
③ I make pastoral visits and do hoondokhae with them.
④ I guide them to come to the events or education sessions hosted by the church.
⑤ I am personally hosting education sessions to train my spiritual children.

13. How do the people in your community perceive you?

① My neighbors don't know what I do.

② My neighbors know me as a member of the Family Federation.

③ My neighbors perceive me as an influential person.

④ My neighbors perceive me as a social leader with great influence.

⑤ My neighbors perceive me as the next-generation leader.

14. What are you doing to spread the mission of heavenly tribal messiah activities?

① I'm not engaged in the activities, so it's difficult to talk to others about engaging in them.

② I am doing the activities, but I do not do them with the people around me.

③ I am actively spreading the word about the activities and asking people to participate.

④ I am engaged in the activities with my children. I am on the path to completing my mission, and I am also helping my children accomplish the same.

⑤ I have already completed the mission, and some of my children have completed their mission as well.

15. How are you recording your religious activities?

① I do not have much of a record that I can pass down to the future generations.

② I am worried about my descendants, so I want to leave something behind.

③ I have always wanted to make records, but I have not been able to actually do it.

④ I have been collecting materials about my past activities, and I am writing my own autobiography based on those materials.

⑤ I have already published a book containing the history of my tribe.

16. How do you envision the future of your tribe or your future tribe?

① I am not at the stage at which I can think about that.
② I am slowly beginning to think about it when I watch my children growing.
③ I am making a plan to create one as I look back at my past and look at my own second-generation children growing.
④ I already have a draft plan and have discussed it with some of the tribe members.
⑤ I already have a document that contains the tribal vision which was created after much discussion and agreement with the tribe members.

17. How are you managing your tribe?

① I am most comfortable handling everything myself.
② I have not been able to give responsibilities to my spiritual children or form an organization after the Blessing.
③ I have given responsibilities to those who are close to me, and I have been working with them.
④ I have given responsibilities to many of my spiritual children when meeting many witnessing candidates. I also have made some adjustments based on trial and error.
⑤ I have staff members, regional directors, and lecturers. We make a plan for each year, we have a person dedicated to managing the finances, and all issues are discussed at a meeting.

18. How are you practicing your leadership in your tribe?
① There is not much leadership.
② All the important decisions are made by me.
③ My spouse and I have our own distinctive roles.
④ My family members and I have our own distinctive roles.
⑤ My family members and the tribal blessed members who have been given responsibilities have our own distinctive roles.

19. How are you carrying out faith education within your hoondok family church or your tribe?
① I don't have the luxury of thinking about education.
② It's difficult to educate them myself, so I'm guiding my children to participate in the education sessions hosted by the church or the pastor.
③ I sometimes guide my spiritual children to participate in an education session hosted by the church, and sometimes I educate them myself.
④ I am wholly responsible for the faith education of my children, but I feel that there are many things that are lacking.
⑤ I have my own lecturers, staff members, lecture plans, education programs, and facilities. We hold education sessions regularly, according to the education program plan we have organized for the tribe.

20. How are you counseling the children in your tribe?
① They do not ask for it, and I don't have much interest either.
② I try to give attention to the children whenever I have time.
③ I carefully listen to what the children tell me and try to help them.
④ The children come to me and ask for help, whenever there is an issue.

⑤ To the children of my tribe, I am their parent and a mentor who provides them with answers to their problems.

21. What kind of activities are you and your tribe members doing to reach out to people in the surrounding community?

① There are no outreach activities other than the church events.
② We are engaged in outreach activities through volunteer service groups.
③ There is a branch of a providential organization managed within the region, and the tribe is actively engaged in spreading the news of the providential organization.
④ There is an organization within the region that is dedicated to conducting activities in the local community.
⑤ We communicate with the region's public organization or leader figures for the shared objective of improving the community.

22. How do you raise the funds necessary for your activities?

① I cannot conduct any activities, because I don't have any funds.
② Either I take a portion of my monthly salary for the activities that month or save some from each month's salary until I have a lump sum to work with.
③ I collect irregular donations from the members of the tribe.
④ I raise funds through monthly membership fees (tithing) from the members of the tribe.
⑤ My tribe has a separate business team that is dedicated to raising funds which are used for the activities.

23. How are you managing the families in your tribe?

① I don't have any Blessing documents, and I don't remember the candidates' faces.

② I keep only the candidates' Blessing documents.

③ I have a record of basic information about the blessed families and visit them sometimes.

④ I properly manage the blessed members, and I know all the facts about their life of faith.

⑤ I have a separate person who manages it, and their information is updated regularly through computers and mobile devices.

Appendix 3 Using the Online Genealogy Service

As the number of families in your tribe grows larger, it becomes more and more difficult to keep track of them using offline methods. Recently a number of free genealogy services have developed on the Internet. You can use one of these to help you manage and care for your tribe. If you use these services effectively, not only will you have a clear and up-to-date record of your tribe but also you can generate various types of statistics profiling your tribe, when needed. Here is some information about some of the online services available.

URL: https://www.familysearch.org

How to sign up

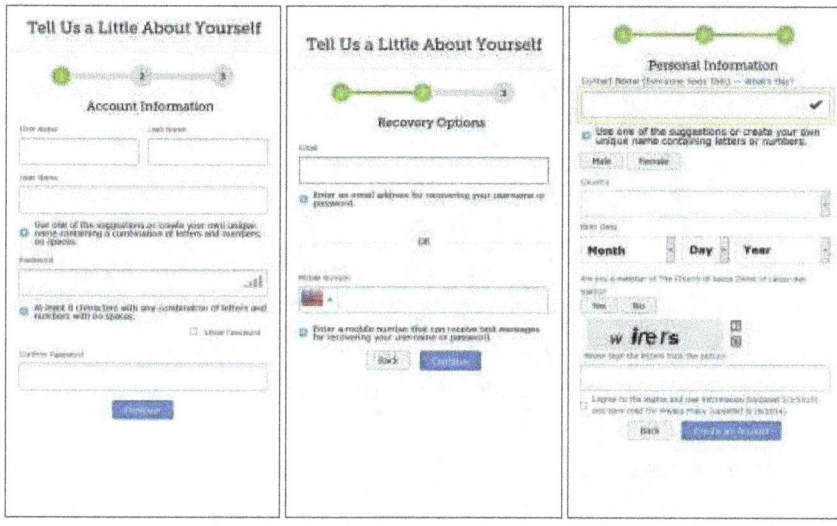

① Enter your first and last name and the user name and password you would like to use.

② Enter an email address OR mobile phone number.

③ Choose your onscreen contact name, gender, country and date of birth. Check the security box, etc.

④ Verify your account through your mobile phone or email account.

Adding family members

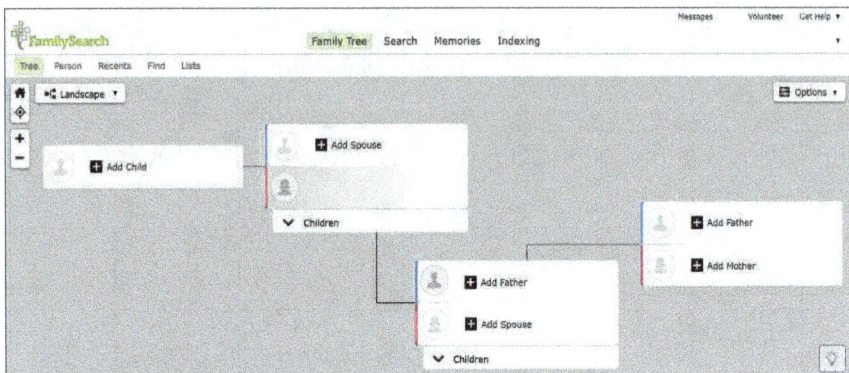

① Enter the date and location of birth for yourself and your spouse.
② Add your parents.
③ Add children.
④ Add grandparents.

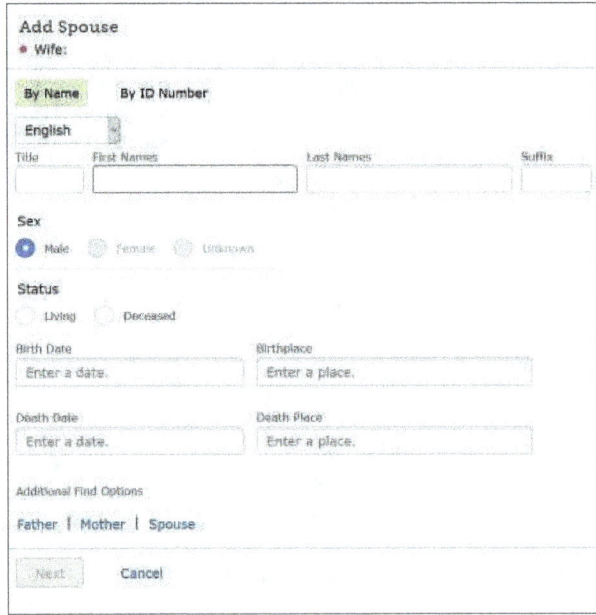

⑤ Keep adding family members in the same way.

Add your personal profile

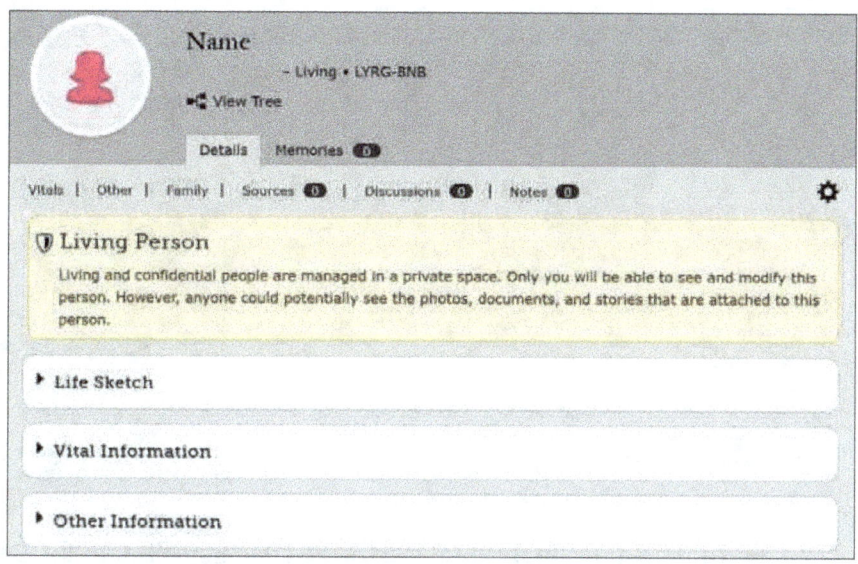

① Click on the face icon next to your name to add a photo.
② Add a summary of your life in Life Sketch.
③ Add more information under Vital Information.
④ Add photos and information for your family members. Appendix . 343

Bibliography

Carson Pue. *Seo Jin-hee, trans.* Mentoring Leaders: Wisdom for Developing Character, Calling, and Competency, Korean Edition. Seoul: Disciple Making Ministries International, 2008 David Finnel, Park Yeong-cheol, trans. Life in His Body, Korean Edition.

NCD, 2000. *Editorial committee for the Collected Sermons of Sun Myung Moon, Ed.* Collected Sermons of the Rev. Sun Myung Moon, vol. 11. Seoul: Sunghwa Publishing, 1961.

Editorial committee. *Sermons, vol.* 13. Seoul: Sunghwa, 1963.

Editorial committee. *Sermons, vol.* 20. Seoul: Sunghwa, 1968.

Editorial committee. *Sermons, vol.* 31. Seoul: Sunghwa, 1970.

Editorial committee. *Sermons, vol.* 48. Seoul: Sunghwa, 1971.

Editorial committee. *Sermons, vol.* 93. Seoul: Sunghwa, 1977.

Editorial committee. *Sermons, vol.* 101. Seoul: Sunghwa, 1978.

Editorial committee. *Sermons, vol.* 110. Seoul: Sunghwa, 1981.
Editorial committee. *Sermons, vol.* 124. Seoul: Sunghwa, 1983.
Editorial committee. *Sermons, vol.* 142. Seoul: Sunghwa, 1986.
Editorial committee. *Sermons, vol.* 150. Seoul: Sunghwa, 1992.
Editorial committee. *Sermons, vol.* 166. Seoul: Sunghwa, 1992.
Editorial committee. *Sermons, vol.* 210. Seoul: Sunghwa, 1990.
Editorial committee. *Sermons, vol.* 219. Seoul: Sunghwa, 1991.
Editorial committee. *Sermons, vol.* 235. Seoul: Sunghwa, 1992.
Family Federation for World Peace and Unification, ed. *Blessed Families and the Ideal Kingdom I.* Seoul: Sunghwa Publishing, 1998.
Family Federation for World Peace and Unification, ed. *Blessing Handbook.* Seoul: Sunghwa Publishing, 1997.
Family Federation for World Peace and Unification, ed. *The Holy Scriptures of Cheon Il Guk: Cheon Seong Gyeong.* Seoul: Sunghwa Publishing, 2013.
Family Federation for World Peace and Unification, ed. *The Holy Scriptures of Cheon Il Guk: Pyeong Hwa Gyeong.* Seoul: Sunghwa Publishing, 2013.
Family Federation for World Peace and Unification, ed. *Teaching Divine Principle to New Members One On One.* Seoul: Sunghwa Publishing, 2013.
Family Federation for World Peace and Unification, ed. *Tribal Messiah.* Seoul: Sunghwa Publishing, 1998.
Family Federation for World Peace and Unification, ed. *The Way of God's Will.* Seoul: Sunghwa Publishing, 2007.
Family Federation for World Peace and Unification, History Compila-

tion Committee, ed. *Etiquette and Rituals*. Seoul: Sunghwa Publishing, 1997.

Family Federation for World Peace and Unification, History Compilation Committee, ed. *Family Federation's Eight Major Holy Days and Important Anniversaries*. Seoul: Sunghwa Publishing, 2001

Family Federation for World Peace and Unification, History Compilation Committee, ed. *Important Ceremonies and Anniversaries of the Unification Church*. Seoul: Sunghwa Publishing, 1997.

Jeon Won-kyun. *Evangelism Marketing*. Seoul: Nuga Publishing, 2007.

Kim Dong-hyun. *Disciples Korean Church Witnessing Small Groups*. Seoul: NCD, 2004.

Kim Sang-hyun. *Change to a Witnessing-Centered Church*. Seoul: Durra-no Press, 2014.

Kim Sang-suk. *I Experienced Miracles Every Day*. Seoul: Word of Life Press, 2010.

Lee Gyu-mok. *A Handbook for Area Lay Pastors*. Seoul: Qumran Publishing, 1999.

Lee Kang-cheon. *A System for Cultivating Happy Church Growth*. Seoul: Green Pastures, 2010.

Lee Sa-guk. *Offerings and Church Finances*. Seoul, Yechan Publishing, 2001.

Lee Yeong-hun. *Evangelism for Fourth Dimension Spirituality*. Seoul: Church Growth Institute, 2010.

Park Jong-gi. *Getting New Believers Settled In*. Seoul: Youngmoon Publishing, 2002.

Park Won-geun. *Theory and Practice of Pastoral Visits*. Seoul: Christian

Literature Society of Korea, 1997.

Yang Pyeon-Seung. *Research on Church Rituals*. Sun Moon University Publishing Department, 2005.

A GLOSSARY OF KEY TERMS

home church :
A style of community ministry that was emphasized in the Unification movement in the 1980s. Each blessed family had the mission to create a model home and family and seek to love and care for 360 families living nearby. Providentially the home church movement had the goal of restoring from Satan the authority of the eldest son.

tribal messiah mission :
The tribal messiah mission was the family ministry that followed home church. Starting in 1991, blessed families were called to return to their home towns and minister to their extended families and others in their home towns. Tribal messiahs worked to bless 160 couples to the Blessing. The tribal messiah age led to the restoration of the authority of parents.

family church / hoondok family church :
The age of hoondok family church was declared in 2005. From this time forward each blessed family was called to establish a hoondok family church, establish

a strong tradition of hoondokhae in their families, and put into practice what they learned through hoondokhae in ministering to their extended families and neighbors. Through hoondok family church the authority of the king was restored.

heavenly tribal messiah mission :
The role of heavenly tribal messiahs was first introduced in March 2012, and True Father emphasized it again in his final prayer. Working in their hometowns or another mission area, heavenly tribal messiahs can shorten the time required for the complete restoration of their lineage from a vertical period of seven generations to as little as one generation, by liberating and blessing 430 vertical generations of their ancestors, and gathering and blessing a horizontal tribe of 430 families, with three generations of their families working together.

home group :
A small group of people, often organized around a few families, who gather regularly as a community of faith, to pray, study, fellowship and minister together. In heavenly tribal messiah activities, a home group sometimes serves as a local pioneer church center.

small group :
see "home group"

midsize group :
A community of faith formed by combining a number of small groups which are in the same vicinity, to work together and support each other, by organizing education programs or community events, for example.

large group :
A larger local church or center which provides opportunities for weekly worship, workshops, and other support services. Parts of the congregation might separate off into small groups and create new pioneer centers.

jeongseong :

An act of devotion, service or care offered to mobilize spiritual support and protection as part of a life of faith. Jeongseong can include prayer, bowing conditions, fasting, taking special care of people, cleaning the church, cooking a special meal, writing letters, and many other types of offering of heart.

"To offer jeongseong means to do your utmost internally and externally. You must offer everything, combining your words, your attitude, your mind and thoughts, all your actions, everything in the internal and external realities of your life." [CSG 11.1.2.1]

hyojeong :

A heart of filial devotion, love given by children in response to the love they have received from their parents, and the exchange of heart between humankind and Heavenly Parent, who also stand in a parent–child relationship. A heart of hyojeong is the starting point of a world that expresses the ideal of creation.

hoondokhae :

Hoondokhae is a meeting where people gather to read, discuss and understand the teachings of True Parents. It is also a time for offering jeongseong of the mind and the body. By engaging in hoondok reading with the whole mind and body, we participate in "hoondok mind-body purification jeongseong."

Cheon Il Guk :

Cheon Il Guk is the shortened name for "Cheonju Pyeonghwa Tongil Guk," which is the "Cosmic Nation of Peace and Unity." Cheon Il Guk is the kingdom of heaven on earth, which we build by practicing what we have learned about love and living for the sake of others.

Seonghwa :

In the Unification movement, the transition from life in the world of air to life in the world of love is call *Seonghwa* (成和: completion and harmony) The end of life in the world of air is nothing to be feared, but is a time of ascending nobly to heaven. When we gather for a Seonghwa Service after somebody has ascended, we celebrate their life up until now, and rejoice for their coming life.

BonHyang Won :

True Father's final resting place above Cheon Jeong Gung is called *BonHyang Won*, which means "garden of the original homeland."

weonjeon / Paju Weonjeon :

Weonjeon is the word used to describe a memorial garden where Unificationists have been laid to rest. The Paju Weonjeon is a special weonjeon in Paju, Korea, for members of the True Family and early church members.

supporters :

Already married couples who received the Blessing through Heavenly Tribal Messiah activities, or other active supporters of FFWPU and/or related providential organizations.

registered members :

Members who attend worship services or donate at least once every six months.

associate members :

Members who donate (tithe if possible) and attend at least two worship services every three months.

regular members :

Members who tithe twice and attend at least six worship services every three months.

Editors
Wonju McDevitt (Head Editor, Chief of Staff, Dr. Hak Ja Han Moon's Secretariat)
Yun Young-ho (Secretary General, FFWPUI HQ)
Yong Jin-hun (Director, FFWPUI HQ Heavenly Tribal Messiah Academy)

Writers
Yoon Do-young (Publishing Committee Chair)
Lee Soon-ju (Sun Moon University)
Lee Bok-jin (FFWPUI HQ Heavenly Tribal Messiah Academy)

Heavenly Tribal Messiah Collection 2 Activity Handbook
Becoming a Heavenly Tribal Messiah

Published June 21, 2018

First edition © 2018
Layout by Sung Hwa Publishing Co., Korea
Published by Heavenly Tribal Messiah Academy
Printed by HSA-Books, New York, NY   June 2019

www.ingramcontent.com/pod-product-compliance
Lightning Source LLC
Chambersburg PA
CBHW050611300426
44112CB00012B/1454